PEOPLE-ORIENTED COMPUTER SYSTEMS

THE COMPUTER IN TRANSITION

EDWARD ALEXANDER TOMESKI
BARRY UNIVERSITY
and
HAROLD LAZARUS
HOFSTRA UNIVERSITY
KONRAD SADEK
WORLD VISION INTERNATIONAL

ROBERT E. KRIEGER PUBLISHING COMPANY
Malabar, Florida
1983

Original Edition 1975
Revised Edition 1983

Printed and Published by
ROBERT E. KRIEGER PUBLISHING COMPANY, INC.
KRIEGER DRIVE
MALABAR, FLORIDA 32950

Copyright © 1975 by
International Thomson Educational Publishing, Inc.
Transferred to Edward A. Tomeski, August 27, 1979
Copyright © 1983 (new material) by
Robert E. Krieger Publishing Company, Inc.

Printed in the United States of America

Library of Congress Cataloging in Publication Data

Tomeski, Edward Alexander.
  People-Oriented Computer Systems.

  Includes index.
    1. Electronic data processing. 2. Computers.
I. Lazarus, Harold.   II. Sadek, Konrad E.   III. Title.
[QA76.T58 1983]   001.64   81-14304
ISBN 0-89874-385-0   AACR2

The happiness of your life depends upon
the quality of your thoughts.

Marcus Aurelius

To
Aurea, my wife, who
constantly renews my
faith in people —
and **ACA,** my daughter,
who is my legacy
to the future.

Why Read This Book?

This book should appeal to executives, in business and government and institutional organizations, who have experienced (and who hasn't) the frustrations of rarely seeing fulfilled the great promises of computerization. Today, many organizations find it difficult to live with computers—but apparently no organization of any size can live without them. For good or ill, they cannot be eliminated. The authors provide insights about the reasons for the unfulfilled promises of computers—particularly the disregard of the "people problems" in computer systems and the low priority given to computerizing the personnel function—and set forth what they find is needed to obtain really effective results from the misdirected tool.

If you consider yourself a humanist (e.g., personnel specialist, psychologist, sociologist, behaviorist) the following pages provide a new perspective on the computer. To date, the hundreds of available books and articles have concentrated primarily on the technical aspects of computers. This book strives to bring a humanistic touch to all phases of computers. This has been a sadly missing ingredient in computer systems, and remains a virtually untapped area for further research and practical application.

If you work in the computer field, either as a vendor or as a user of computers, this book will provide you with a different and helpful view of computers. It suggests that the computer technician must achieve improved interpersonal relations and build such philosophy into his (or her) work. The tarnished image of the computer industry is in no small measure due to the concentration on technical matters and the neglect of people matters.

Faculty and students of many disciplines will also find this book useful and novel. Some of the fields in which its message is pertinent are: business management, public administration, computer sciences, economics, sociology, psychology, engineering, and others. Academic faculties who use a technically-oriented computer textbook might well consider having this people-oriented computer book as a co-text or as supplementary reading. With the current interest of students, faculty, and the public in social problems and human values, it would appear timely that computer curricula should include useful educational materials in these areas.

The revised edition includes updated information and entirely new material which should make the book more useful to the reader. In particular, Chapter 14 strengthens the publication by presenting descriptions of three integrated human resource systems.

EDWARD A. TOMESKI

Preface

The computer is one of the most powerful and well publicized technological developments in history. This modern tool is having increased impact on individuals, families, groups, organizations, and society as a whole.

Our heritage proclaims the central importance of the individual and the great value of human resources. Nevertheless, we see severe neglect of human resources and find organizations damaging (overtly or covertly) people's morale, health, and productivity.

This book's central premise is that the computer's contribution to society has been considerably hindered by an overly mechanistic approach used by both manufacturers and users of computer systems. Many organizations develop computer products and applications with great attention to technical and economic factors—but with minimal attention to the most important resource: people. Yet these very organizations' leaders continually beat their breasts, and ask the following kinds of questions:

- Why is the computer industry faced with so many critics, Congressional investigations, and disgruntled customers?

- Why can't users of computers fully tap the vast power of the new technology?

- Why can't the computer vendors deliver "debugged" and reliable equipment and software?

- Why can't the computer industry and professional groups simplify the tools and techniques (e.g., programming) for ease of use by human beings?

- Why don't they understand us? (Technocrats ask this question about users—and, of course, users ask the same question about technocrats!)

- Why can't we hire a computer professional that understands our real problems?

- Why do our employees have a sullen attitude about the wondrous computer?

- Why is top management becoming increasingly disenchanted with computers?

The authors place the personnel function and the computer function into perspective. They identify critical computer issues in the personnel function and critical personnel problems in the computer function.

The book is eclectic. It contains a blend of concepts and practices, illustrations from government and business, perspectives on personnel functions and people-related challenges of computer systems, and the dilemmas of both computer vendors and users. The authors' analysis and views are derived from experience and research in more than ninety organizations.

While the central theme of the book is simple—the neglect of the human element in computer systems—the facts indicate that organizations are making precious little effort to correct this shortcoming. This is eroding the potential of one of man's greatest inventions. The reader should not misinterpret the authors' views. They are optimistic and enthusiastic about the potential of the computer—but they confess to some disillusionment with the insensitivity of many people in the computer world.

Part I of the book traces the impact of technology on organizations, human resource challenges, and organizations' personnel problems.

Part II summarizes key facets of the systems approach, information systems, and computers. These are viewed from a humanistic rather than a strictly technical stance.

Part III relates computer systems with human systems. Some of the topics explored include: the computer's impact on the management process, personnel function, training and development, employment, privacy, and the design of personnel systems.

Part IV is a brief epilogue.

After each of Chapters 2 through 13 the authors present,

- A summary.
- A list of key concepts.
- Discussion questions.
- Bibliography.
- Chapter 14 describes three computerized human resource systems.

The discussion questions are segregated for different levels of reader interest, i.e., general background, technical and operational, and policy level. Recommendations for research follow the questions.

A series of short cases are to be found at the ends of Parts I, II, and III. These cases should be of particular interest to faculty and students.

The authors hope that this book will facilitate the attainment of a new generation of computer systems—employing a humanistic approach. The intent is that this work will improve the understanding of computers by administrators and personnel staffs—and instill a more sensitive awareness of the human element in computer systems by computer professionals. *The path to a healthier and more productive environment is through genuine concern and positive acts on behalf of people.*

Edward A. Tomeski

Acknowledgments

The authors would like to express appreciation to the numerous organizations and their staffs that, in some way, contributed to the fact-finding and research which formed a basis for the material presented in this book. The organizations included:

- Businesses: Ford Motor, Chrysler, Mobil Oil, Standard Oil (Indiana), Lockheed Aircraft, Chesapeake and Ohio Railway, International Paper, American Can, Ralston Purina, National Cash Register, Weyerhaeuser, CPC International, Inland Steel, American Airlines, Consolidated Edison, El Paso Natural Gas, and Eastern Air Lines.

- Federal Government: Departments of Agriculture, Commerce, Defense, Housing and Urban Development, Justice, Labor, Post Office, State, and Treasury. Also, the Civil Service Commission was most helpful.

- States: California, New York, Pennsylvania, Illinois, New Jersey, Massachusetts, Virginia, Maryland, Minnesota, Iowa, Colorado, Oregon, Arizona, Utah, New Mexico, Rhode Island, Hawaii, New Hampshire, Delaware, Nevada, Vermont, and Wyoming.

- Counties: Los Angeles, California; Cook, Illinois; Wayne, Michigan; Nassau, New York; San Diego, California; Dade, Florida; Kings, Washington; Erie, New York; Milwaukee, Wisconsin; Hennepin, Minnesota; Westchester, New York; Monroe, New York; San Bernardino, California; Prince Georges, Maryland; and Jackson, Missouri.

- Cities: New York, Los Angeles, Philadelphia, Baltimore, Washington, D.C., Cleveland, San Diego, Memphis, St. Louis, Phoenix, Columbus, Seattle, Denver, Kansas City, Atlanta, Buffalo, Nashville, San Jose, Fort Worth, Newark, Tulsa, Honolulu, El Paso, and Tampa.

- Other: United Nations, Port Authority of New York and New Jersey.

While these organizations participated in the authors' studies, this in no way suggests that they endorse any or all of the authors' analyses, interpretations, conclusions, and recommendations which are presented in this book.

A number of colleagues read various sections of the authors' manuscript at different stages of preparation, and made valuable recommendations. These colleagues are: John M. Capozzola, Willard B. Hansen, and Jose G. Miguel, all of New York University; and George Stephenson of Fordham University. In addition, Susan Kliavkoff, John McLoin, and Robert Hopkins, all of Fordham University, provided technical support by providing advice about related statistical and computer analysis of research data.

One of the authors has had the good fortune to have access to the views, advice, and encouragement of members of the Fordham University community. Among these, particular appreciation is expressed to: Reverend James C. Finlay, President; Dr. Joseph R. Cammarosano, Executive Vice President; Dr. Paul J. Reiss, Vice President for Academic Affairs; Reverend William C. Bier; Reverend Joseph P. Fitzpatrick; Dr. Milton Alexander; Reverend William T. Hogan; Reverend Lorenzo Reed; Dr. Marvin Reznikoff; Dr. Harry Rivlin; and Reverend Robert J. Roth. These stimulating relationships have been sources of insights and ideas about administration, humanism, and the role of technology. Sisters Trinita Flood, O.P., and Jeanne O'Laughlin, of Barry University, were constantly encouraging about my research.

The authors' lives have been enriched by their colleague Sidney Mailick, of New York University, whose humanistic approach to administration is a model for many of the ideas developed in this book.

A number of seminal thought leaders have stimulated the considerable research that forms a bases for much of this book. In particular, the following persons are enthusiastically given recognition: John A. Beckett, Timothy Costello, Peter Drucker, Eli Ginzberg, Arch B. Johnston, William Newman, Titus Podea, Leonard Sayles, Pierre Oury, and Sam Gaynor.

Maria Isabel Marin merits considerable appreciation, for she was gracious and dedicated in handling administrative details as well as most of the voluminous and intricate typing of the early, and most difficult, drafts of the manuscript. Ann Elizabeth Sambataro was of meritorious support in the preparation of later phases of the manuscript's development.

The authors are appreciative of the responsiveness and understanding of Barry Nathan, Editor of Van Nostrand Reinhold, who recognized the need for a computer book with "a human touch," and Ann and Robert Krieger for continuing the book's life.

Last, but indeed not least, the authors are indebted to Carl Heyel who—in special response to "old friendship"—read the complete manuscript and provided invaluable (and often very blunt) recommendations for its improvement. The final manuscript undoubtedly has been considerably improved as a result of his earnest concern for the people who will read this book.

The authors, of course, accept complete responsibility for the book and whatever impediments exist in it.

Edward A. Tomeski

Highland Beach, Florida

Contents

Why Read This Book?   vii

Preface   ix

Acknowledgments   xiii

1. A Crisis in Computers?   1

Preparing Employees for Change   1
Ignorance Level Concerning Computers   3
Need for Improved Communication   4
Computers are Still Too Complex   4
Effect of Computers on Work   5
Limited Use of Computers for Personnel Systems   6
Lack of a "Human Touch" in Systems   6
Social and Ethical Concerns   7
Unproductive Use of the Computer   8
Overdependence on Computers   9
To Humanize the Use of Computers   10
Summary   11

PART I. THE HUMAN SYSTEM   13

2. Organization and Technological Change   15

Objectives of the Chapter   15
Technological Change: A Growing Force   15
Technology and the Computer   18
Problems Posed by Technological Change   19
Coping with Technological Change   21
Computers and Change   26
People and Computer-Induced Change   28
Summary   29
Key Concepts of the Chapter   29
Discussion Questions   30
Bibliography   31

3. Scope of the Human Resource Challenge   33

Objectives of the Chapter   33
National Policy and Attitudes   33
Manpower Goals   38
Pressures for Improved Manpower Planning   39
The Government as Employer   40
Patterns of Manpower Change   41
The United States Economy: Looking Towards the 1990's   43
Need for Manpower Forecasts   45
Summary   46
Key Concepts of the Chapter   46
Discussion Questions   47
Bibliography   48

4. The Emerging Human Resource Function   50

Objectives of the Chapter   50
Emerging Roles for Personnel Departments   50
Change in Employees   53
Impediments of and Opportunities for the Personnel Area   56
Computer Challenges for the Personnel Area   60
Needed: A Results Orientation   61
Manpower Planning   62
Summary   68
Key Concepts of the Chapter   68
Discussion Questions   69
Bibliography   70

Part I. Cases   71

Hemisphere Inc.   71
Rockill-Cotton Machine Company   72
Janus Public Authority   72
High Style Co.   73

PART II. THE COMPUTER SYSTEM   75

5. A Systems Approach to Organization   77

Objectives of the Chapter   77
Concept of the Organization   77
The Administrator's Role   78
The Systems Concept   79
Total Systems and Subsystems   81

Integration of Subsystems   83
Implications of Systems in Organizations   86
The Study, Design, and Implementation of Systems   88
Gaining Acceptance of Change   91
Weaknesses in Existing Computer Systems   94
Summary   96
Key Concepts of the Chapter   97
Discussion Questions   97
Bibliography   98

6. Management Information Systems   100

Objectives of the Chapter   100
Status and Trends of MIS   100
Computer-Based MIS   105
Management Science in MIS   110
Planning and Implementing MIS   112
Future Challenges for MIS   118
Summary   126
Key Concepts of the Chapter   127
Discussion Questions   127
Bibliography   128

7. The Computer in Perspective   130

Objectives of the Chapter   130
The "Age of Computers"   130
Types of Processing Systems   131
History of the Computer   134
The Computer Industry   136
Computer Users   139
Highlights of the Computer   144
Computer Trends   148
2001: A Computer Space Odyssey   151
Problems of the Computer Field   155
Summary   159
Key Concepts of the Chapter   159
Discussion Questions   160
Bibliography   161

Part II. Cases   163

Southeast Research Co.   163
Masters Inc.   164
Stuart University   164

Hammerntong Corporation 165
Middle City 166
Pyramid 167

PART III.   COMPUTER SYSTEMS
SERVING SOCIAL SYSTEMS   169

8.   Impact of Computers on Management and Organizations   171

Objectives of the Chapter 171
The Pros and Cons of Computers 171
Management Responsibilities 174
Humanists' Roles in Computer Systems 176
Computers and Decision-Making 176
How the Computer Affects Management and Organization Structure 179
Summary 185
Key Concepts of the Chapter 186
Discussion Questions 186
Bibliography 187

9.   Use of the Computer in the Personnel Process   190

Objectives of the Chapter 190
Status of Computerization in Personnel 190
Personnel Department Attitudes About Computers 193
Approaches to Computerization of the Personnel Process 195
Selected Examples of Computerized Personnel Applications 199
Effectiveness of Personnel Systems 205
Attaining an Effective Personnel System 206
Summary 208
Key Concepts of the Chapter 208
Discussion Questions 209
Bibliography 210

10.   Use of the Computer for Training and Development   212

Objectives of the Chapter 212
New Challenges for Training and Development 212
Traditional Training Techniques 213
Contemporary Training Techniques 216
Management Games 220
Computer-Assisted Instruction (CAI) 224
Summary 228
Key Concepts of the Chapter 228

Discussion Questions 229
Bibliography 230

11. Social Issues and the Computer 232

Objectives of the Chapter 232
Scope of the Social Challenge 232
Some Dehumanizing Results of Computerization 236
Impact of Computers/Automation on Manpower 238
Technology and Work 239
Occupational Patterns 241
The Computer and Changing Job Patterns 242
Use of the Computer in Manpower Programs 247
Privacy and the Computer 250
The Computer as a Criminal's Tool 253
Summary 254
Key Concepts of the Chapter 255
Discussion Questions 256
Bibliography 256

12. Organizing and Staffing the Computer Department 258

Objectives of the Chapter 258
Organizational Structure for Computers 258
Staffing Challenges 261
Education for Computer Professionals 268
Motivation and the Systems Professional 273
Summary 281
Key Concepts of the Chapter 281
Discussion Questions 282
Bibliography 283

13. Designing the Human Resource Information System 284

Objectives of the Chapter 284
Conduct of a Systems Study 284
Understanding the Present System 286
Determining the Requirement for a System 286
Design of the New System 288
Expectations from a Computerized Personnel System 289
People-Related Effects in All Systems 290
Description of an Employee Information System 293
Different Approaches to Information Systems 299
Summary 309

Key Concepts of the Chapter   309
Discussion Questions   310
Bibliography   310

14. Case Examples: Integrated Human Resource Information Systems   312

Objectives of the Chapter   312
The Human Resource System   312
The Personnel Management and Reporting System   315
Super Personnel   319
Summary   332

Part III. Cases   333

Denver Controls   333
Suburban Bank   334
No-Fail Company   335
Crown Company   336
Carter Products   336

PART IV.   EPILOGUE   339

Subject Index   345

Name Index   347

1

A Crisis in Computers?

. . . the new industrial revolution [computers and cybernetics] is a two-edged sword. It may be used for the benefit of humanity, but only if humanity survives long enough to enter a period in which such a benefit is possible. It may also be used to destroy humanity, and if it is not used intelligently it can go very far in that direction.

Norbert Wiener

When you read about the projected characteristics of a planned new computer, you are almost certain to be bombarded by such claims as:

1. Tremendous computer memory devices, based on exotic new technology, which can store billions or even trillions of items of data.

2. Very rapid computing circuits that permit calculations in nano-seconds (billionths-of-a-second) or pico-seconds (trillionths-of-a-second).

3. Software packages (computer programs) which will quickly solve intricate problems that would take many man-years to solve by non-computer means.

4. Tiny computers that are so cheap and so powerful that they will revolutionize home life and each individual's activities.

This "hardware hypnosis" exists in spite of the fact that most computers are under-utilized and that most users have difficulty in coping even with current computer technology.

Human not technical problems are the major obstacles to more effective computer applications. Yet, it is the human problems that tend to be neglected. Because the computer, one of the foremost technological developments of our time, has often been used with little sensitivity to its impacts on people, it has been resisted by many whose cooperation is needed to realize the full benefits that computerization can bring.

PREPARING EMPLOYEES FOR CHANGE

It is virtually impossible to introduce a computer into an organization without creating change in work flow, positions, and organizational relationships.

However, organizations frequently do not prepare employees for such change; rather, a shock treatment approach is used which creates fear, a sense of inadequacy, and alienation in those affected by the computer.

- A large bank computerized a substantial part of the work of one of its trust departments, but little consideration was given as to how the computerization would affect the department's staff. A high percentage of the employees, who had been performing the same routine tasks for many years, dreaded the uncertainty created by the computer. Rumors began to circulate about the computer's absorbing all of the work of the department and eliminating all jobs. A number of key employees, who actually had not been in jeopardy, sought job opportunities in other organizations. Because no regard had been given to the emotions of the people affected, the company lost a group of heretofore loyal employees.

- A city department introduced on-line data terminals for use by administrators and their staffs. Several months after installation, the data terminals were seldom used and were the object of widespread sarcasm. The intended users had never been guided in the appropriate use of the devices and how they related to their work assignments. Because modern, sophisticated equipment was installed without adequately preparing and training the persons affected, a substantial investment lay idle.

These two examples illustrate the need to prepare employees for change induced by the computer. In this connection, pilot and parallel checkouts of new systems are frequently inadequate, and ideas are poorly conceived and implemented without adequately involving all interested parties.

There is need to achieve a balance between rapid technological change and the capacity *and willingness* of humans to adapt to such change. For this reason, the introduction and use of computer technology should take into account not only the technical and economic factors, but also the social factors.

- One large chemical company brought in a new, sophisticated computer to replace a relatively modest-sized machine with the idea that the new computer power could be used for a "total system"—thereby automating complex inventory-billing-shipping procedures that could be handled only piecemeal on the old computer, and which required a large staff of clerks. The new system looked very impressive in the proposals. However, once in operation, after expenditure of hundreds-of-thousands of dollars, it was discovered that the designers had overlooked a number of critical procedures followed by the clerks. The departments responsible for billing, inventory, and shipping had been involved only peripherally in the discussions leading to decisions regarding the new system. The lack of involvement and enthusiasm of the clerks resulted in silent barriers, including the withholding of information about how exception routines were handled. The result was erroneously functioning computer programs (e.g., a carload of goods shipped to a customer who had ordered a single carton) and damaged relations with customers.

IGNORANCE LEVEL CONCERNING COMPUTERS

Although about thirty years have passed since the modern computer was introduced, a surprising amount of ignorance about computers and their use remains. This ignorance is reflected in a wide range of views: At one extreme is the blanket indictment that computers are ineffectual and the cause of organizational shortcomings (e.g., "Our work is always behind schedule because the computer keeps breaking down!"). At the other extreme is the fear that computers are so powerful that they are about to seize control of the world.

Organizations where billing, issuance of checks, or other data-processing have been incorrect have been known to blame the inanimate computer rather than admit to human errors. The uninformed public readily accepts such indictments of the computer when, in fact, many such errors can be traced to human failures in the systems. The computer is an electronic robot having a high degree of reliability and which obediently follows the commands of humans. Of course, if the human commands and the data fed to the computer are faulty, then "GIGO" (garbage-in, garbage-out) brings with it its inevitable consequences.

- The seriousness of prevailing attitudes is evidenced by the fact that the Association for Computing Machinery (ACM), a prestigious society in the computer field, recently set up an ombudsman mechanism to challenge erroneous publicity about the computer. It is reported that one businessman issued a public statement apologizing to his customers for widespread errors in billing; he attributed the mistakes to the computer of the company. The ombudsman, after investigation, ascertained that the organization did not prepare its bills by computer! Can we assume that the businessman issued a public apology to the computer for his unfounded accusation?

NEED FOR IMPROVED COMMUNICATION

Computer technicians too often lack practical understanding about the organization's objectives and practices. They attempt to apply their technical skills (e.g., flow charting, computer programming, mathematical modelling) in an assumed or idealistic world. At the same time, employees whose work is affected by computer, or whose work could be improved by computer use, are too often unable to participate in planning for computerization because they lack understanding about the computer's power and limitations. This ignorance on both sides compounds existing fear of the computer.

- The operations research department of a petroleum company spent several man-years designing and developing a computerized model of the supply and distribution area. The model, when completed, was considered by the supply and distribution staff to be too theoretical and "blue sky" and not applicable to real-world problems. The operations researchers never perceived the down-to-earth issues that the supply and distribution staff considered to be the heart of the problem. The supply and distribution staff, for their part, could not comprehend the sophisticated mathematical models of the operations researchers. Years of work were largely wasted because of ineffective communication.

- A department manager in a non-profit organization spent several weeks laboriously preparing a statistical report. After her work was almost concluded, she discovered that the basic data were already computerized and that the report could have been prepared in less than an hour by the computer.

COMPUTERS ARE STILL TOO COMPLEX

Despite advances in easier-to-use programming languages and improvements in computer design, the first three generations of computers have, by and large, not yet produced programming languages or equipment that are simple enough for people to understand and use. Considerable training and work experience are still required to gain proficiency in using computers.

- Such computer programming languages as BASIC, COBOL, FORTRAN, PL/1, RPG, PASCAL, APL, and others were introduced with the claim that even laymen would be able to write their own programs to solve their problems. The fact remains that most programs are still written by technicians specializing in computer programming. Programs of any sophistication are often beyond the capability of laymen to understand and develop. Further, constantly evolving new computer features (e.g., direct-access disk storage, remote data terminals, operating systems, multi-programming, multi-processing, virtual memory) have actually added substantial degrees of sophistication and complexity to computer programming. These developments tend to make the computer even more remote and mysterious to the average person.

- In graduate schools of business it is found that many entrants have not previously been adequately trained in the basics of computers. This means that secondary schools, undergraduate colleges, and business organizations (where many students work during the day while attending graduate school at night) are not adequately educating students and employees about the most simple features and techniques of computers.

From the above it would appear that there remains a serious gap between the level of computer proficiency, on the part of people who might avail themselves of computer use, and the level of complexity of computer equipment and programming languages.

EFFECT OF COMPUTERS ON WORK

The computer has been used in such a way that it has frequently increased job boredom. This can reduce employee motivation and cause lowered productivity. Computerized applications often require standardization which demands that humans rigorously adhere to routines and specializations. Computer work is often characterized as a "paperwork production line." Humans are expected to adhere to the pace set by the computer's electronic circuits, colorful blinking lights, rapidly spinning disks, humming punched card readers, and clacking printers.

- In one company, budget analysts who formerly did a complete job of preparing budget forecasts were reduced to almost routinely placing numbers in certain blocks on preprinted forms. The data were then punched by keypunch operators (who, to a large extent, did not understand what they were punching), and finally the computer did all the computations and analysis, and printed the reports. What was formerly a dedicated team effort of proud and enthusiastic employees supplying management with valuable reports, changed to a highly automated, dull, and repetitive activity. Little job satisfaction could be derived by the budget analysts from their new mundane tasks. The interesting work had been absorbed by the computer. Errors crept into the computerized system because of the lack of human involvement and understanding about the computer process.

The displacing and replacing of people by computers and automation must increasingly call for careful planning of retraining, job enrichment, reductions through attrition, transfers and rotation to other parts of the organization, and more.

LIMITED USE OF COMPUTERS FOR PERSONNEL SYSTEMS

The computer is extensively applied in such relatively mechanistic areas as production scheduling, inventory control, accounting records, etc. Very limited and prosaic use is made of the computer in the area of human resource systems. For instance, the authors' research revealed that the personnel function was frequently given the lowest priority for computerization (financially-oriented and operations-oriented applications were generally given highest priorities). Personnel department staffs, in many large organizations, are often more absorbed with paperwork-processing than they are with human contact and human resource development. They have created an image of antiquated and unimaginative departments that neither serve the human needs of employees, nor the human resource planning requirements of top management.

The computer should be used to relieve the paperwork burden of the personnel staff so that they can devote more attention to human problems and improved manpower planning.

LACK OF A "HUMAN TOUCH" IN SYSTEMS

Computer technicians, despite their not having any particular training in human relations, design computer systems that have major impact on people and organizational structure. On the other hand, humanists (psychologists, sociologists, and professional personnel staffs) are rarely involved in planning for and implementation of computer systems. Technical and economic considerations of computers appear to be given highest priority, while social and human considerations are frequently ignored.

- A federal governmental agency spent hundreds-of-thousands of dollars in planning a computer system that would centralize heretofore decentralized work. Only after the planning was completed was it determined that there was almost unanimous and vigorous opposition to such centralization from key officials in the decentralized locations. The opposition was primarily articulated on human-factor grounds: interference with local autonomy, undermining of existing responsibilities and control, displacement of long-time employees, forced standardization and uniformity, etc. The plan to centralize the computer systems was largely tabled in spite of the technical and economic soundness of the proposal. Had specialists in human relations been involved in the systems planning, it is likely that there would have been early recognition of the human barriers to the centralization scheme. Such awareness might have permitted early negotiation with the opponents of centralization and a compromise plan, which could have lessened hostile feelings and saved the considerable time and cost that went into the rejected plan.

SOCIAL AND ETHICAL CONCERNS

The social and ethical responsibilities of organizations are of increasing public concern. In this connection, four questions are related to computerization:

1. What is an organization's social responsibility with respect to job displacement caused by computerization and automation?

Various constraints (e.g., unions, public opinion) increasingly impel organizations to give some consideration to the impact of technological change on employment. Persistent pockets of unemployment and unskilled job applicants make the problem a difficult one to solve. However, the government, educational institutions, and business organizations have a growing awareness that training and retraining in marketable skills must be a continuing process.

2. What responsibilities to society do organizations have regarding "dehumanization"?

The computer appears to be part of the trend towards a dehumanizing industrialized society. This trend is abetted by huge and complex organizations that deal in averages and numerical identifications rather than with individuals and personalized situations.

Relationships and loyalties are often transient. The "cold" computer accentuates this atmosphere with its methodical and rational processing. Aside from the impact on workers, anyone who has received computerized dunnings of any kind is keenly aware of the computer's inhuman persistency. It is difficult for a human being to negotiate, compromise, or bargain with the computer system.

3. Computerized data banks and information systems are often designed and installed without full consideration of the human rights and values of the persons who will be affected. What is an organization's responsibilities to protect the privacy of individuals?

Organizations, including the federal government, have contemplated vast integrated data banks containing comprehensive information about each individual. True, much of these data may already be currently available—but they tend to be in highly decentralized locations and forms. Should such information (e.g., education, medical, military, employment, marital, hospital, welfare, internal revenue service, credit, legal violations) be integrated, there is fear that it would place extremely powerful coercive information in the hands of those controlling the data bank, and that this could lead to a society such as that depicted in Orwell's *1984*. Clearly, consideration must be given to ways of protecting the individual's constitutional rights of privacy.

4. Taking for granted the power of the computer, can unscrupulous persons and organizations use the machine for purposes that are harmful to society?

There have been increasing reports of a variety of crimes that at least partially employed the computer as a tool in the criminal acts. The very characteristics of computers (e.g., rapid processing, electronic records, complexity of programming, mysterious nature) can be used to personal advantage by the person with larceny in mind.

- Wide publicity has recently been given to instances involving employees who have manipulated the computer to personal advantage: banks, insurance companies, and stock brokerage houses have been victims. Some losses have been reported to be in the millions of dollars.

In view of the sophisticated nature of syndicated crime, it would not be surprising to learn that the computer may be part of the mobs' arsenal.

UNPRODUCTIVE USE OF THE COMPUTER

Frequently, there is an image in organizations that computers are busy working around-the-clock to full capacity: control panel lights are blinking, magnetic tape reels are spinning, card readers and printing machines are humming.

Behind the scenes investigations reveal that this image is too often a false facade and that, instead, the following are too often true:

1. Inefficiently designed and programmed computer applications waste considerable portions of expensive computer time.

2. There are not infrequent misuses of the computer by computer personnel. Reruns of sloppily handled work, "make-work" jobs to appear to be busy, and even the processing of contraband jobs (sometimes for an under-the-table fee) are not unknown events in a computer center.

The mysterious nature of computers has long protected the field from conventional check-points and controls. Their productive use is, of course, directly related to the quality and abilities of the computer staff and those who manage the computer facility. There is need for improvement in the training, budgetary control, and management audit of the personnel who manage and instruct the computer.

OVERDEPENDENCE ON COMPUTERS

The computer is an instrument that will provide quantitative analyses of problems. This has created an image of computers as rational (if not infallible) tools to replace irrational and frail human decisions. However, there still must be provision for humans and values in the maze of tools and techniques (e.g., flowcharts, coding, compilers, models) that are applied with intricate precision by computer specialists.

• The National Aeronautic and Space Administration (NASA) has spent millions of dollars for computers and programs that provide for minute control over space flights. Even in these most sophisticated computer systems, there is provision for man to take over the system when some failure reveals itself. This reluctance to become overly dependent on computers has even more pertinence in a social system (e.g., a personnel department) where controlled environments are extremely rare.

While the computer can strengthen rationality, its output must be leavened by human judgment. This should be abundantly apparent when one considers that both the computer program and the data used by the computer are products of humans. Thus, the computer's rationality is only as good as the programs and the data that are fed to it by humans. Further, even if the computer could produce completely rational decisions, it is unlikely that it would be wise to accept such decisions mechanistically. Such "rational" decisions are likely to be ill-suited to the real world with its high degree of uncertainty and change (e.g., it is well known that consumers and workers frequently act irrationally and not rationally). At best, the computer can only *aid* rational analysis, with the formal decision left to humans.

There is still inadequate knowledge and research concerning theory and practice related to information-exchange and decision-making. However, systems experts and social scientists are continually devoting more attention to this subject so that computerized information systems, in the future, will be based upon increasingly sounder premises.

TO HUMANIZE THE USE OF COMPUTERS

Many organizations have experienced and are experiencing severe problems with their computer systems. *The authors' research reveals that such problems are usually not solved by merely expending more money or time on computerization. Instead, an effective computer system is likely to evolve from a more humanistic approach to this highly technical area.* Such an approach means that:

, 1. Continual planning is needed to cope with computer change. Such a self-renewal plan includes provision for organization change (as it affects people) as well as technical and economic factors.

2. Continual education about computer limitations and potential is required to cope with this dynamic field. Employers, educational institutions, and computer manufacturers should take a greater coordinating role in this area. Such educational and training efforts should cover human factors as well as technical considerations.

3. More attention to the human element is needed when computer equipment and software are designed. Computer users have been somewhat effective in banding together to place pressure on the computer vendors to deliver faster and more powerful equipment and more versatile programming languages. The computer users and manufacturers have done little to attain such desirable objectives as: simple and utilitarian programming languages, systems techniques that take into account human factors as well as inanimate elements, computer applications designed with human needs and values in mind, and a code of ethics which guides the computer field.

4. The enrichment of jobs and organizational environments should be considered when planning systems for the computer.

5. The computer should be used imaginatively to improve systems dealing with human resources, so as to free personnel staffs for contact with employees.

6. Professionals with human relations skills should be part of the systems team effort, along with computer technicians, when planning and implementing computer applications.

7. Management should be continuously concerned about the quality of computer staffs and the degree of management control exercised over the computer department.

8. Managerial attention should be directed to the social and ethical responsibility issues that are related to computers.

9. Organizations should not have blind confidence in the rationality or output of computers, but should view them as potentially powerful adjuncts to *human* decision-making.

SUMMARY

The great computer issues of the day are not those of computer technology. The critical issues revolve around people and social considerations, such as: displacement of people by computerization and automation, dehumanizing people and organizational environments by twisting them to conform to arbitrary mechanistic concepts and tools, data banks which invade the individual's right to privacy, and the use of the computer for criminal purposes. Computer professionals have rarely constructively faced these issues—either ignoring them or denying their validity. As a result, computers have tended to be far less useful than they could be.

It is largely because the computer vendors and users have poorly handled the human aspect of computers that the computer is so often maligned, is the object of so many derisive jokes, and fails to attain the great promises predicted for it. Computer specialists must learn that the computer must truly *serve people* and not merely *be served* by people.

If the computer field is to become socially responsive, it needs to become more completely humanized. This means a "new generation"—if not of computers, then of computer usage—which places people first and technology second. Up to this point, it is apparent that technology has been given priority over humans.

The next chapter traces the impact of technology, with emphasis on the computer, on organizations and people and suggests more positive responses to the change resulting from technological developments.°

° Chapter 1 was adapted from the authors' article, "A Humanized Approach to Computers," which appeared in *Computers and Automation*, June 1973 (copyright 1973 by and published by Berkeley Enterprises, Inc., 815 Washington St., Newtonville, Massachusetts 02160).

BIBLIOGRAPHY

Tomeski, Edward A. "Building Human Factors Into Computer Applications," Management Datamatics, Volume 4, 1975, pp. 115-120.

———. "The Computer Industry's Social Responsibilities," Computers and People, May 1975, pp. 13-15.

———, George Stephenson, and B. Man Yoon. "Behavioral Issues and the computer." Personnel, July-August 1978, pp. 66-74.

PART 1
THE HUMAN
SYSTEM

This part of the book places the human system of organizations in perspective.

Chapter 2. *Organization and Technological Change* relates technological developments, such as the computer, to human beings in organizations.

Chapter 3. *Scope of the Human Resource Challenge* presents a socio-economic overview of attitudes and policies concerned with the nation's human resources.

Chapter 4. *The Emerging Human Resource Function* analyzes current strengths and weaknesses in personnel departments, and anticipates some broad trends which are reshaping the potential of this function in organizations.

In sum, Part I *establishes a base about human systems which identifies the opportunity areas and challenges for individuals and organizations interested in more people-oriented computer systems.*

2

Organization and Technological Change

In a modern industrialized society, particularly, there are a number of pressures that conspire toward this result [technological change]. First, economic pressures argue for the greater efficiency implicit in a new technology. The principal example of this is the continuing process of capital modernization in industry. Second, there are political pressures that seek the greater absolute effectiveness of a new technology, as in our latest weapons, for example. Third, we turn more and more to the promise of new technology for help in dealing with our social problems. Fourth, there is the spur to action inherent in the mere availability of a technology; space vehicles spawn moon programs. Finally, political and industrial interests engaged in developing a new technology have the vested interest and powerful means needed to urge its adoption and widespread use irrespective of social utility.

Emmanuel G. Mesthene

OBJECTIVES OF THE CHAPTER

This chapter relates technological developments with organizations and the people in organizations. The change caused by the computer, one of the more dramatic of modern technologies, is identified. The challenges of such change are explored and the authors' suggestions about coping with computer-induced change are presented.

TECHNOLOGICAL CHANGE: A GROWING FORCE

There has been more technological change in the last several decades than during the previous recorded history of man. It appears unlikely that such change will significantly subside in the future. Figure 2-1 shows the increasing proportion of the nation's Gross National Product (GNP) that has been allotted to research and development which largely determines the frequency and magnitude of technological developments. In the 1980's the growth rate of R&D has moderated, and some experts attribute economic problems to this development.

Technologies may be defined as bodies of skills, knowledge, and procedures for making, utilizing, and doing useful things. Technology concerns itself primarily with techniques related to physical processes, in contrast to social

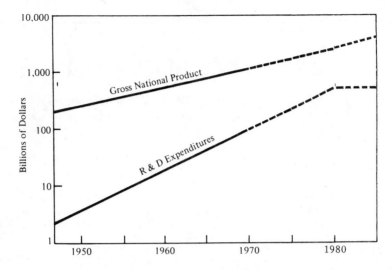

Figure 2-1 **Research and development expenditures.**

and psychological processes. Further, technology is distinguished from science, which strives for acquisition of knowledge. Technology attempts to apply knowledge to meaningful tasks.

Drucker has delineated the nature of modern technology as follows:

> Technological activity during the twentieth century has changed in its structure, methods, and scope. It is this qualitative change which explains even more than the tremendous rise in the volume of work the emergence of technology in the twentieth century as central in war and peace, and its ability within a few short decades to remake man's way of life all over the globe.

> This overall change in the nature of technological work during this century has three separate though closely related aspects: (1) structural changes—the professionalization, specialization, and institutionalization of technological work; (2) changes in methods—the new relationship between technology and science; the emergence of systematic research; and the new concept of innovation; and (3) the 'systems approach'. Each of these is an aspect of the same fundamental trend. Technology has become what it never was before: an organized and systematic discipline.[1]

Advancing technology is, of course, a response to the needs of an evolving, complex society: higher educational levels and generally rising affluence create new and ever-increasing consumer demands. To satisfy this demand, the industrial structure calls for increasing mechanization of production, distribution, and control.

But technology is not only a response to societal change, it is itself a cause of change: need we mention the effect of the automobile on life-style, place of abode, sexual mores, retailing, and physical distribution—or the effect of television on entertainment, news dissemination, general sophistication, and even the "growth culture"? In business and institutional organizations the emergence of technological change has seen the concurrent growth of a new breed of technical personnel (change agents) constituting what Galbraith refers to as the "technostructure." He suggests that such technocrats may become the locus of organization intelligence, decision-making and power.[2] In any event, if we develop a better educated managerial resource capable of coping with more sophisticated techniques, the demand for technology will increase. At the same time, the new technological patterns necessitate a better educated manager able to understand the increasing complexity.

Many of the resultant changes involve major steps, are novel and unpredictable, and collide with established patterns familiar to people and organizations. Technological change thus is a determinant of the human input required by an organization, features of organizational structure and procedure, and individual and group work design.

Several related cases illustrate the impact of technological change on people and organizations:

- Not many years ago, when one visited an oil refinery there was an impressive amount of human activity. A corps of technicians, engineers, and workmen was required to operate and maintain the complex of storage tanks, pipes, valves, gauges, etc. Today, modern refineries are largely under the governance of automatic control devices connected to computers, and are almost eerily devoid of humans.

- The instrumentation and automatic flight controls of the multimillion dollar super jet planes can be entrusted only to pilots with superior training and competence. Many pilots of propeller driven aircraft have not qualified to handle jet planes. But even with the newer breed of pilots, the larger aircraft use computers to provide automated supplement to the pilot and navigator.

- The automobile industry has been a pioneer in automation and the production line, and has mass produced one of the major modes of transportation. However, two unresolved conditions are causing significant problems for the industry. One is the frequent discovery of dangerous flaws in the automobile product after it is in the hands of the consumer, thereby causing expensive recalls. A second problem is the discontent of workers assigned to repetitive tasks paced by the assembly line, as dramatized by the well publicized strike at Chevrolet's Lordstown, Ohio, plant.

TECHNOLOGY AND THE COMPUTER

Herbert Simon views the computer as the fourth greatest breakthrough in history to aid man in his thinking process and decision-making ability.[3] The first was the development of writing, which aided man's memory in recording events and ideas. The other two events prior to the computer were the emergence of the Arabic numeral system and its zero and positional notation, and the invention of analytical geometry and calculus which permitted the solution of complex problems. The modern computer combines the advantages and attributes of all these breakthroughs, along with the feature of very rapid speed; it is inevitable that such a major technological development would have profound implications for society.

Montagu and Snyder identify the computer as one of seven major technological revolutions in the history of man's social development.

1. Discovery and development of toolmaking.
2. Emergence of hunting as a way of life.
3. Discovery and use of fire.
4. Emergence of agriculture and pastoralism.
5. Development of cities and urban civilization.
6. The eighteenth century industrial revolution.
7. Development of the computer.[4]

In less than three decades, the computer has had a pervasive impact on society. There are few workers, managers, professional persons, or citizens who are not either directly or indirectly affected by computers. Some of the areas and types of uses of the computer are:

- Statements, bills, and checks are printed.

- Accounting records are maintained.

- Mathematical analyses, of many kinds, are performed.

- Reservations (e.g., airlines, hotels, entertainment) are confirmed and kept up-to-date.

- Credit status and ratings are instantaneously made available.

- Medical records, diagnostics, and patient monitoring are aided.

- Income tax returns are statistically audited.

- Direct mail advertising is channeled to customers and potential customers.

- Inventory levels are maintained at appropriate levels.

- Air traffic control, at busy airports, is facilitated.

- Law enforcement is strengthened by rapid availability of data about crimes and criminal records.

The variety of uses of the computer is almost endless. Any activity with an informational, mathematical, data processing, or communications nature is feasible for the computer to handle.

PROBLEMS POSED BY TECHNOLOGICAL CHANGE

We are reaching a state now in man's knowledge when the quantity of information being generated in industry, in government, and in the academic world is reaching alarming proportions. The sum total of human knowledge changed very slowly prior to the relatively recent beginnings of scientific thought. It has been estimated that by 1800 it was doubling every fifty years; by 1950, doubling every ten years; and that presently it is doubling every five years!

Ideally, organizations are dynamic systems, internally adjusting and adapting as external conditions and circumstances change. However, the acceleration of technological change has reached a point where it is difficult for organizations to assimilate developments. Besides the difficulty in absorbing the sheer volume of technological change, there are many other immediate and urgent considerations. It is a common experience that organizations and people tend to adhere to established systems and to resist new systems. There is usually a mixed reaction to change, and difficulty in obtaining consensus about it among members of an organization. Established systems are known factors, while new systems are unknown and pose the threat of the unknown. On the other hand, stability encourages stagnation and obsolescence while change, although necessitating adjustment, has the effect of increasing the viability of the organization in dealing with its environment. Argyris has described, in vivid terms, the danger of organizational rigidity:

> The older and more complex organizations in our society—business firms, governmental bureaus, city governments, labor unions, churches, hospitals, schools, and universities—appear to be deteriorating. With every passing day, the human and material costs of providing a product or service seem to be going up, while the resulting quality is either wavering or going down. Organizations are becoming

increasingly rigid and difficult to change; it is almost impossible to induce them to re-examine and renew themselves.[5]

The following statistics indicate the significant upheavals that indeed do take place among organizations.

Of the 20 largest companies in the United States 40 years ago, only 2 are still among the first 20 in size. Of the 100 largest companies 25 years ago, almost 50 per cent either do not exist today or have substantially declined in size.[6]

The interaction between technological change and organizational change is complex and multifaceted. As a result of varying rates of response, technology can produce major changes in some organizations, while organizational constraints will in other instances result in minimal adoption of technology or, indeed, in blockage of uses of technology. In the short run, the nature of social organization is an important determinant of what and how much technology is developed. In the longer run, the effects of technological change on organizations are more profound. Directly or indirectly, a technological change produces alterations in particular organizations, in the general economy, in the political structure of society, and derivatively, in culture and life style.

Technologies have unforeseen consequences since they generate new choices and therefore affect the ordering and intensity of preferences and values. Rapid changes necessitate greater flexibility in values and attitudes; this fluidity can create a sense of alienation. To cope with the loss of the stable state, organizations must evolve into learning systems capable of generating continual self-renewal and adaptation to change. There is apparent need for improved organization and individual response to the evolving technological developments. Toffler indicates the need for balance between rapid change and the limited pace of human response, and emphasizes that "future shock grows out of the increasing lag between the two." [7]

The down-to-earth nature of technological change and its impact on people is dramatized by a simple discussion between a supervisor and an employee.

> The department was increasingly using the computer to process its work. Each employee was exposed to some training so as to orient the staff about how computerization would affect their work.
>
> After the training, an employee said to his supervisor: "I can't understand the computer, no matter how hard I try. It is an instrument for evil. It just makes our work more complicated, particularly for minority people without higher education. The computer is just another

example of making work so technical that the poor people are left even further behind the rich people. Not only that, but the computer has done away with the swell work-group that we had developed in the department. It won't be the same again."

COPING WITH TECHNOLOGICAL CHANGE

There is need for a continuing planned approach to change. This includes providing evaluation and justification of the worth of the planned change. Unplanned change can cause stress and breakdowns; a gradual introduction of technological change seems to be required so that people can make the necessary personal adjustments.

One theory is that change, whether it is for good or bad, is stressful to the biological organism and makes it more susceptible to the onslaught of illness and disease. Some of the personal stresses of adjusting to change are listed in rank order (from that with most stress to that of less stress): fired at work, retirement, business readjustment, change in financial state, change to different line of work, change in responsibilities at work, outstanding personal achievement, begin or end school, change in living conditions, revision of personal habits, trouble with boss, change in work hours or conditions, change in residence, and others.[8]

Some of the methods for bringing about organizational change include: the use of information, skills training, individual counseling and therapy, the influence of the peer group, sensitivity training, group therapy, feedback on organizational functioning, and direct structural or system alteration. The primary target of change may be the individual, the interpersonal relationships between members of groups, the norms of groups, the interpersonal relationships between members of an organization, the structure of a role, the role relationship, or the structure of the organization as a whole. The difficulty with many attempts at organizational change is that the changers have not clearly distinguished their targets.

There are three basic considerations in planning organizational change:

1. Deciding when it is appropriate or necessary to make a change.
2. Deciding what has to be changed—blueprinting the desired future state of the organization.
3. Deciding how to implement the change—solving both technical and motivational problems.

People will often evaluate a technological change based on whether it is personally advantageous or disadvantageous and not on its operating merits. Recognizing the vital aspect of acceptance of change by those affected, the advocates of the behavioral approach contend that organization change is

"You might know they'd use it to replace the only three eligible bachelors in the place!"

best achieved by influencing the values, attitudes, and beliefs of people. A summary of some of the major points made by behavioral scientists follows:

1. *Bureaucratic Organization.* The widely prevalent bureaucracy (variously referred to as authoritarian, closed systems, "Theory X") is relatively unable to cope with change because of its rigidity and adherence to historical legalism, its hierarchal, formal organization structure, and its rational-mechanistic viewpoint. Under this concept, people are viewed as irresponsible: shirking work, responsive primarily to financial rewards and penalties, and needing close direction. To effect change in this traditional bureaucratic world, those in authority, with expert knowledge, plan the needed changes and specify the modifications required in work content, staffing, and structure. It is assumed that those under their authority will then make the necessary adaptations that are decreed.

2. *Organic Organization.* The organic organization (variously called participative, problem solving, democratic, open system, "Theory Y") provides greater organizational flexibility, commitment, responsibility, and effectiveness in adapting to the environment. In such an organization the people are assumed to be responsible, committed, and productive, and to desire a world in which feelings and interpersonal relationship are valued as highly as technology.

The organic organization approach to change involves a continuous, participative environment in which change is discussed, and interpersonal communication is high. Change is effected through development, understanding, consensus, and acceptance. It is interesting to note that McLuhan depicts electronic technology (including the computer) as an "implosive" force with rapid communication which brings people into closer harmony with environment.[9] This insight would seem to indicate that electronic technology has the potential to be a positive force consistent with the theory of the organic organization.

Figure 2-2 summarizes some of the implications discussed above. The bureaucratic organization has certain characteristics (rigidity, formality, departmentalization, authoritarian leadership, etc.) which tend to be barriers to change. Consequently, such organizations are probably not environments that will be receptive to the dynamic developments of systems and computers. On the other hand, the organic organization's characteristics (e.g., flexibility, process orientation, participative climate, etc.) make such entities more adaptable to change. As a consequence, organic-type organizations are probably more suited to absorb the developments of systems and computers and to gain maximum benefits from them.

Within an organic organization, there will be need for a new type of leadership that can create a conducive environment for both human and

Type of Organization	Characteristics	Reactions to Change	Implications for Computerization
Bureaucracy	• Rigidity • Formality • Departmentalized • Authoritarian • Imposed standards • Adherence to rules • Goals set by a few individuals • Rational man assumptions • Sanctions imposed	• Resists change • Slow to adjust to change • Difficulty in corresponding with environment	• Systems are likely to be unprogressive • Systems tend to perpetuate existing patterns • Computer use is likely to result in relatively marginal benefits
Organic	• Flexibility • Informality • Processes • Participative • Self-imposed standards • Personal initiative • Collective goals • Humanism • Motivation	• Adjustable to change • Induces desirable change • Easily corresponds with environment	• Modern, integrated systems are feasible • Dynamic systems tend to induce related changes in the organization • Computer use is prone to result in relatively significant benefits

Figure 2-2 A paradigm of organization type and implications for computerization.

FIRM OF TODAY	FIRM OF THE FUTURE

Archetype Requirements

Leader	Leader
Administrator-planner	Administrative planner
Entrepreneur	Extrapolative planner
	Entrepreneur
	Statesman
	System architect

Timing Priorities Among Archetype Needs

Sequential	Simultaneous

Contents of Decisions

Operating issues, corporate policies	Strategy formulation, design of systems for strategy implementation
Exploitation of firm's current position	Innovation in patterns of firm's products, markets, and technology
Economic, technological, national, intra-industry perspective	Economic, socio-political, technological, multinational, multi-industry perspective

Decision Process

Emphasis on historical experience, judgment, past programs for solving familiar problems	Emphasis on anticipation, rational analysis, pervasive use of specialist experts, techniques for coping with novel decision situations
Personnel-intensive process	Technology-intensive process

Information for Decisions

Formal information systems for internal performance history	Formal systems for anticipatory, external environment information
One way, top down, flow of information	Interactive, two-way communication channels linking managers and other professionals with knowledge workers
Computer systems emphasizing volume and fast response information for general management	Computer systems emphasizing richness, flexibility, and accessibility of information for general management
Emphasis on periodic operations plans, capital and operating expenditure budgets	Emphasis on continuous planning, covering operations, projects, systems resource development. Control based on cost benefits forecasts

Organizational Design Criteria

Continuous emphasis on efficiency, productivity in utilizing current resources and organization. Periodic emphasis on innovation in product-market patterns, technologies	Simultaneous, continuous emphasis on efficiency, productivity, and innovation
Emphasis on economies of scale	Emphasis on flexible, adaptive response
Emphasis on best assignment of task within given organizational structure	Emphasis on best design of an *ad hoc* organization to perform a given task

Figure 2-3 The changing characteristics of general management. (H. Igor Ansoff and G. Brandenburg, "The General Manager of the Future," *California Management Review*, Spring 1969, p. 69.)

technological factors. Figure 2-3 depicts the changing characteristics of the manager. It is envisioned that there will be a growing need for "multi-managers" with simultaneous competence as leaders, administrators, entrepreneurs, statesmen, planners, and systems architects. Are our colleges and universities, and businesses capable of educating and training the needed quantity and quality of such managers?

COMPUTERS AND CHANGE*

Below are listed some speculations about the kinds of change that have been and will increasingly be caused by computer technology:

Impact on Organization Structure

1. *Shift in Managerial Productivity.* As the computer is used more widely as an aid to administrators, it improves coordination of activities and allows the manager to widen and extend their reach.

2. *Consolidation and Shrinkage.* The absorption of work by the computer results in reduced human labor. In any given assignment, an increasing percentage will be computerized, and a decreasing percentage will be handled by humans.

3. *Reduction of Levels.* The number of levels in the organization's hierarchal structure may diminish as a consequence of the computer absorbing certain data processing tasks and routine decision-making.

4. *Reduction of Span-of-Control.* The number of individuals reporting to a supervisor may be affected by computer use. This appears to be situational—in some cases there is an increase of span-of-control while in other instances there is a decrease.

5. *Changes in Departmentation.* There is little question that computer systems cause rearrangements in organization structure.

6. *Centralization.* There seems to be support that computers encourage centralization; that is, they tend to result in concentration of information and organizational control. The computer department absorbs the data and information of multitudinous units, making such intelligence available at one location rather than at scattered points. A contra-development has been distributed data processing which has encouraged the decentralization of computer resources and utilization. In most sophisticated organizations there is some degree of central computer control with considerable decentralization of computer access in the work areas of the organization.

7. *Lateral Shifts.* There is some movement away from traditional functional departments toward new ones of general, broader, and integrative scope (e.g.,

---

* For an excellent source on this material, refer to Thomas L. Whisler, *Information Technology and Organizational Change* (Belmont, California: Wadsworth Publishing Company, Inc., 1970).

administrative services, corporate planning, systems and computers).

8. *Machine Control.* The computer extends the controlling power of man over physical processes and other organizational activities. Computer control car be continuous, with automatic modifications of operations.

Impact on Tasks and People

1. *Individual's Discretion.* Computer technology may tend to make many jobs more routine. There is reduced control by the individual over the timing and approach to his or her work. The human becomes an extension of the computer which requires the discipline of routinized performance. On the other hand, some individuals' responsibilities may be enlarged, as a consequence of having to understand computer systems and take part in their use.

2. *Interaction With Others.* Computer systems tend to require people to communicate more effectively and quickly, since an individual's work increasingly will affect others. Also, there will be more man-to-machine communication causing a relative reduction in the amount of man-to-man communication.

3. *Enrichment of Managerial Task Content.* Computer systems are absorbing much of the computational tasks and routine decision-making. A manager's time will be more greatly devoted to goal setting, pattern perception, and human contact.

4. *Changes in Skills.* The computer will absorb a large part of the routinized clerical jobs and, consequently, will require upgrading of the clerical skills that remain. Since computer systems require precision, greater reliability in human performance is necessary. Entirely new occupational skills have already evolved (e.g., systems analyst, computer programmer, management scientist). Additionally, there is need for a substantial number of people who understand computer technology to communicate with the computer specialists.

5. *Psychological Impacts.* What people cannot understand and/or control causes anxiety and related uneasiness, fear, and indifference.

The numerous organizations with which the authors have had contact give relatively minor attention, during computer planning, to organization and work changes. Such attention that is devoted to change more typically comes after-the-fact, when the computer is operational. As a consequence, computer systems frequently result in unexpected and unnecessary disruptions in organization structure and work environments.

- A billion dollar conglomerate prepared a computer feasibility report. The analysis was almost completely devoted to the technical and economic considerations related to upgrading the organization's existing computer system. During the feasibility study, which lasted about six months, the computer technicians did not coordinate with the personnel department. The work of many units of the company would ultimately be affected by the computer system which was proposed; yet those units provided only minimal input into the feasibility study.

- A county government installed a modern management information system which utilized powerful computers. The key civil servants, having tenure, ignored the new reporting system—and continued to use the old, traditional reports. The county was forced to maintain both the new and the old reporting systems. Considerable hostility developed between the technocrats promoting the computerized information system and the bureaucrats supporting continuation of traditional methods.

PEOPLE AND COMPUTER-INDUCED CHANGE

An example of the way the computer tends to modify organizational work patterns and relationships among people is the drastically shorter time in which information can now be made available. On the other hand, in non-computerized systems, data are often historical and may be a month or more old before it is available. Like the jet aircraft, the computer can tend to disorient human beings' perception of time. People have difficulty in physically and psychologically adjusting to rapid movement in space and time. Real-time information systems, which report results simultaneously with the occurrence of an event, encourage quick responses by humans.

Additionally, the application of computers encourages a process or systems approach. The systems approach (discussed in Chapter 5) entails horizontal and vertical integration of data and information while, traditionally, organizations are compartmentalized by functions and divisions. Integration tends to draw together formerly uncoordinated units, and encourages looking at problems from an organizational viewpoint rather than from a departmental viewpoint. Under the systems approach, traditional relationships and loyalties are bound to be affected.

There is growing concern that while we have advanced technological systems, we are unprogressive when dealing with human systems. Fromm, for example, asks:

> Must we produce sick people in order to have a healthy economy, or can we use our material resources, our inventions, our computers to serve the ends of man? Must individuals be passive and dependent in order to have strong and well-functioning organizations? [10]

Computer equipment is manufactured and used with a primary focus on technical factors. This overemphasis on the technical tends to create an indifference towards human factors (an irreverence for man and life). If man feels ignored or helpless, he develops pathological symptoms such as anxiety, depression, depersonalization, and even violence.

> . . . ultimately, psychological pollution precipitated by arbitrary and unthinking leadership action will become unacceptable and subject to compensation just as physical pollution and contamination are now subject to compensation. Weighing the impact of one's decisions on people's psychological attachments, therefore, becomes not merely a do-gooder interest. It is also an important matter of self-interest.[11]

The computer field, vendors and users, have neglected consideration of the very real costs of change. As a consequence, it is little wonder that the installation of new computer systems is often accompanied by unexpected problems and difficulty in attaining the benefits predicted.

SUMMARY

Technological change is a vital force affecting people, organizations, and society. The computer is one of the main facets of technological change.

Organizations have experienced considerable difficulty in ingesting and beneficially using this technology. Problems arise due to an imbalance between technological capacity and human adjustment.

We need a planned approach to cope with technological change, rather than the prevalent approach of *ad hoc* attempts to respond to unexpected developments.

There are indications that the widely prevalent bureaucratic approach to organization structure impedes adjustment to change, whereas the adoption of organic organization structures may facilitate absorption of such change. The computer, when used in organic organizational settings, can actually improve communications, increase self-actualization, and align individual and organization goals. This is possible since the computer can process and supply information as needed and accurately. It can interact with the individual, and satisfy the information needs of diverse users.

Both computer vendors and users have not given adequate attention to the human factors related to computer technology.

Chapter 3, which follows, presents an over-view of the macro human resource challenges in the United States.

KEY CONCEPTS OF THE CHAPTER

1. Technology is both a cause and effect of change in organizations and the work of people.

2. . The computer, one of the foremost of modern technologies, is a significant variable in organization structures and work environments.

3. Change can be the source of stress and breakdown for organizations and individuals. This is particularly true if the change is unplanned and places excessive demands on those involved.

4. Organic organizations (as defined in the chapter) can more effectively absorb change than can traditional bureaucratic organizations.

5. Computer and personnel staffs do not give adequate attention to computer-induced changes, and how they affect people, when planning for and installing computer systems.

DISCUSSION QUESTIONS

General Background (Seminar/Classroom Discussion)

1. Define what is meant by technological change.
2. Identify how technology has been affecting your life (at home, in school, at work).
3. Describe a specific technological development (other than computers) that has caused revolutionary change in a major industry.

Operational and Technical

1. Identify changes to the work environment and organization structure that have resulted from a recent computer project in your company.
2. How might computer planning anticipate probable changes in jobs and organization structure? Attempt such planning in connection with a current or future computer project.

Policy

1. Does your organization plan for change? What benefits can be derived from such planning?
2. Is your organization closer to the bureaucratic or organic model described in the chapter? What policies and procedures would be required to transform a bureaucratic-type organization to an organic-type organization?

Areas for Research

1. Determine the trend of expenditures for research and development (R & D) in your organization. How does the trend compare with industry and national trends? What is the relationship, in your opinion, between R & D and technological change?
2. In anticipation of a fourth and fifth generation of computers, what technological breakthroughs are possible and what impact are they likely to have on data processing, information retrieval, scientific computations, decision-making, etc.? How will such events affect workers, professional staff, and managers?

3. Develop a comparative analysis of technological change in several nations. For instance, determine the percentage of Gross National Product that is allocated to R & D in the United States, Japan, Brazil, Egypt, Israel, and India. Discuss the significance of the differing emphasis on R & D in those nations.
4. Refer to some of the writings of sociologists and psychologists (e.g., Katz and Kahn, Fromm, Maslow, Skinner, Parsons). What are some of their differing views about effectively introducing change in social systems, and solving problems caused by individuals' reactions against change?

BIBLIOGRAPHY

Argyris, Chris. *Intervention Theory and Method.* Reading, Massachusetts: Addison-Wesley Publishing Company, 1970.

Bennis, Warren. *Changing Organizations.* New York: McGraw-Hill Book Co., 1966.

Boguslaw, Robert. *The New Utopians.* Englewood Cliffs, New Jersey: Prentice Hall, Inc., 1965.

Drucker, Peter F. *Technology, Management & Society.* New York: Harper & Row Publishers, Inc., 1970.

Fromm, Erich. *The Revolution of Hope.* New York: Bantam Books, Inc., 1968.

Galbraith, John Kenneth. *The New Industrial State.* Boston: Houghton Mifflin Co., 1967.

Kahn, Herman and Anthony J. Wiener. *The Year 2000.* New York: The Macmillan Company, 1967.

Katz, Daniel and Robert L. Kahn. *The Social Psychology of Organizations.* New York: John Wiley & Sons, Inc., 1966.

Likert, Rensis. *New Patterns of Management.* New York: McGraw-Hill Book Co., 1961.

Maslow, Abraham, H. *Eupsychian Management.* Homewood, Illinois: Richard D. Irwin, Inc. 1965.

McClelland, David C. and David G. Winter. *Motivating Economic Achievement.* New York: The Free Press, 1969.

McGregor, Douglas. *The Professional Manager.* New York: McGraw-Hill Book Co., 1967.

McLuhan, Marshall. *Understanding Media: The Extensions of Man.* New York: The New American Library, Inc., 1966.

Montagu, Ashley and Samuel S. Snyder. *Man and the Computer.* Philadelphia: Auerbach Publishers, Inc., 1972.

Mumford, Luis and Sackman. *Human Choice and Computers.* New York: North Holland Publishing Company, 1975.

Simon, Herbert A. *The New Science of Management Decision.* New York: Harper & Row Publishers, Inc., 1960.

Toffler, Alvin. *Future Shock.* New York: Bantam Books, Inc., 1971.

Tomeski, Edward A. *The Computer Revolution.* New York: The Macmillan Company, 1970.

Whisler, Thomas L. *Information Technology and Organizational Change.* Belmont, California: Wadsworth Publishing Company, Inc., 1970.

FOOTNOTES

[1] Peter F. Drucker, *Technology, Management & Society* (New York: Harper & Row Publishers, Inc., 1970), p. 55.

[2] John Kenneth Galbraith, *The New Industrial State* (Boston: Houghton Mifflin Co., 1967), p. 71.

[3] Herbert A. Simon, *The New Science of Management Decision* (New York: Harper & Row Publishers, Inc., 1960), p. 34.

[4] Ashley Montagu and Samuel S. Snyder, *Man and the Computer* (Philadelphia: Auerbach Publishers Inc., 1972), p. 19.

[5] Chris Argyris, *Intervention Theory and Method* (Reading, Massachusetts: Addison-Wesley Publishing Company, 1970), p. 1.

[6] L. A. Allen, *The Management Process* (New York: McGraw-Hill Book Co., 1964).

[7] Alvin Toffler, *Future Shock* (New York: Bantam Books, Inc., 1971), pp. 3–4.

[8] "Doctors Study Treating Ills Brought On By Stress," *New York Times,* June 10, 1973, p. 20.

[9] Marshall McLuhan, *Understanding Media: The Extensions of Man* (New York: The New American Library, Inc., 1966), pp. 303–311.

[10] Erich Fromm, *The Revolution of Hope* (New York: Bantam Books, Inc., 1968), p. 2.

[11] Harry Levinson, "Easing the Pain of Personal Loss," *Harvard Business Review,* September–October 1972, pp. 80–88.

3

Scope of the Human Resource Challenge

Manpower is the basic resource. It is the indispensable means of converting resources to mankind's use and benefit. How well we develop and employ human skills is fundamental in deciding how much we will accomplish as a nation.

The manner in which we do so will, moreover, profoundly determine the kind of nation we become.

John Fitzgerald Kennedy

OBJECTIVES OF THE CHAPTER

This chapter presents a macro-view of the nation's human resources. The dynamics of our economy and employment are traced and forecasted. A broad understanding of manpower challenges is essential for an organization's personnel function to plan meaningfully for its own manning needs. Computer technicians, involved in developing personnel systems, require an appreciation of the macro-aspects of the manpower situation.

NATIONAL POLICY AND ATTITUDES

There is growing national awareness of the vital issues related to the employment of people in satisfactory numbers and in work that is consistent with human dignity and socially accepted goals. While in the past we have recognized that human resources are a nation's and organization's most valuable asset, there has been a paradoxical lack of definitive programs to cope with the related problems of unemployment, skills obsolescence, and arbitrary barriers to employment.

Two relatively recent landmark laws are relevant. First, the Employment Act of 1946 recognized the responsibility of the federal government to maintain a high level of employment. Second, the Manpower Development and Training Act of 1962 provided for logistical studies of manpower that will help the nation determine the needs and the priorities required to meet them.

Low unemployment rates and price stability have been a goal of U.S. economic policy and will remain a policy objective in the future. Fiscal and monetary policies remain principal instruments for this task. Manpower policy is an important complement. A quicker adaptation of the labor force to growing and changing needs of production is one way to relieve inflationary pressures and, at the same time, minimize unemployment. Still, the nation has experienced uncomfortable periods of extreme shortages of qualified people, as well as periods of unemployment in both unskilled and skilled categories. This seems to suggest that the nation's existing manpower institutions and practices are not yet able to maintain a desirable balance, consistent with national goals, between the supply of human resources and the demand in the labor market.

- A few years ago there was substantial effort, encouraged by the government, to increase the supply of college trained teachers and engineers. The colleges and universities responded to this apparent need. Changes in national priorities (e.g., end of Vietnam involvement, reduction of space program) and population patterns have lessened the demand for teachers and engineers. As a result, there is personal hardship for those unable to use their talents, and a waste of national resources.

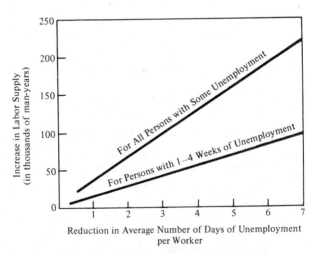

Figure 3-1 Impact of reduced unemployment. (Adapted from *Manpower Report of the President*, Washington, D.C.: U.S. Department of Labor, 1970, p. 9.)

An interesting relationship between the supply of manpower and duration of unemployment is shown in Figure 3-1. For example, if it had been possible in 1968 to reduce the duration of unemployment by one week for all workers unemployed during the year, the effective increase in man-years of employment would have been well over 200,000! If such a reduction in unemployment had been achieved for only the frictionally unemployed (here regarded as those with one to four weeks of unemployment during the year), the addition to the labor force supply would have been close to 100,000 man-years!

Efforts to achieve full utilization of manpower resources involve such programs as educational planning, employment counseling, training and retraining, and methods to encourage relocation from economically depressed areas. The effectiveness of these programs depends, to some large degree, on accurate forecasts of demand and supply of qualified personnel by occupation, industry, and geographic area.

At the federal government level, the U.S. Department of Labor and Department of Health, Education, and Welfare (HEW) have dealt chiefly with the supply side of the manpower problem. Several federal government organizations have a primary interest in the level of employment (from a demand standpoint); these organizations include the Council of Economic Advisors, the Department of Treasury, the Federal Reserve Bank, and the President's Office of Management and Budget (OMB). This segmentation is reflected in the separate and apparently uncoordinated economic and manpower reports of the President. At the Congressional level, this lack of coordination continues; different committees receive and discuss the economic and manpower reports and sponsor legislation which may have only limited integration with any overall policy.

Figure 3-2 depicts an integrated view, developed by the authors, of a model of the manpower supply and demand flow among the various interested components. As the components function, at the present time, there is considerable lack of integration and meaningful information flow. There is no central, integrated data bank containing manpower supply and demand information. What exists is scattered among a variety of agencies and organizations. Further, the existing data have severe limitations because of gaps and lack of common standards; consequently, the data can be misleading or confusing. The communications links in the existing system are at best tenuous. The individual looking for a job and the organization seeking to fill positions do not have easy or helpful access to information from the various governmental bodies dealing with manpower. The nation's manpower effort is, at best, a groping effort that is not yet adequately responsive to the real needs of the individual or local organization.

For some time, social scientists have urged that the Office of the President

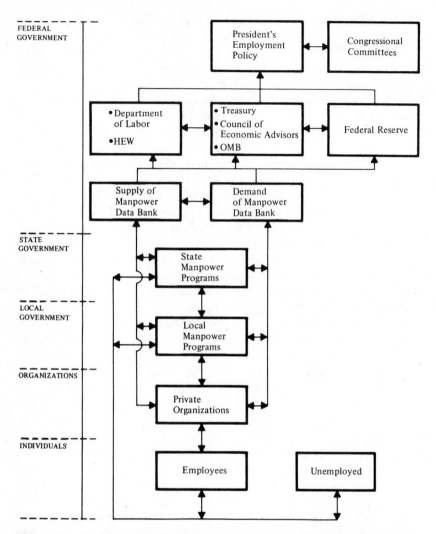

Figure 3-2 An integrated model of manpower supply and demand. (Edward A. Tomeski, "Manpower Planning," in *The Encyclopedia of Management*, 2nd edition, ed. by Carl Heyel, New York: Van Nostrand Reinhold Company, 1973, p. 525.)

and Congress establish a Council of Social Advisors and comparable Congressional committees. The President and Congress have many units devoted to the nation's economic, financial, military, security, and lobby interests. Thus far, the views of humanists (e.g., sociologists, psychologists, philosophers) have not had a prominent voice in government policy-making. *This underscores the propensity, in the United States, to place emphasis on "things" and "programs" rather than "people."*

Our nation's pluralistic, free enterprise system places some obvious constraints on strong central planning and the concentration of the information required for such planning. In several other nations (e.g., Scandanavian countries, Japan, Israel, Germany) that are more planning-conscious, apparently substantial progress has been made toward achieving national manpower-planning policies and programs that are responsive to governmental, organizational, and individual needs.

Our manpower future is shaped by tens-of-millions of individual decisions on the parts of employers, students, workers, union officials, educators, and government officials. While the United States does not pre-plan the future of its working citizens, it is essential to understand the nature and direction of the changing patterns—and to provide a mechanism for coordination which minimizes large-scale diseconomies, misuses, and abuses of the nation's manpower. It is indeed frightening when, for instance, the President or Congress make far-reaching executive and legislative decisions without fully considering the impact on working people. Government programs are cut back or abandoned, in the name of economy, with little or no provision for the hundreds or thousands of people who may lose their jobs. One has but to talk with the many unemployed or under-utilized scientists or teachers to appreciate the very real tragedy that is involved. The laws are made by Congress, they are executed by the Executive Branch, and they are borne by the average citizen.

- Due to lack of opportunities in their areas of training and competence,

    An electrical engineer is working as a clerk in a stationery store.

    A machinery salesman is on welfare.

    An English teacher is doing secretarial tasks.

    A physicist is driving a truck.

- If one discusses this problem with those in power in government, the common response seems to be, "We must deal with aggregates. We cannot deal with individual problems. In a free enterprise economy the individual must fend for herself or himself."

MANPOWER GOALS

The Employment and Training Administration of the U.S. Department of Labor has been a focal point for expanding our meager knowledge of manpower planning and forecasting. One major problem is that the information needed to support a national manpower planning system is inadequate and uncoordinated. The Administration is instrumental in preparing the President's annual *Manpower Report* to Congress; the report describes representative examples of the nation's manpower program and functions.

The Bureau of Labor Statistics of the U.S. Department of Labor is the primary source of statistics on employment, and the Census Bureau of the U.S. Department of Commerce supplies data that is related. However, the statistics, while having improved (including being computerized and available on magnetic tape to the public) in recent years, still are not adequate for many purposes. In fact, little information on occupational employment statistics is available for local organizations; that which is available is often out-of-date, discontinuous, or summary in nature and of little assistance to the local business or government. The inadequacies of the national manpower plans affect local organizations' uses, since the latter are dependent on the national government for broad-based information which is impractical to consolidate anywhere else.

Progressive federal government manpower policy can help advance the nation's economic and social goals. In periods of vigorous economic growth, it can help to reduce inflationary pressures, increase productivity and open up additional employment opportunities by:

- Enlarging and improving the nation's effective labor supply through training or retraining potential workers.

- Reducing skill shortages through selective training and upgrading programs.

- Directing training and employment efforts toward those individuals traditionally bypassed in filling job vacancies.

During economic downturns, federal manpower policy can ease the burden on workers and contribute to renewed economic growth by:

- Extending the duration of unemployment insurance.

- Adjusting the length and content of training programs to correlate with labor market conditions.

- Providing temporary jobs for out-of-work job seekers in public service work that builds skills for subsequent permanent employment.

Under any conditions, a federal manpower policy can help to advance economic and social goals by:

- Improving operation of the labor market through better information and faster job-matching systems.

- Bringing about a more efficient interplay between the institutions that educate, train, and employ workers.

- Working to remove the artificial employment barriers that limit the supply of workers and the availability of jobs.

To date, the federal government's effectiveness in the above mentioned areas leaves much to be desired. It is suspected that this is due to lack of coordinated policy, planning, and integration of interdependent systems.

PRESSURES FOR IMPROVED MANPOWER PLANNING

Numerous dynamic developments make rational manpower planning increasingly imperative:

- There will be continued and increasing mobility and independence of employees.

- Concepts of both individual rights and employer prerogatives are changing. The changes generally appear to weaken organizational and procedural rigidities and give greater protection to the individual.

- The number of workers in the prime 25 to 34 year-old group will increase dramatically. These workers will be better educated than workers of the same age in prior years.

- Slowed growth in the overall teenage labor force will somewhat lessen the magnitude of youth unemployment. However, the sharp increase of young blacks and other minority groups will continue to be a challenge. Blacks and other minorities have entered the 1970's with a larger but still inadequate share in the economy.

- The increasing number of working women underscores the need for day care, continuing training, part-time employment, and equal pay for equal work without regard to sex.

- Employment will continue to shift toward white-collar and service occupations.

- Jobs that require professional and/or technical training, and service occupations, will be the fastest growing employment opportunities.

Shifting priorities, however, will create employment problems in the skill areas affected. For instance, there is great demand for public administrators, health care technicians, and computer systems analysts. On the other hand, teachers and engineers face a situation in which supply exceeds demand.

- State and local governments will have especially rapid employment gains.

- The productivity growth rate in the United States dropped in the 1970's, and was slower than that of other industrial countries. There will be increasing pressure to improve productivity gains.

- The rate of on-the-job injuries is rising, pointing to the need for improvement in workplace environment.

- The challenge of poverty and dependency will continue, with attempts to get such persons into productive work and remove them from welfare.

- Certain groups, such as ex-drug addicts and ex-convicts, have difficulty in participating fully in the economy.

Rapidly advancing technology is accentuating the need for a responsive manpower planning and forecasting approach, since the demand for skills will be more subject to change and, consequently, should be reflected in education and training efforts. For instance, the computer industry has given rise to new occupations (e.g., systems analyst, computer programmer) that are among the most rapidly growing skill categories. Yet, there has been an almost continual shortage, in recent years, of such skills. There is also a major shift in employment growth to the service sector of the economy; this will markedly transform the future profile of the labor force requirements.

THE GOVERNMENT AS EMPLOYER

In addition to the fact that government exerts a unique influence through its policies and programs in the development and utilization of the nation's human resources, government itself is, by far, the largest employer in the nation and, as such, shares many of the problems of other organizations. The increase in government services desired or required by the public has resulted in a rapidly increasing number of workers employed in the public sector. It is estimated that about one-sixth of all employed persons are presently working for government.

The federal government will nevertheless have modest employment growth. The reasons cited for achieving stabilization of federal government employment are: effiiciency and economy efforts, state and local governments' implementation of much new federal legislation, and advances in electronic data processing. The increase in employment will be particularly pronounced at the state and local government levels.

It is generally recognized that state and local governments have not attained efficiency and electronic data processing levels comparable to that of the federal government. Consequently, the state and local governments' employment increases are growing disproportionately faster than that of the federal government. Besides these increases in the number of government employees, the need will probably be for more *highly qualified* employees than has hitherto been the case.

It is generally conceded that the federal government is more advanced in the areas of manpower planning and personnel administration than most state and local governments. This was highlighted in a Senate committee report, which stated that:

> . . . critical is the fact that many of the States and local governments, now and in the foreseeable future, lack the highly qualified administrative, professional, and technical personnel in the number required to plan, innovate, organize, and execute the wide variety of necessary programs.[1]

The human resource problem becomes even more formidable if one considers that the public's attitudes are generally negative about the desirability of employment in government. Several studies have found that the public prefers employment in the private sector rather than working for organizations in the public sector. The reasons for this attitude include an image of the government as being unprogressive, work being very boring, tasks entangled by red tape, and salaries lower than industry.

One example of an attempt to strengthen local government career competence is the Intergovernmental Personnel Act, which provides a combination of grant funds, technical assistance, and intergovernmental cooperation in the personnel area. Particular attention is given to improvement of personnel administration, and more efficient recruitment and training of personnel (with particular emphasis on general administration, personnel staff, financial administration, auditing, and computers).

PATTERNS OF MANPOWER CHANGE

Federal government and other studies[2] provide estimates of employment by industry for 1980, based on projections of the labor force, potential Gross National Product (GNP), the composition and industry structure of GNP, and industry output and output per man-hour. Figure 3-3 depicts an overall model delineating the components and interrelationships.

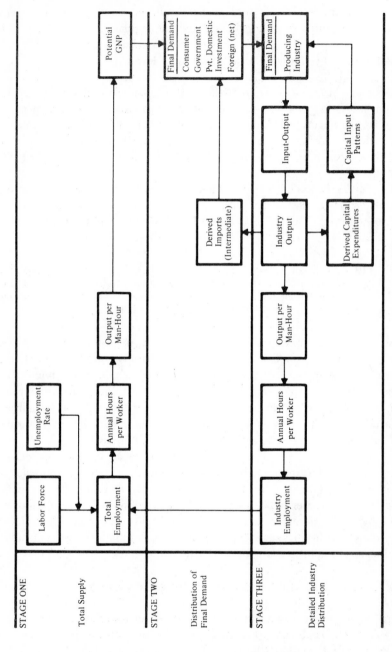

Figure 3-3 Interrelationship of potential Gross National Product, final demand, industry production, productivity, and employment. (*Patterns of U.S. Economic Growth*, Washington, D.C.: U.S. Department of Labor, 1970, p. 54.)

THE UNITED STATES ECONOMY:
LOOKING TOWARDS THE 1990's *

Management cannot base its long-term decisions solely on an examination of and evaluation of short-term trends. Even in a period of world-wide inflation, recession, energy shortage, and threat of another Middle East war, and marked shift to the left in the governments of many of our trading partners, an awareness of the long-term trends is essential and must be balanced against the short-term fluctuations which have immediate impact on sales and profits.

This analysis assumes that we will have no major war, and by the 1990's we will be enjoying relatively full employment (4.75% unemployed), and a modest inflation rate (4%). Under such circumstances we would expect a total national output (Gross National Product) of $4.31 trillion (or in real terms using constant 1973 dollars—$2.08 trillion). The projection is that the U.S. growth rate of the GNP will be 8.4% per year, with real growth of 3.2% per year when factoring in inflation.

Some of the key trends, having a negative weight, that are affecting our economy are:

1. A relatively rapid pace of inflation, with high interest rates.

2. The basic energy shortage will continue to act as a dampener on overall economic growth, and will continue to change our life-style.

3. There appears to be a raw material shortage in many areas, and this will intensify as developing nations begin to industrialize.

4. Growth of U.S. population is slowing to zero rate.

5. There is an increasing tendency for more of today's young people not to get married.

6. Productivity gains will only improve modestly, if at all. This is partly due to relative affluence of American workers and reduced motivation to work hard, and also the shift from high productivity manufacturing industries to low productivity service industries.

7. The slowdown in U.S. research and development has acted as a dampener on new products and improvement.

Key trends, having a positive weight, affecting our economy are:

1. Recent emphasis, in Congress and in the White House, on more responsible fiscal policy and encouragement of capital investment and saving.

2. The Federal Reserve Board's attempt to curb the growth of the money supply and to moderate the inflationary trend.

---

* *The American Economy.* New York: McGraw-Hill Inc., 1975; *The Years of Change.* Washington, D.C.: Chamber of Commerce of the United States, 1978.

3. An increase in the flow of foreign investment in the U.S.

4. It is possible that mainland China and Eastern Europe may provide big and growing markets for U.S. goods, services, and investment.

5. U.S. farm area is becoming the food basket of the world as our agricultural productivity and diversity are superior to any other nation's.

6. The beginning of a search for ways to solve the energy and raw material shortages.

7. Some strengthening in the confidence in the U.S. dollar vis-a-vis other nations' currencies.

The Composition of the Labor Force

Our working population has increased steadily as our total population grows. With the trend towards a zero rate of growth in population, it is likely that the growth in the labor force will also level off. There were about 90 million persons employed in 1977 and it is expected that the labor force will number 100 million by the mid 1980's. Working persons, as a proportion of total population, has fluctuated between 36% and 40%, due largely to changes in our birth rate, as dependent children became a larger or smaller proportion of total population. By 1990 it is expected that 43% of our population will be employed. This increasing proportion reflects both the increasing proportion of women at work and the decreasing proportion of dependent children as families become smaller. One-third of our workers were women in 1960; in the 1970's women comprised two-fifths of the work force. In the 1970's there was some trend towards earlier retirements, but that trend may be blunted in view of recent legislation about extending the mandatory retirement age and also the inflationary pressures placed on retirees.

The educational level of our workers has been constantly increasing. About 75% of our youths graduate from high school. During the 1970's about 25% of our youths graduated from college. The higher educated persons tend to be employed in professional and technical positions, managerial and administrative positions, and sales or clerical jobs. There is increased emphasis on education as a life-long process, and education and training for adults is a growing area of education.

Industry and Occupational Profile

Agriculture employed over 70% of our workers in the early 19th century. By 1910 the figure was 30%, 12% by 1950, and it was less than 4% in the 1970's. The increasing mechanization of farms, emphasis on large-scale farming and decline in smaller farms, and improved farming methods have resulted in increased yields despite the significant reduction in workers in agriculture.

Manufacturing employees have fluctuated between 22% and 26% of total employment since the 1900's. Construction workers have made up about 5% of all employed persons since the 1870's. Transportation, communications, and public utilities organizations employ about 6% of our workers. Personal and domestic service employees number about 12% of the labor force. Wholesale and retail trade employees constitute about 22% of the employed persons. Professional service firms employ about 5% of workers. Government employs about 17% of our working population.

As to the future, it is expected that the fastest growing occupations will be in the following fields: professional and technical personnel, clerical workers, managers and administrators, sales employees, and craftsmen. There is likely to be only modest increases in employment for blue collar workers and nonfarm laborers. There will be a further decline in farm workers as mechanization and large-scale farming reach higher levels of productivity. Certain specific occupations are likely to be in the forefront as far as openings are concerned; they are: medical and health technicians, nurses, system analysts, computer programmers, physicians, among others.

Some industries are going to grow more rapidly than others, and so will likely require relatively more workers. Industries likely to experience high growth rates in the 1980's include: chemicals, plastic products, electric utilities, instrumentation, electrical machinery including computers, coal. Some industries are likely to have little or no growth; these include: lumber, iron and steel, apparel, tobacco, and leather products.

NEED FOR MANPOWER FORECASTS

Reliable and timely manpower forecasts are valuable for various uses:

- Manpower planners need manning projections to anticipate recruiting, training, and development requirements.

- Counselors use projections to provide information to young people, parents, teachers, etc. about employment trends to aid in sound career counselling and choices.

- Vocational educators need projections of employment to set up high school and post-secondary training programs or to provide apprenticeship training.

- Planners of higher education need estimates of requirements for purposes of pinpointing allocation of educational resources.

Without an accurate and responsive manpower system, vital decisions about employment and education are made without a high level of confidence that the choices are likely to be sound.

As this chapter has suggested, a manpower system requires extensive data about supply and demand related to people and positions. These data can be segmented into various categories: occupational group, industry, geographical location, educational background, etc. A manpower system usually must contain a sufficiency of historical data in order to have a base for projections. Because of the numerous variables involved and the uncertainties in a free enterprise nation, a manpower system frequently involves sophisticated mathematical techniques. The extensive data files involved and computational requirements have made the manpower planning application an appropriate one for processing by computer.

SUMMARY

There has been a rather late emergence of any semblance of a formal national policy regarding human resources. *If a major purpose is to employ our human resources fully and to help develop these resources to their highest potential, then our existing efforts are inadequate.*

Technology, including the computer, affects human resources by requiring new skills and making old ones obsolete. As an operational tool, the computer can help meet expanding business and government workloads and help improve the effectiveness and efficiency of administration. In addition, the computer should have increasing importance in processing the vast data and generating information that is required for effective manpower planning.

The new patterns of manpower needs, reflected in projected industry and occupational employment, should be of interest to the manager responsible for human resources and to the technician who creates systems which relate to the personnel function.

The next chapter will move to the micro-aspects of human resources, and will discuss the evolving personnel function in organizations.

KEY CONCEPTS OF THE CHAPTER

1. The United States government has an unintegrated and short-range approach to the nation's human resources situation.

2. There is lack of comprehensive information, at the national and local levels, about manpower supply and demand. This inhibits meaningful decisions and plans regarding manpower.

3. The nation's manpower requirements are experiencing significant shifts;

this is consistent with change caused by technology (as discussed in the previous chapter).

4. Personnel staffs and computer technicians, working with manpower systems, should be concerned with the condition and trends of our nation's human resources. They should have a macro-view as well as awareness of their immediate organizational problems.

5. Because of the voluminous data and complex computations frequently involved in manpower systems, computers are usually integral tools in such systems.

DISCUSSION QUESTIONS

General Background (Seminar/Classroom Discussion)

1. Defend the statement, "The nation's human resources are its most valuable asset." Why is the principle violated in practice?
2. Discuss the scope of manpower planning.
3. In your opinion, how extensive a role should our national government assume in manpower planning? In what ways does a free enterprise economy inhibit such planning?
4. Discuss the difficulties of career planning for the individual, and its relation to changes in our nation's manpower requirements.

Operational and Technical

1. Identify the ways in which several specific occupations have changed (e.g., work content, skill requirement, level of responsibility) during the last several years.
2. Explain how the computer can be an invaluable tool in manpower planning.
3. Why are the changes in an organization's manpower mix important to the staff member involved in planning, designing, and implementing computer systems?

Policy

1. How do governmental manpower efforts affect the individual organization's manpower programs? Has your organization established points of contact with manpower offices of the federal, state, and local governments?
2. Is there someone in your organization responsible for overall manpower planning? What use is made of macro-manpower information from the government and other sources?
3. What formal policies does your organization have to cope with pressing manpower challenges (e.g., minorities, women's liberation, veterans)?
4. What changes in technology, products, or services might alter the nature of your organization during the next five to ten years? How will this affect your company's manpower mix? How does your organization plan for such contingencies?

Areas for Research

1. Determine how the state and city in which you work forecast labor supply and demand trends. What use does the state or city make of the federal government's manpower data? Ask the state or city officials about any specific manpower data which they think are vital but which are not readily available.
2. Does the industry of which your organization is a part have available industry-wide manpower information? What is, or could be, the value of such information to your company?
3. Contrast the United States government's manpower data with those of another nation (the authors suggest using Japan, a Scandinavian nation, West Germany, or Israel).
4. Describe several computerized mathematical models used in macro-manpower planning. What transferrence, of concepts or methods, could be made to micro-manpower planning?
5. The President of the United States has personal advisors in matters of economics, management and budget, science, defense, and security. Congress has committees for various areas: finance, particular interests (e.g., farmers), military, technical, geographical, etc. Justify the following statement: "There is urgent need for a Council of Social Advisors in the Executive Office of the President, and a Joint Congressional Committee on Social Conditions." Contact thought leaders (e.g., your congressmen, political action groups, educators) about their reaction to such a Council, and how citizens can promote the idea.

BIBLIOGRAPHY

American Economy: *Prospects for Growth to 1988*. New York: McGraw-Hill, Inc., 1975.

Chamber of Commerce of U.S. *The Years of Change*. Washington, D.C., 1978.

Ginzberg, Eli. *Manpower Agenda for America*. New York: McGraw-Hill Book Co., 1968.

Lecht, Leonard A. *Manpower Needs for National Goals in the 1970's*. New York: Frederick A. Praeger, Inc., 1969.

Lester, Richard A. *Manpower Planning in a Free Society*. Princeton, New Jersey: Princeton University Press, 1966.

Patten, Jr., Thomas H. *Manpower Planning and the Development of Human Resources*. New York: John Wiley & Sons, Inc., 1971.

U.S. Department of Labor. *Employer Manpower Planning and Forecasting*. Washington, D.C., 1970.

U.S. Department of Labor. *Manpower Report of the President*. Washington, D.C., 1971.

U.S. Department of Labor. *Patterns of U.S. Economic Growth*. Washington, D.C., 1970.

U.S. Department of Labor. *The U.S. Economy in 1980: A Preview of BLS Projections*. Washington, D.C., April 1970.

FOOTNOTES

[1] U.S. Senate, Committee on Government Operations, *Intergovernmental Personnel Act of 1969.* (Washington, D.C.: U.S. Government Printing Office, 1969), p. 1.

[2] U.S. Department of Labor, *Patterns of U.S. Economic Growth* (Washington, D.C.: U.S. Government Printing Office, 1970); U.S. Department of Labor, *The U.S. Economy in 1980: A Preview of BLS Projections* (Washington, D.C.: U.S. Government Printing Office, April 1970); Chamber of Commerce of U.S., *The Years of Change.* Washington, D.C. 1978; American Economy: *Prospects for Growth to 1988.* New York: McGraw-Hill, Inc., 1975.

4

The Emerging Human Resource Function

The limitations of Personnel Administration are not hard to perceive. They are indeed admitted by most of the people in the field—at least by implication. The constant worry of all personnel administrators is their inability to prove that they are making a contribution to the enterprise . . . the personnel department as a rule stays away from the management of the enterprise's most important human resource, managers . . . It also generally avoids the two most important areas in the management of workers: the organization of the work, and the organization of people to do the work.

Peter F. Drucker

OBJECTIVES OF THE CHAPTER

This chapter is an exploration of some of the trends, strengths, and weaknesses of the personnel function in organizations. Particular attention is devoted to the growing importance of manpower planning at the micro-level. The personnel administrator can benefit by a more analytical view of his department. The computer specialist, involved in designing personnel systems, must have sound understanding of the personnel department's mission and operations. The authors foresee the evolution of the personnel function into a broader, modern, human resource function.

EMERGING ROLES FOR PERSONNEL DEPARTMENTS

The primary resource of an organization is the human resource. All other resources, such as financial and technical, should be supportive of the human resource. *However, while there is a swelling concern, in society, about people-related problems, in actual practice organizations still appear to give higher priority to non-human resources and, indeed, sometimes virtually ignore human resources.* The following illustrations indicate the lack of people-orientation on the part of our organizations and society:

- Professionally trained persons (e.g., teachers and engineers) may have some difficulty in finding positions that use their talents.

- Some veterans, discharged after overseas duty, cannot locate employment.

- Minority groups have continuing difficulty in attaining the employment levels and work status of mainstream citizens.

- The federal government eliminates support of programs and thus abruptly causes pockets of unemployment.

- Women are generally not represented in the highest paying positions, even if they have the necessary qualifications.

- In many organizations, workers lose accumulated pension rights when they leave before retirement.

- Large numbers of young people are idle, and turn to activities that are harmful to society.

Consider some of the possible emerging and expanding roles for the personnel staff:

1. Personnel departments will logically become human resource centers that help manage change and extend human potential.

2. Personnel staffs will collaborate with physicians, psychologists, sociologists, social workers, and human engineers to create a healthful work environment that will help reduce all forms of occupational pollution (excessive noise, stress, etc.) and maximize the quality of life on-the-job.

3. Personnel programs will be concerned about offering appropriate challenges to the individual rather than thinking merely in terms of averages. Creative persons who may be nonconformists will be provided a receptive environment.

4. Underdeveloped human resources will be given more attention: women, minority groups, retarded and handicapped employees, persons being rehabilitated from mental hospitals or prison, etc.

5. In many organizations, the personnel professional will take a world-wide view as enterprises become international in scope.

6. Since training is a life-long process, progressive organizations will provide mechanisms for renewing their human resources.

7. New occupations will appear (e.g., those working in outer space or on the floor of the ocean), and others will decline or disappear with increasing rapidity.

For some time, Likert has pointed out that while organizations consider buildings, equipment, and securities as assets, there is little comparable asset accounting of investment in people. Likert cogently remarks that:

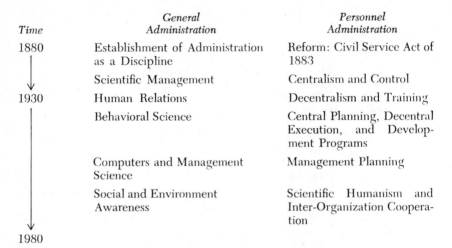

Time	General Administration	Personnel Administration
1880	Establishment of Administration as a Discipline	Reform: Civil Service Act of 1883
↓	Scientific Management	Centralism and Control
1930	Human Relations	Decentralism and Training
	Behavioral Science	Central Planning, Decentral Execution, and Development Programs
	Computers and Management Science	Management Planning
	Social and Environment Awareness	Scientific Humanism and Inter-Organization Cooperation
↓ 1980		

Figure 4-1 Evolution of administration.

Human beings design or order . . . equipment; they decide where and how to use computers; they modernize or fail to modernize the technology employed . . . Every aspect of a firm's activities is determined by the competence, motivation, and general effectiveness of its human organization. Of all the tasks of management, managing the human component is the central and most important task, because all else depends upon how well it is done.[1]

The vital nature of the human resource, to the organization, makes it imperative—in Likert's view—that it be considered as more than an expense. Yet, most enterprises have not adopted human asset accounting.

While progressive personnel policies received earlier attention in the federal government (the Civil Service Act of 1883 was a landmark for objective and modernizing personnel practices), there is some indication that non-government organizations have progressed substantially in the personnel area and, indeed, may have in some practices surpassed that of government (particularly local government). Figure 4-1 traces some of the movements that have taken place in general administration and personnel administration. Conceptually, the authors feel, administration is moving from a technical era (e.g., formal planning and the use of computers) to an ecological era concerned with social and environmental factors.

Increasingly, modern personnel organizations are focusing on a manpower approach to human resources. Manpower planning is a process which translates organizational goals and operational needs into a strategy to provide the human resources to fulfill these requirements. Manpower forecasting is an assessment of current human resources, the capabilities of existing human resources, and the prospective sources of supply. Fundamental to manpower planning and forecasting is coordination with the organization's other plans: financial, facilities, economic and marketing, research and development, etc.

Manpower utilization concerns the effective use of the organization's human resources, and requires that employees be made available wherever and whenever they are needed. It demands managerial understanding of complex motivational factors—both monetary and non-monetary, individual and group—in attaining effectiveness through deployment of employees. Manpower development makes available training and education to improve skills, versatility, growth, motivation, and effectiveness.

The Civil Service Commission of the federal government is the largest non-military personnel effort, affecting more than two million employees of the government as well as tens-of-thousands of individuals that are needed each year to fill vacancies. The importance of modern personnel practices can be seen from the Commission's organizational chart (Figure 4-2). Reporting to the Commission's chairman are the following responsibilities: federal executive institute (for training and development of top officials), bureau of executive manpower, and bureau of manpower information systems. In 1968 the Commission established a formalized manpower information systems effort. This bureau is responsible for coordinating all of the Commission's computer-based information processing activities. Figure 4-3 details the bureau's organizational mission. It is developing an overall plan for an integrated information system for all government personnel records—which are now scattered and unstandardized in the many federal government departments and agencies.

CHANGE IN EMPLOYEES

Changes in people will be a cause of the personnel department's evolving character. Some of the important people changes include the following:

1. Employees are better educated and better informed, more affluent, and more sophisticated.

2. Employees expect more of life and work. As they move to higher levels in the hierarchy of human needs, former incentives become inadequate.

3. As indicated in Chapter 3, fewer people will be employed in menial tasks, as machines displace these activities. A relatively greater number of people will be engaged in various professional, technical, and service-type jobs.

4. People are increasingly mobile. Fewer people are willing to serve long periods in a particular job, in one organization, at a single geographical location.

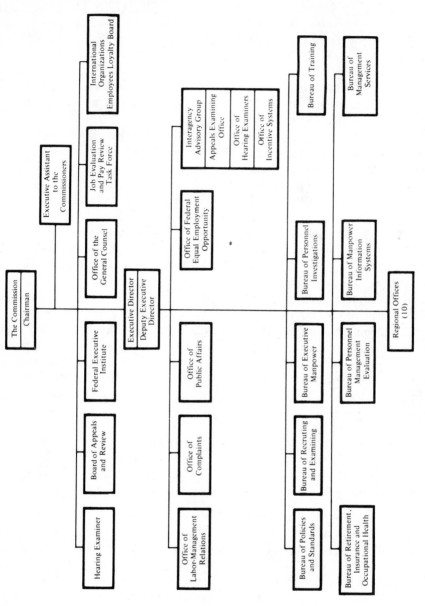

Figure 4-2 U.S. Civil Service Commission.

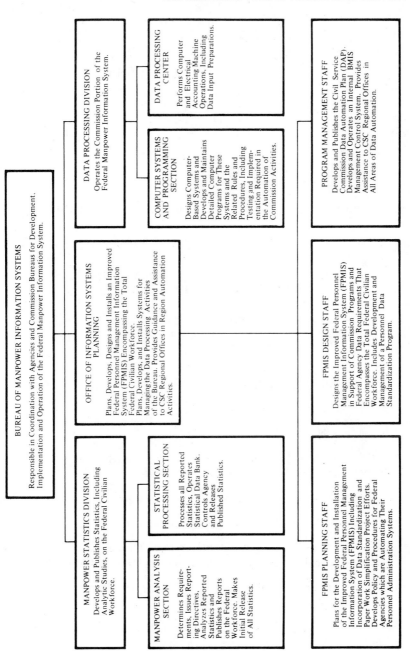

Figure 4-3 U.S. Civil Service Commission: Bureau of Manpower Information System.

5. People are growing more loyal to their profession or skill, and less loyal to the organization in which they work.

6. There will be an alarming number of persons who suffer from alienation and "future shock" because of the accelerated pace of change (discussed in Chapter 2).

7. Employees are spending less time on their jobs, and have more time for recreational, intellectual, and cultural activities.

8. Workers want an increasing voice in decision-making affecting their work and future.

One indication of the need for high level and broad response to such changes is the Government Employees Training Act of 1958 which gives emphasis to career development and training. It helps assure that adequate numbers of employees, with required skills, be available to fill future positions and that they will be able to cope with emerging techniques and tools.

IMPEDIMENTS OF AND OPPORTUNITIES FOR THE PERSONNEL AREA

Drucker, critically appraising the personnel function, concluded that the field was ". . . certainly insolvent, certainly unable to honor with the ready cash of performance the promises of managing worker and work it so liberally makes." [2]

A group of graduate students provided these perceptions of the field of personnel administration:

- It is a dull field.

- There is too much emphasis on procedures and techniques and not enough emphasis on human behavior.

- Its status is low in universities, businesses, and government.

- Individuals of low ability can succeed in the field.

- Personnel departments are not progressive. They do not use modern techniques, such as the computer, or the latest research developments.

- It is concerned with minor questions, and does not deal with broad, conceptual problems.

- Personnel management is not sufficiently humanistic. Everything is done from the point of view of the organization and not from that of the employee.

Consider some not uncommon complaints, gathered by the authors, from employees.

- A manager of an operating department said, "I recruit for my own staff and the personnel department rubber stamps my decisions. They are unable to move quickly, and they don't understand our operational problems."

- An ambitious, talented young staff person indicated, "I have been offered much better jobs outside. I would prefer to stay, but the personnel department just gives me a run around."

- The supervisor of a staff department was alienated from virtually all of his employees. One subordinate decided to discuss the intolerable conditions with the personnel department. The subordinate later commented, "You can't trust those guys in personnel. I should have known better. Someone said that they immediately labeled me as a trouble-maker and informed my supervisor. You can't beat the organization, even if it is in the wrong. I expect to be given a real rough time, and I'll probably have to start looking elsewhere."

Some criticisms of the personnel function, and related areas needing improvement include:

1. The personnel function is not management-oriented. It is absorbed with segmented, immediate problems (e.g., hiring employees on a crisis basis), and does not have the planning horizon that is needed at the management level. The lack of personnel planning generally means inferior manpower actions. Even organizations that do have some manpower planning efforts tend to approach planning in a segmented, discontinuous, and short-range way.

There is need to have the personnel function evolve to the point where it more fully participates in the top management planning process. In the broadest sense, the personnel function should become the focal point for manpower planning which is integrated with the other organizational plans (financial, research and development, etc.). The personnel function itself must be viewed as an integrated entity—and not as a series of separate, isolated activities such as recruitment, classification, training, compensation, etc. Figure 4-4 depicts this integrated view of personnel activities.

2. The personnel function is not adaptable to change. It is prone to accept conditions as it finds them, and consequently often appears to be antiquated and unresponsive to organizational needs. If the personnel function is to service the organization's needs and demands, it must become adaptive and innovational. Personnel people should be prepared to be active change agents

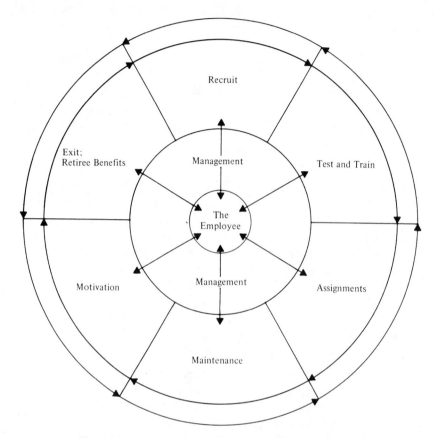

Figure 4-4 Personnel system: servicing human resources.

for introducing new concepts (e.g., job enrichment) and new technological advances (e.g., computers) requiring human adjustment.

3. The personnel function is overly absorbed in relatively unimportant tasks such as record-keeping. Consequently, it does not adequately provide for its central mission of planning for and developing the human resources of the organization.

No longer should the personnel function be content to be regarded as a clerical activity. Rather, it should win recognition as an important function which aids management. Where feasible, the personnel function itself must employ the new technologies to improve its own effectiveness.

4. However, the personnel department should be careful not to usurp the prerogatives of managers. The personnel staff is intended to be an aid to

management and not a substitute for a manager's responsibilities of managing employees and work. The personnel function is not a specialty of the personnel staff alone; every manager has an important personnel responsibility.

In this regard, there is likely a need for strengthening managers' abilities to cope with changing personnel conditions. Top managements are often misinformed about how their managers are managing people. They do not realize that managers often do not know how to manage people, and that there is a need for more imaginative management development.

5. Studies have indicated that administrative offices may be functioning at low levels of productivity (perhaps as low as 50 per cent), while many are not measured against meaningful standards.[3] This suggests a lack of motivation on the part of employees and a weakness of management in bureaucracies.

The adoption of an organic organization (as explored in Chapter 2) to replace the bureaucratic organization might more effectively relate individual and organization goals. A pilot study in the federal government provided evidence that productivity can be increased by the use of motivational approaches and productivity measures.[4]

A study in a large company has indicated the potential for cost effectiveness programs applied to the personnel function.[5] While personnel staff costs may range from 1 to 2 per cent of the organization's total payroll, it may have considerably greater leverage. Manpower constitutes 40 to 70 per cent of many organizations' total costs. Effectiveness increases resulting from personnel programs (e.g., job enrichment, improvement in systems) can significantly impact revenue, cost, and profit.

6. As mentioned in Chapter 3, employment in government has been regarded in the United States as being somewhat less desirable than in other types of organizations; this attitude appears to be particularly pronounced among well-educated technical and professional people. This poses a considerable problem for public personnel administration faced with the problem of unprecedented need for recruiting and developing talented employees. The old bureaucratic image of government will require transformation so as to appeal to the new generation of better educated, more socially conscious, and less organization-oriented workers.

7. Increasingly it appears that the public is taking an anti-bureaucratic attitude, whether the bureaucracy is in the public or private sector. One survey indicated that about 60 per cent of the public sampled has a low regard for large companies, about 30 per cent had moderate approval of them, while only 10 per cent had high regard for large businesses.[6] It is suggested that all large organizations, private or public, require a reappraisal of their goals and images; the public seems to be demanding organizations that are more humanistic and socially aware. Unfortunately, most large

organizations tend to be essentially mechanistic and extremely self-interest motivated, displaying only token concern for people and social responsibility.

COMPUTER CHALLENGES FOR THE PERSONNEL AREA

It is the authors' position that the personnel function should move from its conservative and narrow view of its mission, to a level that is dynamically progressive and having a broad view of its role in its organization. *Such a transformation would require a personnel department that is: management-oriented, adaptable to change and a designer of change, focused on people rather than paperwork, dedicated to manpower planning and development, capable of providing employees and environments conducive to high productivity, and capable of projecting an attractive image to various publics (particularly employees and prospective employees).*

- The authors' studies of personnel departments revealed that not many organizations came close to attaining the levels indicated above. In the specific area of computer use, most organizations have made only modest progress in modernizing their personnel systems. Few personnel departments have developed overall plans and objectives for such systems. Instead, halfhearted and relatively haphazard efforts appear prevalent.

The computer can be used beneficially in exactly the areas where many personnel departments are having problems. Thus:

1. Routine decisions can be programmed and carried out reliably and rapidly by the computer. This can free the personnel staff for planning and higher-level decisions. Further, the computer can be utilized to process more sophisticated mathematical models (e.g., manpower planning models).

2. The meaningful use of the computer would encourage the personnel staff to reconsider the objectives, policies, and procedures of the function. This would occur if the organization adapts an overall systems approach (discussed in Chapter 5) to its personnel applications, rather than a piecemeal approach. In this same vein, the personnel department has an opportunity to be part of meaningful change in other parts of the organization. This can be accomplished by having the personnel staff take an active role in computer planning and projects.

3. A considerable amount of the routine paperwork of personnel departments can be computerized, thus releasing the personnel staff for contact with management and employees.

4. The computer can be used to improve productivity. The rapid and

accurate processing capability of the computer provides the potential for increasing output while containing labor costs. Further, as indicated in Chapter 2, an imaginatively designed computer system can strengthen such areas as organization communication and morale (e.g., relieve the worker of boring, routine work).

5. By attaining the benefits identified above, the personnel department can project an improved image to management, employees, and outside publics (e.g., prospective employees, recruiters, etc.). The image would be that of a personnel function that is modern, practicing management-by-objectives, people-oriented, and responsive to the needs of the organization.

NEEDED: A RESULTS ORIENTATION

Staff functions such as personnel often are not subject to the rigors of meeting specific objectives, as are operational units. The most important consideration in a managerial situation is getting results; results cannot be evaluated without some prior expectation (standards) against which to measure them. Management-by-objectives (MBO) satisfies both requirements in that it concentrates first on setting objectives and determining the means to achieve them, and then sees to it that results are forthcoming. A vital consideration in MBO is that the organization's objectives should, as much as possible, parallel the personal goals of the individuals whose performances will be measured.

The personnel function can be measured by a variety or combination of standards. Some of these are:

- Reduction of labor turnover.

- Quality of new employees hired and retained.

- Minimizing unions' work stoppages.

- Effectiveness of supplying manpower as needed.

- Facilitating higher productivity among employees.

- Ratios which compare the personnel department's budget with the organization's total budget, and which contrast with industry standards where the latter are available.

A more rigorous results orientation would likely encourage staff departments such as personnel to be more alert to self-improvement opportunities and meaningful operations that contribute to organizational goals.

MANPOWER PLANNING °

Manpower planning is an integral segment of the total management process of transforming resources (human effort, information, and material) into programs that will attain the goals of the organization. The term, "manpower resources" (or "human resources") displaces the more traditional "personnel" so as to eliminate the notion of merely seeking bodies to fill slots. People should be considered as changing sets of interests, skills, motivations, capabilities, and attitudes. Managers should attempt to match people with programs so that, ideally, everyone is working up to potential and no one is overqualified, underqualified, or misplaced. Any waste of human talent ultimately reduces organizational effectiveness.

- The authors' research indicated that federal government departments and large business organizations generally do have some kind of manpower planning effort. However, it appears that most manpower planning is given relatively low priority and lacks comprehensiveness and integration. States and local governments have made only very modest strides in the area of manpower planning. Those manpower planning efforts that do exist tend to be quite simple; few organizations are successfully using mathematical models for such purposes.

Most frequently, manpower planning in the individual firm, if formalized (as in some larger organizations), is segmented and specific, or if informal (as in most smaller organizations), is haphazard and disjointed. Although there is great variation in both policy and practice of manpower planning, these non-systematic and disjointed characteristics are pervasive.

Some Basic Considerations

A manpower planning system should provide information necessary for the determination of: recruiting requirements, impact of technological changes, effect of anticipated changes in the organization (e.g., new products or services, relocation of offices or plants), and educational and training programs.

The planning must take into account the several levels that are normal in an organization: top administrators, staff and line supervisors, professionals; technical, clerical, and other salaried personnel; skilled hourly employees; semi-skilled hourly employees; and unskilled hourly employees. The various levels present differing problems in the way of recruiting or education and training.

° For an excellent source of this material, refer to Thomas H. Patten, Jr., *Manpower Planning and the Development of Human Resources* (New York: John Wiley & Sons, Inc., 1971).

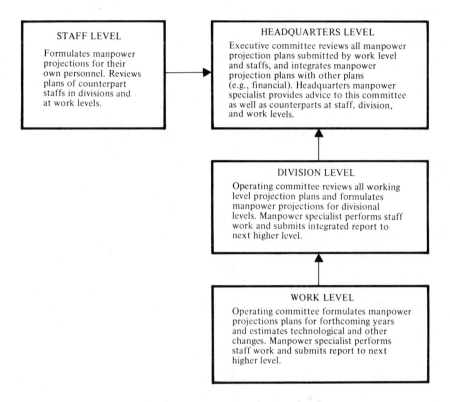

STAFF LEVEL

Formulates manpower projections for their own personnel. Reviews plans of counterpart staffs in divisions and at work levels.

HEADQUARTERS LEVEL

Executive committee reviews all manpower projection plans submitted by work level and staffs, and integrates manpower projection plans with other plans (e.g., financial). Headquarters manpower specialist provides advice to this committee as well as counterparts at staff, division, and work levels.

DIVISION LEVEL

Operating committee reviews all working level projection plans and formulates manpower projections for divisional levels. Manpower specialist performs staff work and submits integrated report to next higher level.

WORK LEVEL

Operating committee formulates manpower projections plans for forthcoming years and estimates technological and other changes. Manpower specialist performs staff work and submits report to next higher level.

Figure 4-5   Manpower planning levels.

Most planning would be very general and broad for horizons of two years or beyond (perhaps up to ten years); this is so because change and uncertainty make specific long-range plans of questionable value. The long-range manpower plan is usually supported with quite specific one or two year plans.

Figure 4-5 provides a visualization of the way in which manpower planning might operate, beginning at the work level and moving upward through the divisional and headquarters levels. It is important to note that the operating line organization provides data to manpower specialists; the manpower specialists analyze, supplement, refine, and integrate the data.

Figure 4-6 illustrates how a manpower projection plan for a unit may be summarized. The various rows relate to the functions and levels of the employees. The columns provide for numeric entries which itemize the organization's demand for employees and probable source.

The manpower specialists provides the following staff support to the various levels of organization:

UNIT OF ORGANIZATION	Current Employees (date)	Anticipated Number Employees on (date)	Net Difference (between 1 and 2)	Total Employees Required	Total Employees Made Available	Promoted from Within	Transferred from Inside Organization	To Be Recruited
	1	2	3	4	5	6	7	8
A. Production								
Managers								
Supervisors								
Professional								
B. Finance								
Managers								
Supervisors								
Professional								
C. Marketing								
Managers								
Supervisors								
Professional								
D. Engineering								
Managers								
Supervisors								
Professional								
E. Total Management (A + B + C + D)								
F. Other Salaried - Non-Exempt, Non-Supervisory, Technical, and Clerical Employees								
G. Hourly Employees								
Skilled								
Semi-skilled and Unskilled								
H. Total (A + B + C + D + F + G)								

Figure 4-6 Manpower projection plan. (Adapted from Thomas H. Patten, Jr. *Manpower Planning and the Development of Human Resources,* **New York: John Wiley & Sons, Inc., 1971, p. 64.)**

1. Reviews and analyzes information on the organization's manpower situation and the developing trends.

2. Assists managers in identifying assumptions upon which estimates will be based.

3. Develops a common set of factors such as economic and labor market conditions, technological changes, etc.

4. Integrates estimates to eliminate contradictions.

5. Presents information uniformly to facilitate review.

Each higher level of management reviews the manpower plans, and makes decisions appropriate to that level. Once decisions have been made, there is need for staff follow-up to make any modifications of the plan as changing conditions occur. The plan must result in actions that effectuate the decision-making process. Finally, there is need to evaluate the effectiveness of the plan in action, and its results.

While this example of manpower planning is simplistic, it is intended to establish basic tenets, since interest in manpower planning is of recent vintage and is still emerging in many organizations.

Difficulties in Manpower Forecasting °

Since there is a complex of internal and external labor factors, a systems approach (see Chapter 5) is needed to seek a rational solution to the large number of variables. What has been traditionally a series of separate and apparently unrelated manpower decisions needs to be tied together in a way that maximizes decision options and cost-benefit trade-offs.

Computers can handle many variables and manipulate massive amounts of data. Given input parameters, a computer can yield projections of manpower needs for an organization for each of the years in the future (e.g., ten year forecast). Obviously, certain constraints have to be taken into account: size of the organization, assumptions regarding individual attributes affecting manpower supply, growth rates, etc.

Planning is based on assumptions and judgments. Changes occur that modify the mix of human resources needed in an organization. Some of these changes are: new products or services, improved techniques of production, modernized marketing techniques, etc. Changes and future states must be anticipated, so that required training, education, and recruitment can proceed. Thus, it is important to specify the factors or variables that represent change. The manpower model, Figure 4-7, depicts the dynamics of some of the key variables that influence manpower requirements of an organization.

In the model, the dependent variable, manpower requirements, is defined as the number of replacements and additional employees needed, and is expressed in terms of occupation or skill level. The independent variable, product demand, is estimated by forecasting sales or by forecasting workloads. It includes all goods, services, and activities performed or produced within the employing unit.

Relationships between product demand and manpower requirements are influenced by the following intervening variables: financial resources, external labor supplies, and internal labor supplies.

° For an excellent source of this material refer to the U.S. Department of Labor's *Employer Manpower Planning and Forecasting,* 1970.

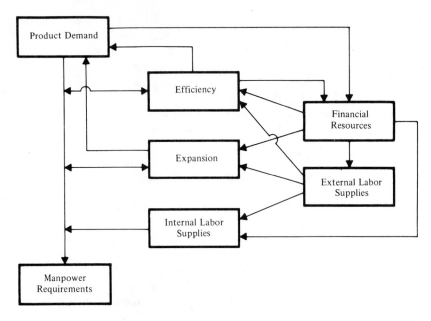

Figure 4-7 **Micro-model of manpower forecasting. (Adapted from *Employer Manpower Planning and Forecasting*, Washington, D.C.: U.S. Department of Labor, 1970, p. 10.)**

Efficiency refers to technological and administrative changes which modify labor productivity, consequently affecting manpower requirements per unit of output. In most cases, manpower requirements generally will be lowered as efficiency improves. It is hypothesized that increases in efficiency which lead to price reductions will result in increases in sales and, consequently, in manpower requirements. The net effect of increased efficiency depends largely on the price elasticity of product demand and on the magnitude of the increase in labor productivity. Increased efficiency is expected to increase financial resources.

The next intervening variable, expansion, includes facilities expansion and new products. Expansion affects product demand and also may have an impact on the relationship between product demand and manpower requirements.

Internal labor supplies include both the quality and skills of an organization's labor force and the number of employees. The former is estimated by skills inventories and forecasts of employee development and the latter by turnover figures.

Increased financial resources are assumed to have a positive impact on internal labor supplies, external supplies, expansion and efficiency. As financial resources increase, more training can be given to the current labor force, thus increasing the quality of labor. Higher wages can be paid, which will tend to reduce separations and increase the external supply of labor. More financial resources also facilitate capital investment.

The last intervening variable in the primitive model is external labor supplies, defined as the manpower, by occupation or skill level, available to the firm from its various labor markets. It is postulated that large external labor supplies of the type currently used by an organization will restrict the introduction of labor-saving innovations, but will increase the likelihood of expansion (assuming sufficient product demand). If an excess external labor supply exists, labor costs will be less than would otherwise be the case.

It is predicted that, as product demand increases, pressures for increases in efficiency are greater, the likelihood of product line and facilities expansion increases, and financial resources become larger.

Needed Improvements in Manpower Planning

The decade ahead is likely to see vastly greater organizational involvement in manpower planning than ever before. Top management is likely to find that long-range strategies for manpower development are as essential as financial, research, marketing, production, or capital planning.

Meanwhile, there is a good deal that remains to be developed and understood regarding both macro- and micro-manpower planning. There is need for better insight regarding:

1. Methods of projecting manpower needs.
2. Accounting for jobs and vacancies at the organization level.
3. The way in which manpower constraints fit into the other facets of planning.
4. Data on occupational distributions.
5. Coordination between government, business, and educational institutions.
6. Lags in the period of production, so that people can be educated and trained for occupations that are marketable.

Organizations differ with respect to their missions, resources, technologies, and environments. This necessitates a variety of approaches to manpower planning even though the ultimate goal—making the best use of people to achieve an organization's objective and the social good—is basically the same for all.

SUMMARY

The personnel function appears to contain a series of paradoxes. While most of us believe that our most valuable resource is people, that resource seems frequehtly to be given lower priority (both in government and business) than resources of a nonhuman variety. The personnel function, which should obviously be people-oriented, is often set within an organizational environment inimical to individual growth and satisfaction. Further, *the personnel activity should help individuals in organizations to adjust to change. Yet, by and large, the personnel function is itself not adequately geared for change.*

Computers can facilitate manpower planning by relieving the personnel function of paperwork burdens and by improving productivity while providing a basis for measuring it. *Rather than the computer being a dehumanizing instrument, it can help to humanize the organization by permitting the personnel staff to attend to its most important role: development of human resources.*

The next chapter considers the systems approach to organization. The term "systems" is very much in vogue. It has particular significance in the computer field where such an approach is required for the analysis of problem areas, and the design and development of computer applications.

KEY CONCEPTS OF THE CHAPTER

1. While lip service is paid to the idea that people are the organization's most valuable resource, in practice this too often does not seem to be the case.

2. The changing needs and drives of employees, and concurrent environmental changes, call for a more adaptive personnel function. To date, the personnel departments appear to have lagged behind developments rather than served as change agents.

3. In many personnel departments, a series of impediments have restricted contribution to organizational objectives and to facilitation of the development of human resources.

4. Generally, the personnel function has not imaginatively taken advantage of the capabilities of computers—which could enhance that function's role in its organization.

5. One of the most promising areas of computer application, manpower planning, has been neglected at the micro-level as it has been at the macro-level (described in Chapter 3).

6. Modernization of existing personnel departments would result in a function making a more decisive contribution to society; the authors

anticipate the emergence of "human resource" departments, replacing the narrower and conservative personnel units.

DISCUSSION QUESTIONS

General Background (Seminar/Classroom Discussion)

1. Differentiate between what is meant by a "personnel approach" and a "human resource approach."
2. How has the personnel department's activities changed over the last several years? What activities are increasing in importance, and which are decreasing in importance?
3. Why do organizations consider such things as land and buildings as assets, but view human resources as expenses? (Refer to Rensis Likert's work on human asset accounting.)

Operational and Technical

1. How has your organization's employee mix changed in the last several years? Consider such items as education level, sex, age, minorities, professional and salaried versus hourly employees, etc. How do such changes alter the services that should be rendered by your company's personnel function?
2. In what way can mathematical models be used in manpower planning? Has your organization made any such use of management science techniques?

Policy

1. How can your organization's personnel function make a more significant contribution to company planning and policy matters?
2. Does your organization have a long-range plan for manpower? If not, how might such a plan improve your organization's effectiveness?
3. In what ways do you think your organization's personnel function can make a greater impact on organizational effectiveness? How must the personnel function change to make such a contribution?

Areas for Research

1. What percentage of your organization's total cost can be attributed to human resources (salaries, benefits, training, etc.)? How does this compare with other organizations in your industry? Explain the differences.
2. Determine what some other organizations, comparable to yours, are doing in the way of manpower planning. How do those organizations use computers for manpower planning applications?
3. Develop a questionnaire and conduct a survey to determine the level of esteem, of managers and employees, for the personnel department(s) in one or more organizations. How might the staff of the personnel department strengthen the personnel function's image?

BIBLIOGRAPHY

Ackoff, Russell L. *A Concept of Corporate Planning.* New York: John Wiley & Sons, Inc., 1970.

Drucker, Peter F. *Managing for Results.* New York: Harper & Row Publishers, Inc., 1964.

————. *The Practice of Management.* New York: Harper & Row Publishers, Inc., 1954.

French, Wendel. *The Personnel Management Process.* Boston: Houghton Mifflin Co., 1964.

Golembiewski, Robert and Cohen, Michael, eds. *People in Public Service.* Itasca, Illinois: F. E. Peacock, Publishers, Inc., 1970.

Katz, Daniel and Kahn, Robert L. *The Social Psychology of Organizations.* New York: John Wiley & Sons, Inc., 1966.

Likert, Rensis. *The Human Organization.* New York: McGraw-Hill Book Co., 1961.

McGregor, Douglas. *The Human Side of Enterprise.* New York: McGraw-Hill Book Co., 1960.

Patten, Jr., Thomas H. *Manpower Planning and the Development of Human Resources.* New York: John Wiley & Sons, Inc., 1971.

Stahl, O. Glenn. *The Personnel Job of Government Managers.* Chicago: Public Personnel Association, 1971.

U.S. Department of Labor. *Employer Manpower Planning and Forecasting.* Washington, D.C., 1970.

FOOTNOTES

[1] Rensis Likert, *The Human Organization* (New York: McGraw-Hill Book Co., 1967), p. 1.

[2] Peter F. Drucker, *The Practice of Management* (New York: Harper & Row Publishers, Inc., 1954), p. 287.

[3] "Measuring How Office Workers Work," *Business Week*, November 14, 1970, pp. 54–60; Bruce Payne, "Clerical Cost Control," *Business Automation*, November 1968, pp. 52–55; Thomas H. Patten, Jr., *Manpower Planning and the Development of Human Resources* (New York: John Wiley & Sons, Inc., 1971), pp. 251–277; Rensis Likert, *New Patterns of Management* (New York: McGraw-Hill Book Co., 1961), pp. 192–221; Rensis Likert, *The Human Organization* (New York: McGraw-Hill Book Co., 1967), pp. 128–145; Stanley P. Powers and Annette Hartenstein, "Improving City Hall's Human Resources Management," *Nation's Cities*, August 1970, pp. 24–26; Dan Cordtz, "City Hall Discovers Productivity," *Fortune*, October 1971, pp. 92–96, 127–128.

[4] U.S. Bureau of the Budget, *Measuring Productivity of Federal Government Organizations* (Washington, D.C.: U.S. Government Printing Office, 1964), pp. 3–18. Also, see: Bertram M. Gross, "What Are Your Organization's Objectives?" *Human Relations*, August 1965, pp. 195–216; "Check Your Management Costs," *Nation's Business*, January 1962, pp. 218–221.

[5] Logan M. Cheek, "Cost Effectiveness Comes to the Personnel Function," *Harvard Business Review*, May-June 1973, p. 97.

[6] "America's Growing Antibusiness Mood," *Business Week*, June 12, 1972, pp. 100–103.

Part I Cases

HEMISPHERE INC.

ROCKILL-COTTON MACHINE COMPANY

JANUS PUBLIC AUTHORITY

HIGH STYLE COMPANY

HEMISPHERE INC.

Dr. Tony Slimline, director of manpower and organization development for Hemisphere Inc., retained Dr. Anne Ashe to undertake a consulting assignment relative to identifying goals for the enterprise.

After investigation and discussions, Dr. Ashe proposed the following:

Five-Year Goals for Hemisphere Inc.

1. Establish within Hemisphere a recruiting, selection, and development process which will enable it to fulfill the short-term and long-range manpower requirements necessary to attain strategic goals. This process must take into account all sources of manpower: minorities, women, handicapped, and others, as well as the mainstream individuals.

2. Create the capacity to analyze and respond to manpower and organizational development requirements. This includes establishing an in-house consulting service with professional skills in management development, manpower planning, behavioral sciences, etc.

3. Provide a vehicle for the continuing appraisal of the various management systems (e.g., compensation, training, etc.) and determine their impact on organizational and individual performance. As an outgrowth of the appraisal methodology, identify ways to improve existing systems and/or establish new systems.

4. Develop an information system that supports the human resource area of the organization. This includes the ability to assess the effectiveness of human resources (e.g., rate-of-return on investment in manpower planning and development).

5. Coordinate with the communities in which Hemisphere is located, and make a

meaningful contribution in establishing the communities as better places in which to live and work.

6. Provide a continuing organizational planning activity as it relates to manpower and organization development. This effort should be integrated with the overall goals and strategies of Hemisphere Inc.

QUESTIONS

1. What types of analyses is required to set appropriate goals or objectives for a specific organization?
2. How do you appraise the practicality of Dr. Ashe's suggested five-year goals for Hemisphere?
3. What types of policy decisions and resources would be required by Dr. Slimline if his department is to attain the suggested goals?

ROCKILL-COTTON MACHINE COMPANY

Mr. Rockill, chairman of the board and founder of the company, was concerned about the organization's ineffective use of computers. He had heard from executives of other organizations that they had reaped substantial benefits from computerization. Mr. Rockill suspects that the shortcoming in his organization emanates from middle management's lack of enthusiasm about computers. A management consultant recently recommended that Rockill-Cotton should upgrade its computer, and Mr. Rockill is considering signing a contract for a new computer with Big Machines Corporation. Before doing so, however, Mr. Rockill calls Mr. Jack Carson, personnel director, into his office. He tells Mr. Carson that he is thinking about holding a meeting with all the personnel concerned to inform them that anything less than complete cooperation with the computer effort would not be tolerated, and might result in dismissal.

QUESTIONS

1. Why might middle management have, in the past, resisted computerization in Rockill-Cotton?
2. Do you agree with Mr. Rockill's proposed method of gaining employees' cooperation for the computerization effort?
3. If you were Mr. Carson, what recommendations would you make to Mr. Rockill?

JANUS PUBLIC AUTHORITY

The Janus Public Authority had responsibility for public transportation in three adjacent states. Its problems were becoming more acute due to increased use of automobiles, highway construction not keeping pace with traffic, decreased use of buses and trains, population growth in the suburbs, and rising concerns about air pollution.

The director of the Authority, after consultation with his aides, decided that a transportation model (which mathematically represents the area's traffic patterns and facilities) was needed for planning solutions to the complex situation. The director asked the manager for planning to hire specialists to build such a model.

The manager of planning provided the personnel manager with a personnel requisition for two model builders (management scientists). After interviewing about ten candidates sent to him by the personnel manager, the manager of planning commented as follows:

"The personnel department is of no help to us. They don't understand technical problems and staffing.

The ten persons sent to me weren't qualified to build mud pies, let alone a transportation model.

Certainly, somewhere in this city there must be some talented model builders who understand practical problems and who can apply advanced mathematical techniques. But the personnel department can't find them."

QUESTIONS

1. What action would you take if you were the manager of planning?
2. What are some of the possible underlying causes of the failure of the personnel manager to satisfy the request of the manager of planning?

HIGH STYLE COMPANY

High Style Co. offices and plant are located in Boston. It manufactures a line of basic consumer goods. It employs about 500 persons and has a sales volume of about $5 million.

In the summer of 1972, the High Style Co. was preparing for the installation of its first computer, and management suspected it might have personnel ramifications.

A computer committee, consisting of the controller, the cost accountant, and an industrial engineer, conducted a computer feasibility study. After studying computers of several manufacturers, the committee decided to rent, with an option to buy, a medium-sized computer. Cost factors, displacement of personnel, and personnel training for the new operations were all included in the committee's considerations. In their report to the president, the committee recommended that employees be assured that they would not lose their jobs. The committee felt that normal turnover would eventually compensate for the displacements, while some employees might have to be transferred to other jobs.

The president decided not to follow the committee's advice, and drafted a notice which communicated the following facts to all employees:

1. The organization had ordered a computer.
2. The computer would not be delivered for 12 months, and no one would be released during that period.
3. After the computer was installed and operative, certain jobs would be eliminated while others would be reclassified.

4. The organization would try to transfer employees whose jobs were eliminated. Training programs would be made available for employees needing new skills.
5. No one would be terminated without three months advance notice.

The message was transmitted to the employees by means of the employees' bulletin board.

QUESTIONS

1. Discuss the pros and cons of the recommendations of the computer committee about not eliminating employees, and the president's position on the matter.
2. What were the likely outcomes of the president's bulletin to the employees?
3. How can such outcomes, as identified in the previous question, affect the success of the computer system that is to be installed?
4. If you were a member of High Style's top management, how would you have handled the situation?

PART 2
THE COMPUTER SYSTEM

This part of the book places computer systems, as related to human systems, in perspective.

Chapter 5. *A Systems Approach to Organization* explores the nature and importance of the systems approach, and its impact on people and organizations.

Chapter 6. *Management Information Systems* describes the characteristics of MIS and their effect on employees and their work. It also discusses the problems faced by those planning the introduction of computer-based information systems.

Chapter 7. *The Computer in Perspective* surveys the scope of the computer industry, the people in the computer field, computer users, trends in computer technology, and some of the social considerations related to the industry.

In sum, Part II *places the computer in focus and highlights people, group, and social factors that are related to the efforts of computer manufacturers, computer users, and computer professionals.*

5

A Systems Approach to Organization

If someone were to analyze current notions and fashionable catchwords, he would find "systems" high on the list. The concept has pervaded all fields of science and penetrated into popular thinking, jargon, and mass media. Systems thinking plays a dominant role in a wide range of fields from industrial enterprise and armaments to esoteric topics of pure science. Innumerable publications, conferences, symposia and courses are devoted to it. Professions and jobs have appeared in recent years which, unknown a short while ago, go under names such as systems design, systems analysis, systems engineering, and others. They are the very nucleus of a new technology and technocracy; their practitioners are the "new utopians" of our time . . . who—in contrast to the classic breed whose ideas remained between the covers of books—are at work creating a New World, brave or otherwise.

Ludwig von Bertalanffy

OBJECTIVES OF THE CHAPTER

The systems approach, a basic concept for coping with large-scale and complex problems, is discussed in this chapter. Two ideas stressed are the importance of avoiding a narrow perspective when analyzing problems and the imperativeness of considering the human element when designing new systems. Planners, designers, implementers, and managers of computers require a systems philosophy if they are to apply technology in a way that takes maximum advantage of computers and gains acceptance of those affected by change.

A later chapter (Chapter 13) deals with the more practical aspects of designing a personnel system.

CONCEPT OF THE ORGANIZATION

There are various ways of placing a frame around the concept of the organization. For our purposes, we shall consider the organization to be a human entity tied together by a common purpose and having definite boundaries. However, an organization becomes a vital instrument only when it has a suitable balance of its three resource elements.

Human resources are, of course, by definition, the indispensable ingredient. In most organizations they also constitute the most valuable element—although this too frequently appears to be overlooked under various pressures. Perceptive analysis, thinking, imagination, inspiration, creativity . . . individuality, ambition, competition, conflict . . . these make the human resource one of great plasticity, and present an exciting challenge to administration.

Physical resources encompass a host of items including: plant and equipment, land, materials and supplies, energy, money, and markets. The physical resources, unlike human resources, are subject to precise definition. One challenge is to maintain a best mix of the physical resources in changing environments.

Information resources are data, records, files, and reports—formal and informal. These include all the recorded history within the organization: reports on current status, descriptive reports, formal accounting reports, etc. Also included are the data pertaining to uncontrollable outside forces impinging upon the organization—economic climate, competition, political developments, technological advances, and the like. Only with the advent of the computer and related communications technology have the possibilities of an *integrated management information system* been recognized, and its development as an organizational resource been made possible.

These resource elements are joined together, in both a formal and informal sense; this can be considered the organization structure. In dynamic interplay, the human, physical, and information resources are combined in the operational activities of the organization; they are provided with required inputs and they generate outputs.

The systems approach is concerned with the most appropriate quantity and quality of these organizational resource elements and their structure and dynamic operation, for the purposes of the organization as a whole. The intent is thus to attain best use of resources in order to achieve desired goals.

THE ADMINISTRATOR'S ROLE

We shall define the administrator as the individual charged with the responsibility, and given the authority, to manage the organization, or a bounded segment of the organization having a charter which specifies purposes and overall goals.

The administrator has a primary task: to communicate and coordinate effectively, linking the administrative and the organizational resources. He or she must be an accepted leader and must competently carry out administrative functions: policy formulation, planning, decision-making and control. As a leader, the administrator has the challenge of motivating diverse individuals toward common goals. This entails making best use of organizational resources to attain overall objectives. Communication and coordination include two-way interaction with superiors, colleagues, subordinates, other units of the organization, and various external publics. Further, recognition must be given to both formal and informal types of communication and coordination.

THE SYSTEMS CONCEPT

The concept of system is of increasing importance in coping with the magnitude and intensity of technical and social change occurring in society. Broadly, the systems approach involves attaining an overview of a set of elements (subsystems) which are interrelated and which together constitute an entity (a system), having a specific purpose, and existing within a definable environment. Systems eventually become static and entropied unless they are renewed so that they adjust to changing conditions.

Von Bertalanffy and Boulding have shown the wide applicability of the systems approach. They have developed a unifying and integrating framework for the scientific disciplines to overcome the communications impediments caused by increasing fragmentation and specialization.[1] James G. Miller, building on von Bertalanffy's and Boulding's ideas, has classified living systems as follows:

- Cells are composed of atoms and molecules.

- Organs are composed of cells aggregated into tissues.

- Organisms are made up of organs.

- Groups (e.g., families, teams, tribes) are collections of organisms.

- Organizations consist of groups.

- Societies are made up of organizations, groups, and individuals.

- Supernational systems are coalescings of societies and organizations.

- The world system encompasses all supernational systems, organizations, societies, etc.[2]

The more particular systems constitute subsystems of broader systems, and so on in the hierarchy. It is important to determine the level in the hierarchy that may be appropriate when using the systems approach. The level should be consistent with the need to cope with a specific problem to be solved, while maintaining sufficient scope so that any solution is not severely sub-optimal in a broader framework.

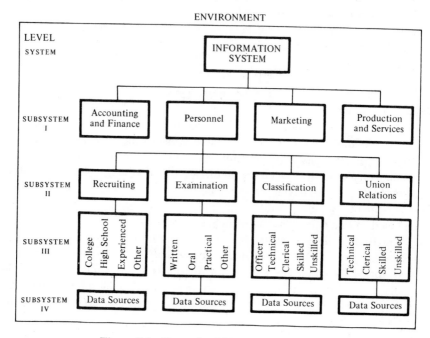

Figure 5-1 Example of hierarchy of systems.

The boundary between a system and its environment poses another danger, since frequently the environmental factors are less identifiable and controllable when compared to the internal factors of the system. Figure 5-1 depicts a system hierarchy. In the illustration, the total system is the information system. The information system is composed of four subsystems—accounting and finance, personnel, marketing, and production and services. Each of the major subsystems are, in turn, built upon lower subsystems (only those in the personnel area are detailed in the figure). The personnel subsystems are recruiting, examination, classification, and union relations. These subsystems are further differentiated (see subsystem level III). Finally, the ultimate data sources for each subsystem form the base for the example. The illustration should communicate the idea of an architectural design approach to the relationship of subsystems, in contrast with the prevalent view of considering each subsystem in isolation from any other.

Since systems theory focuses on the dynamic interrelationship and interaction of entities, information and communication are important elements. Wiener saw communication and information theory as a basis for describing and analyzing organizations and human groups. He drew parallels between computers and living beings: both have the capacity for collecting information, storing it, and using it as a basis for action.[3] Further, they have the potential for comparing actual performance with expected performance and to correct deviations by sending messages (feedback) which can change the behavior of the recipient. For this feedback and corrective process he coined the term *cybernetics* (which is derived from a Greek word meaning steersman or governor).

TOTAL SYSTEMS AND SUBSYSTEMS

The concept of system stresses that "best" subsystems can be created and can function only when related to all other subsystems in the organization, as well as to the bounded environmental conditions in which they all exist collectively. This overview approach employs optimization—although in real life one often can only approach or approximate an optimal solution. Although it is desirable to identify the ideal total system, in the implementation and operational phases, compromise is frequently required to compensate for such restraints as time and cost pressures.

The object function of a system is usually some measure of worth or value of the system. The process of systems optimization consists of two phases:

- The formulation of a value which is desired to be maximized, and
- The variation of the system in such a way as to accomplish the maximization.

One of the difficulties lies in the intricacies of even relatively simple systems. For instance, if a system has only seven elements, it has forty-two relations within itself. If we define the state of this system as the pattern produced in the network when each of these relations is either in being or not in being, there will be 2^{42} different states of the system. This is more than four million millions! This is the reason why the rigorous and exhaustive study of systems is so difficult, and why it remains as much art as science.

Of course, in real life many of the options in systems are immediately obvious. Many, if not most options, are uneconomic, technically not feasible, or beyond the threshold of acceptance in society.

The minimum human involvement obviously occurs in a system whose components are largely mechanical and whose operation is largely determined by the laws of science (e.g., guided missiles, automated refineries). Many systems, however, are not highly mechanistic; such systems cannot have predefined rules to cover all possible variations. Here, the human is essential to making decisions that modify the system to new conditions. These systems are referred to as being *adaptive*.

Systems means a continued effort to think in terms of the good of the entire organization and not segmented units of the organization. The administrator frequently faces a formidable task in getting subordinate managers fully to accept this notion, since people have the tendency to think in terms of their immediate environment and vested interest. This is a provincial, narrow, and shallow approach. On the other hand, the systems approach encourages depth and breadth of vision.

Admittedly, the total systems concept often involves grossly simplifying very intricate elements of the organization. This is frequently necessary for comprehension and for reduction of complexity to manageable dimensions, and does not preclude more minute study of manageable subsystems.

A system should not be viewed as closed or self-contained, but rather as an open one that is affected by its environment and, indeed, that affects the environment. Each organization has an internal event chain but it also has a vital external event chain that should be taken into account. Unfortunately, members of an organization will, by and large, give recognition only to their own immediate, internal environment and little or no attention to impinging external matters (e.g., those related to competitors, the realities of the market, government, social responsibilities, etc.).

Any subsystem exists as a matter of convenience or suitability (e.g., geographic, functional, project). Any such segmentation of the total system implies a certain degree of uncoupling which tends to create undesirable states (e.g., queues, friction, idleness, noise, disequilibrium). The objective is to minimize the undesirable conditions for the organization as a whole. In this connection, it is well to point out that subsystems can function independently very efficiently while tending to bankrupt the total system.

The total system must be a proper fit for both the internal requirement and the external world. In other words, the total system must be realistically proper—not idealistically desirable. When the system does not match the realistic world, the organization exists at reduced vigor. In a sense, the organization continues to survive and carry out its functions in spite of poor systems. In other words, rational consequences ensue from irrational factors.

The systems approach attempts to bring order and structure to chaos, segmentation, and complexity. It does this with the recognition of the dynamics of change and of the indeterminacy of many events in the universe.

An example of the realistic pressures which often prevent application of the systems approach follows:

- Leo was assigned the project of computerizing the organization's benefit plans, including the pension area. Several months passed, and the controller asked Leo if the computer program was ready. Leo replied, "No. I am still trying to understand the current system and the complex relations between the benefits plans, payroll, and the accounting procedures. Also, I want to evaluate several alternative ways of designing the new system." The controller was very irritated and contacted Leo's boss, Richard Moor. He said to Moor, "Let's get Leo on the stick. He is spinning his wheels. I want that darn benefit plan computerized *now*, not in two or three years!"

INTEGRATION OF SUBSYSTEMS

The designing of a total system necessitates integration of subsystems. This means active and concerted participation of all operations, resources, and administrative tasks of the organization. Traditional and artificial boundaries must yield when systems integration takes place. Systems require both vertical and horizontal integration; the latter is often difficult to achieve because of traditional functionalism.

Horizontal integration is in contrast with vertical integration where, traditionally, each function operated in its own world without particular concern for its surroundings or its influence on the total system. By linking the organization resource elements (information, physical, human) together in an operation flow pattern that cuts across the traditional functions, a system can be designed that will best support the administrative tasks. Such an approach tends to improve communication and coordination, since a common and uniform data source is used throughout the organization. This approach also tends to shorten the information time cycle, thus providing more responsive capability. (Figure 5-2 illustrates two approaches to systems.)

In unintegrated systems, information resource elements are frequently out of phase with the physical and human resource elements. Therefore, inappropriate information may be used by the administrator in planning, decision-making, and control. Even the most competent administrator will perform at less than capacity under such circumstances.

In integrated systems, the organization resource elements (information, physical, and human) move in a continuous operational flow—sequentially or parallel—toward a common and explicit goal.

- While some significant strides have been achieved in the development of integrated systems in the financial and operations areas of organizations, the authors' research revealed that few organizations have attained highly integrated personnel systems. The federal government's departments appear to have made most progress in this direction. Business and state governments are developing plans for integrating their personnel systems. Local governments are lagging in this movement towards integration.

A. VERTICAL INTEGRATION

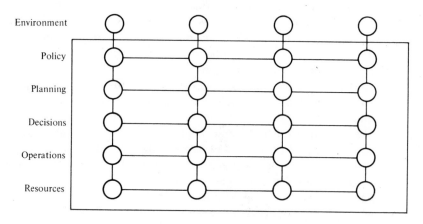

B. VERTICAL AND HORIZONTAL INTEGRATION

Figure 5-2   Approaches to systems.

A. CONVENTIONAL ORGANIZATION CHART

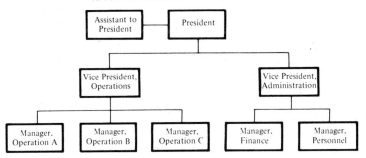

B. SYSTEMS APPROACH TO ORGANIZATION RELATIONS

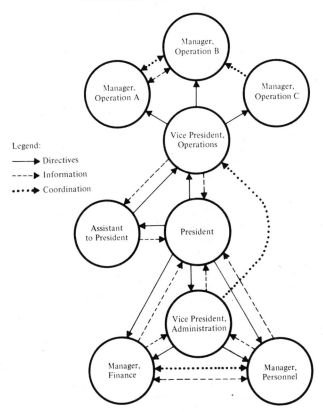

Figure 5-3   Systems approach to organization charts.

A highly desirable outcome of the integrated systems approach is the realignment of the organization structure. Such realignment would reflect the realistic underlying needs of the organization and its operations, resource elements, and administrative tasks. Many organization structures have evolved over the years, and they reflect patchwork accumulation of history rather than logical patterns for coping with dynamic conditions. Figure 5-3 compares a conventional organization chart with one developed using a systems approach.

The conventional organization chart is static and only represents formal relationships. The systems approach chart attempts to indicate a more realistic view of interrelationships, which may be of an informal kind as well as of the formal variety. A systems analyst who depended on the formal depiction could be seriously misled and, consequentially, could design a system that is out-of-phase with reality.

IMPLICATIONS OF SYSTEMS IN ORGANIZATIONS

The systems approach is, to a large extent, the antithesis of the bureaucratic (in business as well as government) approach, while it is largely consistent with the organic organization approach. Bureaucracy emphasizes, among other things, the chain-of-command, formalized communications, well-defined procedures, etc. The systems view presumes an open rather than closed organization, interactions at numerous points, dynamic responses to a changing environment, etc. While bureaucracy focuses on individual functional goals, the systems approach stresses integrated subsystems and total system performance. Simultaneous action of separate but interrelated parts can together produce a total effect greater than the sum of the individual parts. *This synergistic characteristic is the essence of system.* Figure 5-4 depicts some of the facets of the systems approach by viewing some planning activities (including manpower planning) and how they relate and integrate into an overall coordinated pattern.

While organizations are open systems faced with uncertainty, the use of the systems approach is intended to reduce the degree of uncertainty and to add rationality to decision-making. Besides the objectivity that is sought in a systems model, consideration must be given to the human requirement within the system. Rather than being a dehumanizing factor, the systems concept can improve the effectiveness of the organization and provide opportunity for increased human expression and self-fulfillment. Figure 5-5 is a model of organization as a system.

While the human element is recognized as vital in the dynamic systems concept, there unfortunately appears to be a contemporary tendency to view man as a predictable robot. While robotic theory is sometimes denounced, it

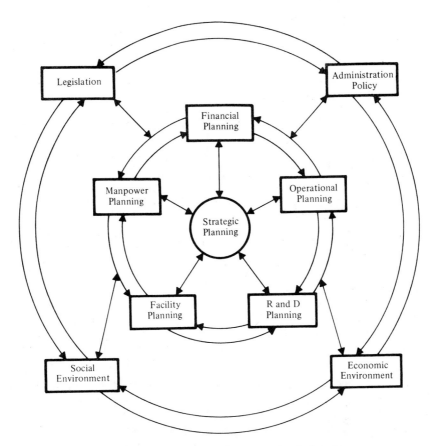

Figure 5-4 Systems view of organizational planning.

remains quite widely accepted in psychological research, theory, and engineering (e.g., social scientists who pattern human behavior on the model of rat or pigeon behavior). The image of man as a robot closely corresponds to the mythology of mass society and to the glorification of machine and profit motive as being prime sources of progress.

There is need to consider a new model of man: a model that emphasizes humanistic psychology. Such a view stresses the creative side of human beings, the importance of individual differences, and aspects of life that are non-utilitarian and beyond the biological values of subsistence and survival. Thus, man is not merely a passive receiver of stimuli, but in very concrete ways creates his world. This view of man encourages systems that are molded for the benefit of people, and discourages mechanistic approaches which

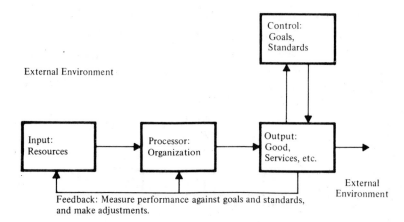

Figure 5-5   The organization as a system.

either ignore the human element or attempt to force humans to suit the system.[4]

Under the systems concept, the organization is viewed as a series of parts which include the individual, the informal work groups, the formal organization, and the environmental factors. These parts are integrated through such processes as communication, information, and decision-making.

THE STUDY, DESIGN, AND IMPLEMENTATION OF SYSTEMS

The systems concept is increasingly relevant in our world because of the growing complexity of our society, the large size of many organizations, the shrinking of time and space, the explosion of information, the inter-dependency of operations, and the diversity of ideals and goals. A few examples will indicate the types of problems that call for the use of the systems approach:

- Planning for the "best" balance of transportation facilities (highways, automobiles, railroads, rapid transit, etc.).

- Allocating the federal government's financial resources for national defense and domestic programs.

- Determining an appropriate blend of public and private education facilities, and allocating resources for particular educational purposes (e.g., health, science, urban planners).

- Instituting environmental protection programs while, at the same time, assuring adequate power for industry, government, homes, etc.

Problems such as those mentioned above are complex mixtures of technical, financial, economic, social, and political considerations. There are four broad phases in studying, designing, and implementing a system:

1. Understanding the present system.
2. Determining the requirements for the new system.
3. Designing the new system.
4. Gaining the acceptance of the new system.

Chapter 13 illustrates in some detail the application of these phases to a personnel system.

A thorough systems effort includes the study of such factors as:

- History of the organization.
- The organization's creeds and policies.
- Plans and objectives of the firm.
- Organization structure.
- Responsibilities and authorities of positions.
- Resources of the organization.
- The organization's place in its industry and in the economy.
- Existing operational procedures.
- Government regulations and other constraints.
- Social and other external influences.

Gross suggests that the key points in systems analysis involve gaining understanding of organizational structure and performance. In discussing organizational structure, Gross provides the following delineation:

> The structure of any organization or unit thereof consists of (1) people, and (2) non-human resources, (3) grouped together in differentiated subsystems, that (4) interrelate among themselves, and (5) with the external environment, (6) and are subject to various values, and (7) to such central guidance as may help to provide the capacity for future performance.[5]

Gross then says that the performance of an organization consists of activities that:

> (1) satisfy the varying interests of people and groups by (2) producing outputs of services or goods, (3) making efficient use of inputs relative to outputs, (4) investing in the system, (5) acquiring resources, and (6) doing all these things in a manner that conforms with various codes of behaviour and (7) varying concepts of technical and administrative rationality.[6]

The systems analyst must observe both the formal and informal system.

Thus, he must study organization charts and job descriptions in order to learn about authority and responsibility, decision-making locus, and the nature of work performed. However, these formal documents are often unrealistic oversimplifications. Therefore, it is essential to determine such things as the actual communication lines—which may vary considerably from the formal chains of command.

Usually there is little recorded information about the informal environment; the analyst must ferret out such conditions through observation, investigation, and interaction with people. The analyst must also recognize that the environment is constantly changing: systems should not be analyzed or designed on the assumption that they exist in a stable state.

The analyst must always remember that the systems he is analyzing or designing affect people. He must try to understand possible reactions to the system and the reasons behind them, even if they appear to be irrational. Two pitfalls the analyst himself must avoid are: generalizing from non-representative cases and assuming cause and effect from a correlation.

A simple model of job performance (Figure 5-6) provides a basis for the manager's understanding of the ways in which he can influence individual behavior. The model shows that job performance is a function of two primary elements—the individual's ability and his motivation. Ability, in turn, depends on mental capacity, experience, education, and training. An individual's motivation depends on his personal needs and the ways in which

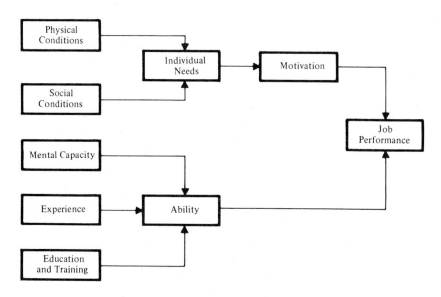

Figure 5-6   Job performance model.

his physical and social surroundings satisfy him. The elements which the manager can affect are at the left of the diagram. Although he cannot affect the basic abilities or needs of the people who function in his organization, the manager can try to select people on the basis of their needs, mental capacity, experience, education, and training, and he can provide physical and social conditions which contribute to the fulfillment of individual needs.

GAINING ACCEPTANCE OF CHANGE

The analyst must consider the possible causes of employees' resistance to change. These include:

1. Fear of: losing one's position, loss of status, and inability to cope with new work.
2. Reduced interest in the work.
3. Suspicion of management's motives in proposing the change.
4. Resentment of change because it is assumed to be a personal criticism.
5. Social disruption caused by rearranging work relationships.

Following are some of the effective ways of overcoming such resistance:

1. Inform people in advance of the reasons and benefits of changes.
2. Provide opportunity for employees to participate in the consideration of change.
3. When possible, provide employees with some personal reward connected with the change.
4. Provide training and education to make certain that employees are prepared to cope with changes.
5. Carefully schedule the timing of the change (e.g., decide whether it should be introduced in gradual stages, or quickly).
6. Cultivate the "habit of change." Help people to see the need for change in a viable organization, and show how the change can bring them personal rewards.
7. Where possible, provide models or examples of how the change has been beneficial and successful elsewhere.

- The authors found, in their study of organizations, that much of systems work is done in isolation from the real world. The analyst may have some limited discussions about the problem area with a few key persons. A considerable amount of the analyst's time is spent in relative isolation—closed in his work area. The analyst has difficulty in communicating with the people in the problem area. Conversely, those people have difficulty in communicating their needs to the systems

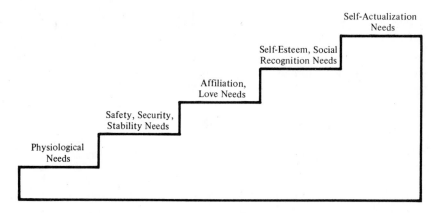

Figure 5-7   Hierarchy of human needs.

analyst. Further, the analyst tends to concentrate on the non-human facets of the system (e.g., reports, paperwork, organization charts, controls). This results in systems that do not consider the organization's most vital resource: people!

In this connection, *awareness of the needs of people is highly important to the systems person, since systems changes must coincide, as closely as possible, with employee benefits as well as organizational objectives.* A. H. Maslow's widely quoted hierarchy of needs (Figure 5-7) is one illustration of how human needs shift from the most basic (e.g., food and shelter) to the highest (e.g., personal development, moral and spiritual growth). People are motivated by unsatisfied needs. As their lower-level needs are satisfied, they tend no longer to motivate. High-level needs take over and are the bases for motivation.

Figure 5-8 presents a facetious comparison of two flow chart systems for "getting to work in the morning." One system is overly generalized and does not consider many human elements. The second system is more detailed and takes into account the human factors.

A systems designer cannot design the behavior and attitude of people, nor can he program people as he would a computer. Each individual has a unique personality. What the designer can do, however, is to consider the characteristics and features of the organization—both formal and informal—which will contribute to getting the most for and from individuals and groups. He can then design a facilitating system—one that will serve as a fertile environment for new ideas and for productive, satisfying effort.

SYSTEM WITH HUMAN FACTORS

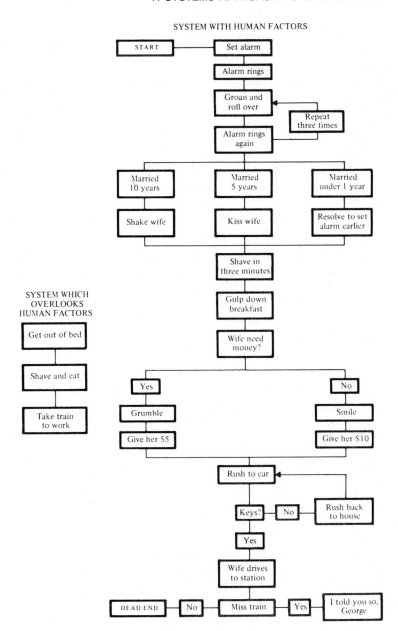

Figure 5-8   How to get to work in the morning.

WEAKNESSES IN EXISTING COMPUTER SYSTEMS

In actual practice, many systems appear to ignore the foregoing insights about human needs and motivation. Instead, systems are designed which

1. Do not incorporate the ideas and experiences of those with many years experience in the problem area.
2. Emphasize the technical and economic aspects, and largely ignore human elements.
3. Solve idealized or overly simplified versions of the real problem.
4. Contain inflexible routines which prove unadaptable to changing conditions.
5. Concentrate on a restricted problem area solution which may improve a local condition while creating even greater problems in related areas.

Argyris' research findings are confirmed by the authors' experience in practice:

. . . the nature of the organizational structure, managerial controls, executive leadership styles, personnel control systems (for example, practices in human relations and communication), and the values executives hold about effective human relationships are all synchronized to decrease the probability that the conditions for systems competence will be optimally fulfilled when the system is dealing with nonroutine, innovative, and potentially threatening problems. There is a built-in tendency for most systems to create in the lower levels psychological failure minimal essentiality, and acceptance of oneself as an object rather than as a human being (to be "market-oriented," to quote Eric Fromm). There is also the tendency for most systems to increase at the upper levels an attitude of closedness, conformity, and mistrust, and the need to play it safe and to distort and censor information going to the top. These two tendencies produce organizational dysfunctions such as (a) management by crisis, by pressure, and by detail; (b) destructive intergroup conflicts; and (c) ineffective problem solving, decision-making, and implementation.[7]

To overcome such existing weaknesses in systems, Argyris suggests that:

. . . a high frequency of psychological success, shared leadership, expressed concern for the effectiveness of the group as a system, continual examination of group processes to reduce blocks, reduction of the gap between leader and members, and continued attention to the accomplishment of challenging group tasks will tend to increase the probability that the group will tend to manifest a high degree of system competence. These conditions will also tend to provide opportunities for individuals to increase their self-acceptance, feelings of confirmation, and essentiality. These, in turn, will increase the member's identification with and concern over the group which, in turn, will tend to increase the focus on stimulating even further opportunities for psychological success, shared leadership, and all other criteria of effective groups . . .[8]

Most manual and mechanical ways of performing work are based on specialization and fragmentation. The use of a computer can set in motion a systematic re-evaluation of what the organization is and how it can operate more effectively. A re-evaluation can expose the real problems which are often related to fragmented decision-making and information inadequacies. Such an exposure can lead to establishing systems that will provide information needed for coordinated decision-making. Electronic technology can thus help us handle large-scale, interrelated problems on an integrated basis.

- The authors discussed, with a senior systems analyst, the personnel systems in one of the larger states. The analyst said, "Although this is the central computer facility for the state, we don't have anything like the control we need. Even in our department, the personnel records are not integrated; for instance, there are totally different files for payroll and personnel statistics. Then, the retirement and benefits board works almost completely independently as far as their data processing is concerned. The Civil Service Commission has their own small computer, for recruitment and other uses. The state educational records are outside of our system. We are a long, long way from anything like integration and a total system for our personnel records."

Too frequently, it is assumed that the brute power and speed of the computer will resolve the problems of an organization. This assumption, although widely held, is naive. *The effective use of a computer is dependent, to a considerable degree, on the imagination and sensitive awareness of the systems people who create the blueprint of the programs which are to be executed by the computer equipment.* Unfortunately, systems work is too often done on a provincial basis, rather than with the systems approach. Almost invariably, such narrower applications perpetuate or magnify problems. For instance, in a poorly designed manual system the employees will often develop informal procedures to compensate for unworkable procedures. On the other hand, the computer will, unthinking, carry out the poorly designed programs and do so at speeds and with methods that are difficult to audit and correct by humans.

- Not infrequently during their research, the authors heard the following comment,

  "We just don't have time for systems planning and design. We are under too much pressure to get our applications running on the computer."

It is apparent that many organizations short-circuit systems work and, consequently, often do not understand the real nature of their problems and have not pre-planned the best system. Instead, work is hastily programmed and turned over to the computer.

Because of the mysterious characteristics of the computer, often incorrect computer processing can evade detection for long periods of time and can result in serious losses (financial and human) to the organization. Managements that want to achieve more effective use of computers must be committed to a substantial investment of time and talent in systems planning, design, and development, prior to placing applications on computers. The organizations that bypass the systems phase are undoubtedly the ones in which management is perplexed as to why their computers fail to live up to expectations.

SUMMARY

The systems approach entails taking an overview of any matter that is under study; that is, attempting to perceive the "big picture" before concentrating on a smaller, manageable sector. The approach encourages identification of how the various components (subsystems) of a larger system are related and interact. One of the pressing general problems of our time is that when we think we solve one problem (e.g., increasing our fuel supply by opening new oil fields) we, too often, create other problems (e.g., ecological damage). By using the systems approach, the expectation is that harmful sub-optimization will be avoided and wiser decisions can be made.

In many computer installations, the claim is that "there is no time for integrated systems work." As a consequence, unintegrated and sub-optimal computer applications appear to be the rule rather than the exception. Is it little wonder that there have been so many disappointments with computer performance?

Those systems concepts and techniques that are employed have, unfortunately, by and large taken a coldly rational approach to problems. This has resulted in many unrealistic or poorly received computer applications. *The systems approach must factor in the human element if computer applications are to work well in our society*. Too little attention has been devoted to providing systems people with the training, methods, or support to achieve the goals of the integrated systems approach.

Chapter 6, which follows, surveys the nature of management information systems, and discusses the challenges involved when planning and implementing such systems.

KEY CONCEPTS OF THE CHAPTER

1. The systems approach involves having both the "big picture" of the organization and insight about the interrelationships of the smaller components (subsystems) of the organization.

2. When designing computer applications, the systems approach should be used to avoid harmful, sub-optimal computer programs.

3. Systems work cannot be successfully accomplished in a vacuum. The person doing the systems work must have, in addition to technical competency, an appreciation for the practical aspects of the business' objectives and operations.

4. Imaginatively designed systems can be supportive of organic organizations (discussed in Chapter 2).

5. Systems work often fails to consider the needs and motivations of the people affected.

6. The widely used practice of circumventing the systems approach has resulted in sub-optimal computer applications and unenthusiastic attitudes about computers and computer technicians.

DISCUSSION QUESTIONS

General Background (Seminar/Classroom Discussion)

1. What is the "systems approach"? Why is it important and useful?
2. How might the systems approach be used in a phase of your work or personal life?
3. Of what value is the general systems theory of von Bertalanffy?

Operational and Technical

1. Identify a system which has recently been designed or one in the process of being designed. Determine the extent to which human factors were taken into account when designing the system. How does one build a system which balances technical, economic, and social factors?
2. Prior to designing a system, is concerted effort made to relate that system to other systems and to the "big picture"? Why are these steps important?

Policy

1. Try to depict, on paper, your organization as a system. Do not adhere to conventional vertical functionalism or divisions but, rather, trace the natural flow of goods, services, information, etc. Why is such a systems approach important to an executive?
2. Does your organization make efforts to discover and integrate systems which are

fragmented and uncoordinated? What are the barriers to attaining such integration?

Areas for Research

1. Discuss the practicalities of the total systems concept. Obtain the views of several systems analysts. What are the pros and cons of the concept?
2. Study a formal organization chart of a unit with which you are familiar. Indicate the weaknesses of the chart (e.g., what relationships are not shown). Develop a more realistic picture for displaying the organizational relations.
3. Analyze the amount of man-hours devoted to systems work and computer programming in your organization. Do you think your organization devotes a reasonable balance to both of the activities? Compare your findings with the experiences of several other organizations. Explain any significant differences.
4. Discuss, with people affected by a systems change, what their reactions are to such change. How can systems change be made more acceptable to people?

BIBLIOGRAPHY

Argyris, Chris. *Intervention Theory and Method.* Reading, Massachusetts: Addison-Wesley Publishing Company, 1970.

Beckett, John A. *Management Dynamics.* New York: McGraw-Hill Book Co., 1971.

Churchman, C. West. *The Systems Approach.* New York: Delacorte Press, 1968.

Cleland, David I. and William R. King. *Management: A Systems Approach.* New York: McGraw-Hill Book Co., 1972.

Couqer, Daniel and Knapp. *Systems Analysis Techniques.* New York: John Wiley & Sons, Inc., 1974.

Daniels, Alan and Donald Yeates. *Systems Analysis.* Palo Alto, California: Science Research Associates, Inc., 1971.

DeGreene, Kenyon B., ed. *Systems Psychology.* New York: McGraw-Hill Book Co., 1970.

Emery, James C. *Organizational Planning and Control Systems.* New York: The Macmillan Co., 1969.

Glans, Thomas B., et al. *Management Systems.* New York: Holt, Rinehart, and Winston, Inc., 1968.

Kast, Fremont E. and James E. Rosenzweig. *Organization and Management–A Systems Approach.* New York: McGraw-Hill Book Co., 1970.

Laszlo, Ervin, ed. *The Relevance of General Systems Theory.* New York: George Braziller, Inc., 1972.

Lucas, Henry. *Toward Creative Systems Design.* New York: Columbia University Press, 1974.

Optner, Stanford L. *Systems Analysis for Business Management.* Englewood Cliffs, New Jersey: Prentice-Hall, Inc., 1975.

Seiler, John A. *Systems Analysis in Organizational Behavior.* Homewood, Illinois: Richard D. Irwin, Inc., 1967.

Tomeski, Edward A. *The Computer Revolution.* New York: The Macmillan Co., 1970.

Tomeski, Edward A. "Systems and Management Concepts, in Computers in Business." San Francisco: Holden-Day, Inc., 1979, pp. 2-43.

Von Bertalanffy, Ludwig. *General System Theory.* New York: George Braziller, Inc., 1968.

―――. *Robots, Men and Minds.* New York: George Braziller, Inc., 1967.

Weinberg, Gerald. *An Introduction to General Systems Thinking.* New York: John Wiley & Sons, Inc., 1975.

FOOTNOTES

[1] Ludwig von Bertalanffy, *General System Theory* (New York: George Braziller, Inc., 1968), pp. 28–38; Kenneth Boulding, "General System Theory—The Skeleton of Science," *Management Science*, Volume II, 1956, pp. 1–10.

[2] James G. Miller, "Living Systems: Basic Concepts," *Behavioral Science*, July 1965, p. 213.

[3] Norbert Wiener, *The Human Use of Human Beings* (New York: Doubleday & Co., Inc., 1954), pp. 48, 57–64, 78–80; Norbert Wiener, *God and Golem, Inc.* (Cambridge, Massachusetts: M.I.T. Press, 1964).

[4] Ludwig von Bertalanffy, *General System Theory* (New York: George Braziller, Inc., 1968), pp. 188–197.

[5] Bertram M. Gross, "What Are Your Organization's Objectives?" *Human Relations*, August 1965, pp. 197–198.

[6] Ibid., pp. 197–198.

[7] Chris Argyris, *Intervention Theory and Method* (Reading, Massachusetts: Addison-Wesley Publishing Co., 1970), pp. 77–78.

[8] Ibid., p. 45.

6

Management Information Systems

Information flows are as important to the life and health of businesses as the flow of blood is to the life and health of an individual.

George A. Steiner

Theoreticians may debate the topic fruitlessly, but a management information system has become an absolute necessity for successful operation of a large and complex business enterprise.

Terrance Hanold

OBJECTIVES OF THE CHAPTER

This chapter discusses the nature, scope, and challenges of management information systems (MIS). Particular attention is devoted to the problems in planning for and installing such systems. Some of the behavioral and political considerations related to MIS are considered. Administrators and technicians, interested in using the computer for more than a processor of routine data, should become familiar with the prospects and difficulties of MIS.

STATUS AND TRENDS OF MIS

A management information system is an assemblage of data (facts, opinions, etc.) so processed (summarized, categorized, projected, etc.) that it constitutes intelligence (information) for purposes of managerial decision-making and the attainment of organizational goals.

Organizations that are very small, such as the neighborhood retail store, may function well with an informal information system. Such a system may have information stored in the mind of the owner and on scraps of paper. Even in these cases, however, government taxes necessitate some kind of formal record-keeping and reports. As an organization grows in size and diversity, informal information systems no longer suffice. Lack of information and improper communication of it can cause organizational breakdowns.

Large organizations must have some kind of formal information systems, which provide a basis for managing records, operations, and functions. An information system is a major method of communications between humans in an organization, and serves as linkage with the external environment. Besides the formal information system, each organization has an informal information system based on personal contacts, observations, the "grapevine," etc. According to Drucker:

> Information has been unbelievably expensive, almost totally unreliable, and always so late that it was of little if any value. Most of us who had to work with information in the past, therefore, knew we had to invent our own. One developed, if one had any sense, a reasonably good instinct for what invention was plausible and likely to fly, and what wasn't. But ·eal information just wasn't to be had. Now, for the first time, it's beginning to ↲ available—and the overall impact on society is bound to be very great.[1]

It is estimated that as much as 50 per cent of the costs of running our economy may be related to information costs. Obviously, sound decisions are based upon the adequacy and accuracy of the information used, as well as the decision-makers' sense of timing.

Two citations will indicate the tremendous magnitude of the paperwork explosion in the United States.

- It is estimated that there are about two quadrillion pieces of paper filed in offices and storage areas, and that about two million persons spend a large percentage of their working time handling and maintaining this paper avalanche. (By the way, a quadrillion is a number followed by 15 zeroes!)

- The Federal Reserve Board of the federal government has indicated that about 26 billion paper checks are written each year, and the number will increase to 54 billion by 1985 if the present rate of increase is continued.

Traditionally, management information has not received high priority, and has usually represented a relatively loose amalgamation of data and reports having no overall consistent pattern. Such information invariably is generated to fulfill basic accounting and legal requirements, and does not focus on supporting managerial decision-making. Figure 6-1 contrasts routine data processing characteristics, prevalent in most organizations, with the emerging MIS approach.

One large organization analyzed the output of its computers and determined that 96 per cent of the volume could be classified as routine data

According to our research department, our public opinion polls, our sampling of potential users, our forecasts of marketing trends, our estimates of consumer reaction, and our statistical model manipulations, we overcooked the vegetables."

© DATAMATION (Reproduced with permission)

Data processing frequently has the following characteristics	*MIS frequently has the following characteristics*
• Routine	• Non-routine and novel
• Procedurized	• Difficult to procedurize
• Accounting orientation	• Extends beyond accounting
• Internal data	• External as well as internal data
• Mechanistic	• Requires some human judgment
• Basic computations	• Complex computations
• Historical or current data	• Predictive
• Precision recordings	• Estimates
Examples of Data Processing	*Examples of MIS*
• Payroll	• Collective bargaining strategy
• Man-job matching	• Manpower forecasting
• Labor cost accounting	• Human resource accounting

Figure 6-1   Contrast of data processing and MIS.

processing, while the remaining 4 per cent was information that might aid management's decision-making!

Sheer volume and complexity of information patterns in today's organizations have revealed the inadequacies of the traditional approaches to information. They include such impediments as information overload, irrelevancy, lack of timeliness, and inaccuracies. These information limitations have caused decision-making to be based upon arbitrariness, inadequate analysis, and uninformed judgment.

There are a number of reasons why management has a growing interest in information systems:

1. There is less time today between the presentation of a problem to management and the time needed for a solution. The complexity of organizations, and the sheer volume and size of problems, require information systems that can facilitate sound and timely decision-making.

2. Change in public attitudes towards organizations and authority creates need for information systems. The executive must be able to respond more sensitively to the inquiries and requests of various active publics: government, consumer groups, stockholders, researchers, investigatory units, etc.

3. Organizations, as previously indicated, are increasingly staffed with sophisticated, better educated employees engaged in work related to higher technology processes (e.g., research and development, science-oriented organizations, automation and computer systems, market research). Executives must be able to provide leadership for such human resources, including assessing their activities and information.

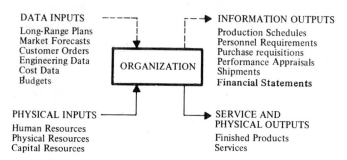

Figure 6-2 An organization as an input-output system.

The role of top management, related to information systems, can be defined as follows:

One of management's most important responsibilities is to create a climate of support throughout the organization for the systems that are being undertaken. This supportive climate includes: recruiting qualified persons, education of management about modern technology, involvement of the users affected by modern technology, and leadership by top management. "Top flight people," says Gaylord Freeman, "will be the most important factor in the success or failure of your MIS." [2]

Information flowing through a system may take many forms:

- Operating documents used in routine activities of the organization (e.g., paychecks, invoices, requisitions).

- Directives used to guide the actions of others (e.g., budgets, schedules, plans).

- Performance and status reports (e.g., accounting statements, actual expenditures compared to budget, inventory status, productivity levels).

- Environmental data (e.g., demographic analysis, economic forecasts).

Figure 6-2 contains an overview of an organization system, showing the inputs and outputs of the system. Physical inputs are converted by the organization into outputs of products and services. Data inputs are converted to information outputs.

Gardner has provided some pertinent cautions about information systems:

As organizations (and societies) become larger and more complex, the men at the top (whether managers or analysts) depend less and less on firsthand experience, more and more on heavily 'processed' data. Before reaching them, the raw data—what actually goes on 'out there'—have been sampled, screened, condensed, compiled, coded, expressed in statistical form, spun into generalizations and crystallized into recommendations.

It is a characteristic of an information processing system that it systematically filters out certain kinds of data so that these never reach the men who depend on the system. The information that is omitted (or seriously distorted) is information that is not readily expressed in words or numbers, or cannot be rationally condensed into lists, categories, formulas or compact generalizations by procedures now available to us.

No one can run a modern organization who is not extraordinarily gifted in handling the end products of a modern information processing system. So we find at the top of our large organizations (and at the top of our government) more and more men who are exceedingly gifted in manipulating verbal and mathematical symbols. And they all understand one another. It is not that they see reality the same way. It is that through long training they have come to see reality through the same distorting glasses. There is nothing more heartwarming than the intellectual harmony of two analysts whose training has accustomed them to accept as reality the same systematic distortions thereof.

But what does the information processing system filter out? It filters out all sensory impressions not readily expressed in words and numbers. It filters out emotion, feeling, sentiment, mood and almost all of the irrational nuances of human situations. It filters out those intuitive judgments that are just below the level of consciousness.

So the picture of reality that shifts to the top of our great organizations and our society is sometimes a dangerous mismatch with the real world. We suffer the consequences when we run head on into situations that cannot be understood except in terms of those elements that have been filtered out. The planners base their plans on the prediction that the people will react in one way, and they react violently in quite another way.[3]

COMPUTER-BASED MIS

MIS can be handled primarily by manual means, mechanical methods, by computer—or some combination of the three. Recent technology has provided the basis for significant potential improvements in MIS. This potential has aroused considerable interest about computer-based MIS, although it appears that wide implementation of such systems is still largely in the future.

- A study of ninety organizations, by the authors, revealed that the most extensive computerized applications in the personnel area tend to be highly routinized (e.g., payroll, employee benefits). On the other hand, the uncomputerized areas include those less subject to standardization but which might be more vital to management decision-making (e.g., collective bargaining, manpower planning).

- The authors' studies indicate that while personnel administrators in the federal government, state officials, and executives in many businesses do use computer-generated information for decision-making—there is an awareness that much more remains to be done in this area. On the other hand, the findings indicate that local government officials have received little aid from computers.

The features of the computer, discussed at length in the next chapter, which make an MIS more feasible are:

- Accurate and rapid processing of data.

- Vast storage and prompt retrievability of information.

- Performance of computations and logical operations with very high reliability.

Without the computer, sophisticated and even unsophisticated information systems would be difficult to attain in today's complex organizations. Such organizations may deal with data in the following kinds of magnitudes:

- Thousands, tens-of-thousands, or hundreds-of-thousands of employees.

- Many hundreds, thousands, or even millions of customers or clients.

- Hundreds or thousands of different products and/or services.

- Numerous vendors.

- Thousands, tens-of-thousands, or hundreds-of-thousands of stockholders.

- Numerous facilities, equipment, inventories, etc. in many different locations.

- Thousands or even millions of different records and reports.

An organization can be viewed as a super-system containing three kinds of systems:

1. The process system, consisting of stations where work is performed and the paths along which the work flows.

2. The decision system required to make the work flow, or which is in response to the work flow.

3. The information system which consists of the flow of internal information between work and decision, and external information related to the outside world which is connected to the decision system.

An effective information system should have certain characteristics that permit:

1. Selection of information that is relevant to particular situations (management-by-exception), preventing either an excess or inadequacy of information.

2. Comparison of current information with plans (feedback) to discover deviations and, if needed, trigger corrective action.

3. Immediate access to information to support management decisions in unpredictable situations.

4. Delivery of information in a timely fashion to facilitate decision-making.

5. Horizontal and vertical dissemination of needed information so that all affected persons will be properly informed.

A computer-based MIS can have particular value in an organization that is committed to management-by-objectives (MBO). The computer's rapid processing can permit the persons interested in results to trace, on a real-time basis if that is desirable, performance versus set standards. The person being measured can find this useful, since it alerts that individual when and where performance may be lagging. Properly applied, the MBO approach can be strengthened by MIS. Improperly applied, a real-time follow-up of performance can appear to be an insidious intelligence scheme to place undue pressure on employees. Further, since there is an understandable fluctuation of performance in many types of work, a continuous tracing of performance can be a waste of managerial time and effort.

Figure 6-3 depicts the management information systems concept. Several key elements should be mentioned. A planned data base constitutes the foundation of the MIS. The data base contains rigorously selected and defined data elements that represent the activities and goals of the organization, as well as pertinent external inputs. Considerable care is given to assuring that the data elements, which collectively make up the data base, are accurate, consistent, and up-to-date. In essence, the data base is a supra-file with flexibility, quick retrievability, and expandability. The data elements in the data base can be combined and manipulated to provide any combination of integrated information. The integrated information can be filtered, based upon any set of rules, resulting in selected information. The levels of the MIS are planned to be responsive to the levels of responsibility in the organization. Thus, the data base provides routine reports to appropriate persons responsible for the work performed by the organization. Managers and staff have access to integrated information in order to facilitate their plans and decisions. Policy makers have access to selected information. This representation indicates the need, in MIS, for an architectural structure for the

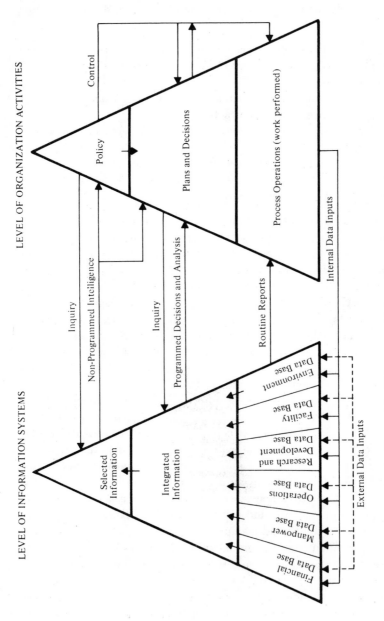

Figure 6-3 **Management information systems concept.**

Equation	Linear Equations			Nonlinear Equations		
	One Equation	A Few Equations	Many Equations	One Equation	A Few Equations	Many Equations
Algebraic	Trivial	Easy	Essentially Impossible	Very Difficult	Very Difficult	Impossible
Ordinary Differential	Easy	Difficult	Essentially Impossible	Very Difficult	Impossible	Impossible
Partial Differential	Difficult	Essentially Impossible	Impossible	Impossible	Impossible	Impossible

Figure 6-4   Classification of mathematical problems and their ease of solution by non-computer methods. (Adapted from Ludwig von Bertalanffy, *General System Theory*, New York: George Braziller, Inc., 1968, p. 20.)

information system as well as defined linkages between the organization activities and the MIS.

MANAGEMENT SCIENCE IN MIS

Management science (or operations research) is a discipline which promises to add sophistication to MIS. It usually involves extensive computations and its development has been parallel with that of the computer. The computational power provided by the computer has brought reality to management science approaches that were previously impractical theories.

Von Bertalanffy has shown (Figure 6-4) that without the modern computer it would be difficult, if not impossible, to perform the mathematics for some classes of problems. Management science applications can involve scores, hundreds, or thousands of variables and interrelated computations.

In addition to relying on the computational power of the computer, the management science techniques are dependent on an information system to provide the data elements identified as the known variables. Without such data, the elegant mathematical formulas are inoperative.

Management science involves:

1. Constructing mathematical, economic, and statistical descriptions or models of decision and control problems to treat situations of complexity and uncertainty.

2. Analyzing the relationships that determine the probable future consequences of decision choices, and devising appropriate measures of effectiveness in order to evaluate the relative merit of alternative action.

Following are examples of management science use in various areas of an organization.

Purchasing. Management science can be used to develop rules for buying raw materials whose prices are either stable or vary.

Production. Management science can be used to aid in the design and site selection of plants, to determine how many plants of what size and mix capabilities are required, to what extent they should be automated and how, and what number and types of different kinds of equipment should be installed.

Marketing. Management science has been used to determine where distribution points should be located, how large they should be, how much they should stock of what, and whom they should supply. Also, it has been used to determine how large a sales budget should be and how the budget should be allocated to direct selling, sales promotion, and advertising.

Research and Development. The management science approach can be applied in determining what the budget for research and development should be, how this should be divided between basic and applied research, and which projects should be supported.

Personnel. The technique has been employed to determine what mix of age and skills among workers is most desirable, what causes accidents and how they can and should be prevented, and what causes absenteeism and labor turnover and how they can be minimized.

Finance and Accounting. Management science has been used to design accounting and auditing procedures which minimize the sum of the cost of the procedure and error.

A simulation approach to management science has been particularly attractive to organizations. Instead of trying out a new plan or action in the real world, it can be tested by manipulating a mathematical model. Simulation can provide a better understanding of the area under study, and can identify alternatives that are likely to fail or succeed before committing the organization to a particular choice.

Management science quantitative techniques make it possible to program decisions that heretofore have not been programmable, to refine decision-making, and to explore implications of alternative courses of action.

Following are short descriptions of two specific management science models:

PERSYM is an operational entity-simulation system designed explicitly to permit observation and selective control of system dynamics of a military personnel system under a variety of policy alternatives. The functions simulated are procurement, assignment and reassignment, promotion and loss. While not explicitly simulated, necessary training outputs and transients are identified and reported. . . . The simulated population is introduced and maintained in the form of individual records and individual people (the entities). Each entity is characterized by as many attributes as is desired. Some of the attributes will also be used as indices of personnel inventories and manpower requirements which are maintained in the computer in aggregated form. Other attributes, not directly relevant to require- ments but bearing on some of the change-of-status probabilities, appear nowhere but in the entity records and as indices of probability tables. The primary operational objectives of the model is the management of the inventory (in accordance with a set of decision rules and constraints) so as to satisfy or attempt to satisfy the current manpower requirement. Those requirements, the decision rules, the constraints, or any of the parametric values are subject to modification by the user either before or during a simulation; in addition, the model may be programmed to accomplish self-adaptive modifications to some of these.[4]

A Markovian Model for Projecting Movements of Personnel Through a System. A large centrally controlled organization needs an accurate projection of future personnel requirements. A computer-processed mathematical model is developed which simulates movements of personnel through the system, with the movements based on empirically derived probabilities, the transition rates. Significant variables are selected—such as career field, length of service, grade—that distribute the system members in a vector of states upon which a probability matrix operates to produce the estimated distribution of personnel at the end of the next time interval—say a year. By iteration, the model can provide estimates for any number of years in the future. Proposed policy changes (e.g., accelerated promotions) can be entered into the system to forecast their effects. In establishing a model, the basic decision is the selection of variables that will characterize the members. The first requirement is that reliable input data be available for the current and preceding time intervals.[5]

Several conditions have restricted wide adoption of management science.

- Usually it is a costly endeavor because there is need for high-priced management scientists, mathematical models can take many man-years to build, often extensive data must be collected to be processed by the mathematical model, and such models require extensive computer time.

- Some of the management science efforts, in the past, have been exercises in theory—with only limited pertinence to the real world.

PLANNING AND IMPLEMENTING MIS

The planning and implementation of MIS can be time-consuming, costly, and complex. Since information is a product, and like any product has cost associated with it, the value of information must outweigh the cost if it is to be justified. Experience has shown that an organization may spend millions of dollars on information, with little understanding of the real costs and benefits.

Planning MIS

Ideally there should be an organization-wide approach to the design of MIS, since all subsystems should be integrated to assure that the overall system will function in the best interest of the organization as a whole. The authors concluded, as a result of a survey of 90 large organizations, that many organizations are investigating integrated MIS; however, most attainments are some years away.

While it is desirable to have an overall MIS design, actual implementation can proceed by subsystems, since it probably would be impractical to implement all subsystems of the MIS simultaneously. MIS planning should be a continuing effort, since organizations and information should be responsive to change. While there are some general MIS principles that are useful in most organizations, specific MIS design must be suitable for the individual organization.

The complexity of a comprehensive computer-based information system is accounted for by a number of factors:

1. It typically deals with very large quantities of input data. Collection of data and error protection methods are expensive, and affect numerous units of an organization which originate data.

2. Large volumes of data must be maintained more or less permanently in data files, and there must be a method of linking related data.

3. A variety of computer programs must be written to provide for the desired output and performance of the MIS.

4. Computer programs and their output are intimately linked to an organization's practices and management style. This reduces the extent to which standardized procedures can be transferred from one organization to another.

5. On-going operations must continue, thus necessitating careful conversion from an existing system to a new one (often over the course of a year or more).

6. Many parts of the system must tie together into an integrated whole.

7. The efforts of many persons must be closely coordinated over a considerable period of time.

- A vice president, who had sponsored a study of his organization's MIS needs, lamented: "Every year the computer department management claims it needs an expanded budget for more equipment, more programs, and more staff. Yet, we have yet to obtain any management information. What information we do get is too often of questionable value. The other day I received some forecasted data regarding the next year's sources of revenue. Some of the figures were absurd. I won't spend a nickel more on the operation until the mess is cleaned up."

There is need for flexibility and open-endedness in such systems, since it is difficult to anticipate all changes and needs of users and how technology will specifically evolve.

Numerous decisions may be required each day. Each decision process can be viewed as a transformation of information inputs into decision outputs. The designer of an information system must thus concern himself with three major aspects of the decision process:

1. The information inputs for the decision.
2. The decision process.
3. The decision outputs and the way it results in action.

The preparation of inputs and outputs permit considerable formalizing. Formalization of the decision process usually necessitates the development of a mathematical decision model which represents the significant characteristics of the decision. The transformation of inputs into outputs is usually expressed in symbolic form as a series of mathematical equations in a computer program.

Formalization of routine decisions is fairly simple. It becomes increasingly difficult to formalize decisions as one considers those which are not routine, but which are qualitative and subjective rather than quantitative. Under these circumstances, the formal system may be, at best, a limited aid to the human decision-maker. However, it is well to mention that the continued advances in computer technology and MIS techniques are constantly improving the feasibility of tackling heretofore unmanageable problems.

Implementing MIS

The implementation of an MIS assumes that those who are to use it, the managers, are sufficiently familiar with it so that they can use it meaningfully for decision-making purposes. This implies that management development and training is a vital part of the MIS effort. It must be emphasized that MIS can be a substantial aid to decision-making, but that it does not supplant human judgment—it aids it. Further, the formal MIS should be only part of the information flow that will influence managerial decision-making. The manager will also have to take into account such things as discussions with superiors, colleagues, and subordinates, sensory impressions of human situations, intuitive and creative insights, etc. Some of these factors, not a part of the formal MIS, may be as important in the decision-making process.

The design of a management information system requires the determination of the manager's information needs based on his responsibilities, authorities, and relationships. The decisions made by managers largely define the kinds of information required and, hence, set the parameters of the system itself. Since this is the case, the design of MIS should entail involvement of the managers in identifying decision patterns. Some decisions, particularly at the higher levels of management, are difficult to anticipate since they are novel, usually not repeated, and may be based more on qualitative rather than quantitative factors.

Ackoff has indicated the difficulties in designing information systems, by challenging a number of basic assumptions which are often built into such systems.

1. *Assumption:* The critical deficiency under which most managers operate is the lack of relevant data.

Critique: It is likely that most managers receive much more data (if not information) than they can absorb; hence, they suffer more from information overload rather than information underload.

A controller in a conglomerate remarked,

"There is no lack of information. If anything, we have paperwork pollution generated by the computer. Computer print-outs are sent to our offices by the pound, and every day. They are stacked on desks, window sills, file cabinets. We don't have time to digest one, and we get another. Something has to be done to control this avalanche of information caused by computers and reproducing machines."

2. *Assumption:* The manager is the only one who can determine what information he requires for decision-making.

Critique: Managers often have weak conceptions of the decision-making models they use; consequently, it is difficult for such managers to know what information is needed for decision-making.

3. *Assumption:* A manager does not have to understand how his information system works, only how to use it.

Critique: MIS should not be installed unless the managers for whom it is intended are knowledgeable enough to evaluate and participate with it rather than be controlled by it.[6]

The challenge in establishing an effective MIS is dramatically indicated by Downs, who offers certain principles:

> The quantity and detail of reporting required . . . tends to rise steadily over time . . . Each official tends to distort the information he passes upward in the hierarchy, exaggerating those data favorable to himself and minimizing those unfavorable to himself . . . When information must be passed through many officials, each of whom condenses it somewhat before passing it on to the next, the final output will be very different in quality from the original input; that is, significant distortion will occur . . . In a bureau hierarchy, information passed upward to the topmost official tends to be distorted so as to more closely reflect what he would like to hear, or his preconceived views, than reality warrants . . .
>
> Successful high-level officials develop whole networks of outside information sources through which they can verify the reports made to them by their subordinates.[7]

Regarding public policy decision-making, Schlesinger also indicates the political barrier to MIS:

> . . . rationality of information systems and systems analysis often conflicts with the rationality of politics. While system analysis takes a long-run view and involves careful calculations of the resources required to implement real alternatives, politics takes a short-run view and is committed to the appearance of effort in numerous directions in order to satisfy diverse interest groups.[8]

These observations indicate that management information systems should not be designed in a purely theoretical fashion; pragmatic politics in organizations are crucial determinants of the effectiveness of any MIS.

The United States Defense Department, the largest single user of computers, has been prominent in the forefront of computer-based information systems. Robert McNamara, when he was Secretary of Defense, introduced a plethora of advanced management techniques including computerized planning-programming-budgeting systems (PPBS) which appraised missions on a cost/benefit basis, rather than on the old line-item basis.

Notwithstanding, the Defense Department has continued to experience some frightful inefficiencies (e.g., cost overruns on new jet aircraft and nuclear powered ships). Further, when some of the Defense Department's techniques were transplanted and applied in other departments and agencies, it was discovered that the results were not terribly productive. For instance, there was an attempt to install PPBS throughout the federal government; the experience has resulted in severe cutbacks in these original orders. In particular, it was discovered that techniques which might be appropriate in an organization like the Defense Department might not be germane to the Department of Health, Education, and Welfare—where social concerns and not technical matters should have highest priorities. To date, our ability to quantify social priorities is in the infancy stage.

People Considerations in MIS

To obtain the technical benefits of MIS, it is often necessary to solve problems stemming from people. Reactions to the installation of MIS may range from lack of enthusiasm to sabotage. Figure 6-5 identifies three types of dysfunctional behavior—aggression, projection, and avoidance—as they were revealed among various groups in one study.[9] It is interesting that operating management, the group that should enjoy most of the MIS benefits, goes further than any other group in its resistance to MIS. Figure 6-6 provides some of the specific reasons for resisting MIS. Noteworthy is the fact that the study shows that even top management tends to resist MIS. *This clearly indicates that systems people and computer technicians have to cope, not only with the formidable technical barriers, but also with people's attitudes, related to management information systems.*

There is some indication of growing interest in using MIS in areas that are the province of personnel administration. As indicated in Chapter 4, manpower planning is to some considerable degree dependent on a sound information system containing data about existing work force and skills, organizational operations plans, supply and demand conditions in the labor market, etc. Subsequent chapters will look, in more depth, at MIS uses in the personnel function.

Organizational Subgroup	Relation to MIS	Probable Dysfunctional Behavior
Operating personnel		
Nonclerical	Provide system inputs	Aggression
Clerical	Particularly affected by clerical systems; job eliminated, job patterns changed	Projection
Operating management	Controlled from above by information systems; job content modified by information-decision systems and programmed systems	Aggression, avoidance, and projection
Technical staff	Systems designers and agents of systems change	Little
Top management	Generally unaffected and unconcerned with systems	Avoidance

Figure 6-5 Dysfunctional behavior related to MIS. (Adapted from G.W. Dickson and John K. Simmons, "The Behavioral Side of MIS," *Business Horizons*, August 1970, p. 63.)

	Operating (nonclerical)	Operating (clerical)	Operating Management	Top Management
Threats to economic security		X	X	
Threats to status or power		X	X	
Increased job complexity	X		X	X
Uncertainty or unfamiliarity	X	X	X	X
Changed interpersonal relations or work patterns		X	X	
Changed superior-subordinate relationships		X	X	
Increased rigidity or time pressure	X	X	X	
Role ambiguity		X	X	X
Feelings of insecurity		X	X	X

Figure 6-6 Reasons for resistance to MIS by work groups. (Adapted from G.W. Dickson and John K. Simmons, "The Behavioral Side of MIS," *Business Horizons*, August 1970, p. 68.)

FUTURE CHALLENGES FOR MIS*

We are moving rapidly into the area of macro systems which are national and/or international in their scope. These systems will infringe upon all organizations (in the private and public sectors) as well as all citizens. Systems such as EFT (Electronic Fund Transfer), POS (Point-of-Sale), CARDIS (Cargo Data Interchange System), the various governments' systems, and the electronic transfer of mail are now here. These systems are only the tip of the iceberg, for as time goes by newer and larger ones in scope will be developed.

The present discussions on these systems are extensive, but each takes place independently of the other (i.e. the disjoint set approach is taken). These macro systems do interface with each other, with all organizations (directly and/or indirectly), as well as all citizens (directly and/or indirectly), meaning that the systems do not operate in isolation of each other, . . . the omission of any one sub-system would imply that it was not subject to uncertainty and to variation in performance level.

This article will discuss the importance of conceptualizing the total environment; recognizing the interface areas; the need for systems simulation; and the challenges these systems create for the MIS Department and all members of management. Since these macro systems do become part of our daily lives, management scientists, systems analysts, operations researchers, management, and experts from other fields must find a way of integrating all macro systems into the internal environment of an organization. The following three sections will give a basic outline of EFT, POS, and CARDIS; then the total environment; the need for systems simulation; and finally, some behavioral implications of the macro systems will be discussed.

The Electronic Fund Transfer System[10]

The introduction of the cheque was similar to the introduction of the EFT system. The cheque replaced the physical transfer of money from one firm to the next. If both firms have an account with the same bank, the bank merely adjusts the balance on the respective balance sheets. The physical quantity of money within the bank does not change, hence the EFT system is similar to the cheque. The system only speeds up the process. This is an over-simplified statement, but in essence the EFT system will accomplish this result. Because of the many benefits and social implications, the discussions on the system are accordingly varied.

Large corporations have complex internal systems which interface with EFT, and the systems department should make itself aware of the parameters of the

---

* Adapted from the authors article "Future Challenges for MIS," which appeared in Journal of Systems Management, July 1979.

EFT system as the systems department will be the one which will be called upon to integrate the external with the internal environment. In other words, the systems department must consider each internal system as well as the macro systems as sub-systems of the total, and integrate them so they will serve the firm's best interests.

The transfer of information is not a simple one for there is a conflict of interest between the various systems. For example, the accounting department wants to see a speed-up in the collection of cash, but it also wants to hold back payments to the last possible minute so it can receive benefits from the invested cash. That is, the accounting department wants the money from the customer at the earliest possible time, and the EFT system will accomplish this as the cheque does not have to be mailed to the firm, and during this time when the cheque is in the mail, the firm cannot use the money for its own purpose. But when the firm has to make a payment, the firm may want to send the cheque by mail, as the firm can keep the money in the bank until the cheque is cashed and receive interest from this amount. This results in a conflict of interest within the accounting department, and therefore, the internal systems must be sufficiently flexible to incorporate the additional constraints. Thus the accounting department must have fully operational supporting systems so it can maximize the benefits to the firm and, as the accounting department interfaces with the total organization, the supporting systems must also interface with all departments on a formal and/or informal basis. Several corporate EFT systems are discussed in the Oct. 1977 edition of the EDP Analyzer.[11]

Additionally, the need for more complex decision systems (systems simulations) will bcome apparent as the accounting department must find the best possible answer from a set of alternatives.

The Point-of-Sale System[12]

The POS system is rapidly becoming part of our daily environment and the full potential of the system will only be utilized efficiently sometime in the future. The change from the present environment to the POS one takes time and money but the system is here to stay. The benefits, costs and social concerns of the system are many, therefore the points of view vary with each individual. The greatest misgiving by the public is that the stores will no longer display the prices and hence the customer will not be able to shop competitively. However, as time goes by this issue will also be overcome.

Some of the benefits of the POS system will be: "1. Increased 'front-end' productivity at the point-of-sale, 2. More effective utilization of personnel at the check-out stations, 3. Improved control over inventories, leading to reduced inventory investment, 4. Automatic verification of customer credit, leading to fewer bad cheques and illegal use of credit cards, 5. Improved checking and control of cash received, 6. Reduced employee training costs, 7. More precise buying practices, leading to faster inventory turnover and reduced markdowns, 8. Increased sales and gross margins, 9. Increased customer loyalty, 10. Better information for management."

For example, a new product is introduced and heavily advertised. The manufacturer of the product may have spent many years on its development. The product goes on the shelf on Monday morning, and the POS system monitors the product's sales. The store will have set a minimum selling quantity so as to maximize the revenue of the shelf space and management will remove the product from the shelf the moment its sales drop below the set minimum. The store does not receive revenue from slow moving items and, therefore, the product may go on the shelf on Monday, reach a peak on Thursday, and on Saturday fall below the set minimum, and be removed from the shelf. The product may not even have had a chance to receive sufficient consumer exposure. The POS system will keep track of each item sold and hence, the store will be more efficiently managed, which in turn will increase the pressure on the manufacturer.

The Cargo Data Interchange System[13, 14]

CARDIS is being designed by the Canadian Department of Transport's Office of Facilitation. The scope of the system is to reduce the quantity of documents which must be generated when a shipment takes place nationally and especially, internationally. The system should speed up the exchange of information between the shipper, receiver, and all firms and organizations involved which may serve the shipper and/or receiver, as well as the government. The paperwork which is presently needed per year for the shipment of goods is in excess of $1.5 billion in Canada, and as traffic increases so will this figure (a similar system is being designed in Canada under the name COSTRO—Canadian Organization for Standardization of Traffic Procedures). The quantity of documents required to prepare an international shipment is staggering and varies with the nation which is the receiver and the kind of goods being shipped. Thus, various governments from the shipping as well as the receiving countries need documents depending on the make-up of the goods in question. As CARDIS and COSTRO will interface, they should speed up the international shipments between Canada and the USA.

The system will accomplish the following data: data switching trade centers and transportation terminals (also international in its scope); documents can be seen on CRT's and hard copies can be originated from the system; the in-house terminal will display the national and international documents required to prepare a shipment; a regional directory of trade and transportation companies and organizations together with their services; a directory of government departments and agencies; and many more services. This system will interface with all companies as well as the governments involved.

CARDIS will readily integrate with a firm which is geographically distributed across the nation, or which ships nationally and/or internationally. The materials management department of any firm will be interested in this system and the systems department must investigate methods of integrating it within the firm to maximize the benefits derived from the system.

The Total Environment

Many have discussed the total systems concept and the advantages over the sub-system design. The total systems theory is not only a concern of the systems professionals, economists also advocate the concept. The macro systems will expand the total systems concept, since they will encompass the nation, and for some firms, they will be international in their scope. That is, the macro systems will set parameters for the individual, and the individual will have to conform to those constraints. At present, discussions concerning these macro systems occur in isolation of each other. In other words, the interested parties who design these systems, adapt them to their advantage to best meet their own particular needs. We can read how EFT, POS, and CARDIS will benefit a firm, but there is no discussion on how these systems interface. Large information systems have been developed and are operating on an up-to-date basis. They are systems which consider the economy of a nation, as well as systems which encompass many different cultural and occupational groups.

The internal systems of any firm interact with all three (four if we include the government) macro systems. For example, a store sells a product. At the time that the sale is registered, the POS system recognizes the re-order condition, and concurrently handles the financial forecasting (i.e. how many funds are required on a given date to pay for the goods, import duty if required, transportation cost, etc.). Additionally, through CARDIS, POS recognizes the lead time (i.e. elapsed time for transporting the goods from the supplier to the store). Perhaps the store is a few thousand miles away from the home office which does the purchasing. In this case, the elapsed time between recognizing the re-order condition, mailing the information to the home office, then analyzing the data from all stores and finally, placing the order, will be reduced (i.e. the information generated by a clerk in the store does not have to be handled several times by different people before the order is placed.) Therefore, the store does not have to keep a large safety stock to cover the lead time and can keep the cash invested, thus gaining interest from the cash in the bank, which is tracked through the EFT system.

Furthermore, the information received from each store will be very valuable to the suppliers, since they will know instantaneously if a product is selling or not; in which geographical region to increase or decrease advertising; and how much raw material to re-order. This information will improve production planning and inventory control functions, and therefore, effect improvements in financial planning.

The supplier ships the goods and, through CARDIS, all interested parties will be informed of the shipping date and the name of the transportation firm. The status of the shipment can be monitored during transit for expediting, etc. and, when the cycle is finally completed, all parties involved will be paid through EFT.

In order to remain competitive, a firm's internal systems must respond immediately to any request by all decision-makers. The internal systems must be able to counteract the external forces, for if the firm is not capable of accomplishing this, the external forces will continuously alter the firm's parameters. A firm which wants to remain in a competitive position must respond to the total environment. That is, if the internal systems are fragmented, i.e. do not interface with each other, and there is no smooth transmission between them, then the interaction with the macro system will also be fragmented. It will become even more critical that information flows freely and uninhibited between all organizational units. For example, if a certain condition arises within one macro system and it is recognized by an internal system it may stop there; since there is no continuation from one internal system to the other, there may be an overall negative effect on the firm.

The firm which recognizes the problem and deals with it efficiently can set parameters for all other firms. As soon as the firm recognizes the problem, it has a set of alternatives from which it can choose (i.e. the firm had the foresight and simulated the condition earlier) and thus it can benefit, or at least minimize the impact to itself. By doing so, the firm may set parameters for the external systems and the rest of the firms may have to accept the leader's conditions. By the time the other firms have found a solution to the problem, the parameters from the macro systems may have changed again and they will still be behind the leader firm (i.e. the leader who sets the parameters will have control over the followers).

These stated examples are over-simplified, for there are many sub-systems within each firm which interface with the macro systems, as well as systems of other firms and various organizations and agencies. As the systems we develop become increasingly complex, the intuitive approach in solving various business problems will also become increasingly intricate, and therefore, the systems developers must design models to support the decision makers. Since such a vast amount of data is available, the decision-makers must first determine which data is important in order to formulate alternatives. However, the fallacy is that with the need for more information by the requesting decision-makers, the increase in information may not necessarily decrease the communication gap between decision-makers and the people who should follow or respond to their proposals. Furthermore, there seems to be a point where the accuracy of the decision makers' predictions reaches an optimum and towards the end of the information gathering process most people become overconfident but do not increase the prediction accuracy. Zeleny advocates we should build models and let them do the decision-making to a certain extent, since as it has been proven by him and others, the models' predictions are better than those of the average human being.[15] Therefore, the information exchange must be properly balanced in order to make it an efficient information system. The macro systems will generate a large amount of information, but the necessity of all of this information required by the decision-makers is questionable.

The preceding discussion illustrates that the systems department will be called upon to integrate the sub-systems with the macro systems so that the total environment serves the best interests of all parties involved. Additionally, EFT and POS are rapidly becoming part of our daily lives and CARDIS will be with us shortly. Firms which take the time and look ahead, may develop skills now to enable them to cope with the complexities when they arise. In doing so they will be able to exploit the total environment to their own advantage.

Some firms plan five years ahead for their systems department (i.e. hardware requirements, priorities of projects, etc.). If this is done, the systems department should consider the impact of the macro systems. If it does not, perhaps some projects which are undertaken now will have to be revised considerably before they are even completed.

The Need For Systems Simulation

The interface areas of all three macro systems will encompass the total firm, thus affecting all departments to varying degrees. Since these systems also include all other firms, the transfer of information will speed up tremendously. When this happens, the decision-makers will also have to increase the speed of their decision-making, i.e. the decision-makers will not have time to sit back and analyze given information for a prolonged period of time but will be forced into the position of reaching a decision within minutes. This situation will not only demand one answer, but rather a set of alternatives must be originated from which the decision makers may choose—a choice which must benefit the firm. This will only be accomplished through systems simulation.

The complexities of the interrelationships between all external and internal systems will increase and from this total environment the decision-maker must be able to extract answers which will help him to formulate strategies. In order to accomplish this, systems simulation will be the only alternative to the present one step at a time approach. That is, the simulation applications must encompass the total environment, and from within this total a model must be built, one which serves the decision-maker's needs. If it does not, the alternatives chosen by the decision-maker may serve his needs, but if all the departments of the firm are considered, the decision may have negative effects upon the firm as a whole.

Hence, the systems department will continue to play a more important role in helping to develop strategy formualtion for the firm, but in order to accomplish this, the strategy planning for the systems departments will also become increasingly important.

Models are built and used to aid decision-makers in their daily activities, and for the benefit of the firm. Examples of various specific model applications and how some companies use them are given by Boehm. For example, through the POS system the stores in a particular region increase the purchase of a product. The manufacturer must decide whether to increase production, but before he does this through an econometric model and gaming, he forecasts demands and marketing strategies for the total nation. The econometric model should reveal whether this increase is only seasonal, regional, etc. Perhaps the increase in demand in one region is offset by a total reduction in demand for the product nation wide. Hence, the marketing strategies translate into production and inventory planning. Here various techniques of mathematical programming applications are used (e.g. linear, dynamic, integer programming, etc.) to balance production lines and warehouse space. If new equipment has to be purchased, PERT and CPM are used to determine the best possible start-up date of production, and during the whole process, EFT is utilized for financial planning (i.e. funds available and/or required, interest rates, etc.). When the product is finally ready for shipping, a mathematical programming technique tests the transportation problem in conjunction with CARDIS in order to determine the minimum cost for shipping, and lead time. Queuing is used to determine the customer service level at various warehouses. All of these management science techniques are used through the computer, and perhaps the simulation model will encompass all or some of these above mentioned techniques. Management will use the simulation models to study the cost/benefit of whether to increase production, transfer goods from one warehouse to another, or to stop production of the goods, since the total nation's demand is forecasted to fall below the set minimum.

In order to study the effects of changes in one of the parameters in one of the macro systems, systems simulation is by far a better approach than a set-of-the-pants decision. The simulation model can encompass the total environment, but abstracted to the important variables and parameters, i.e. a predictor of the consequences of a proposed alternative; whereas a decision maker in isolation primarily comprehends only what happens to the system with which he is involved. Not only should the simulation model replicate that actual events from real life, but it should also include some of the optimization techniques in order to give the best possible solution to changes in various parameters. Such an intricate simulation model is described by Svetka and the model incorporates . . . "a multiple salesman travelling algorithm, a bottleneck assignment algorithm, a dynamic program algorithm, regression models, various heuristic routines, and report generating programs, all interrelated to generate coherent solutions".[16]

Another such complex simulation model is reported by Sheppard, and Crane, Knoop, and Pettigrew.[17] All of these models show the decision-makers the best possible solution(s) from a set of alternatives. It must be remembered that in the interface areas of all systems, there are usually a whole set of alternatives from which the decision-maker may choose.

Simulation models are only abstracted from real life, but in order to build meaningful models, the users and systems designers, (computer scientists, system analysts, management scientists, operations researchers, management, and specialists from other fields) must interact. The structure of a good simulation model has been given by Wyatt.[18]

Behavioral Implications of the Macro Systems

An individual or organization is distinct from others by the actions, attitudes and habits he/it displays . . . he/it develops its own way of doing things, its own climate of judgement about what is acceptable and unacceptable. The macro systems are ones which will integrate, to a degree, the total economy of a nation. When this happens, a certain amount of individuality (flexibility to do things) will be lost by all and certain functions of our daily lives will be governed by procedure so that these macro systems can function effectively.

Management's ability to cope with these additional constraints will bring challenges, which many people may be unwilling to accept. These constraints will demand that management both understand the total environment, and has the ability to simulate decisions which span the internal as well as external environment, so that the decisions will benefit the firm.

Additionally, the increase in applications of the macro systems will, of necessity, result in an increase in the use of management sciences applications by business — applications which will become increasingly more complex. That is, not only one specialist will be able to develop models, but a team of them will be involved to develop them. Hence, management at all levels must be willing to accept these techniques and know how to use them to simulate overall systems changes.

Some organizations experience a very low turnover in employees and these firms must make themselves especially aware of the macro systems and their implications for the firm. As these systems will have a major impact upon all firms, the firms with a low turnover may require a different kind of employee. Managers must make themselves conscious of this situation, and when an employee leaves the firm, an employee with improved skill must be hired. If the manager replaces the employee with one who has identical skills, the behavioral implications could become enormous when the macro systems become part of the firm. In fact, the firm may have to dismiss some employees in order to make room for better qualified ones.

However, there is a conflict of interest within the foregoing statement in that if the new employee is better qualified than the one who left, the manager may feel threatened. He may fear that he will remain in his present position while the newly hired employee will advance as the overall functions increase in complexity, and hence, the manager may be inclined to replace the leaving employee with one who has identical skills. Conversely, if a better qualified employee is hired, he may feel that his potential is not realized immediately and may not be willing to wait until the more challenging tasks are available.

Consideration must also be given to the unions and the government. These organizations are requesting increased job security and, therefore, all firms should prepare themselves now so they can minimize conflict at a later stage. Also, since these macro systems encompass a nation, careful thought must be given to the environment inputs, i.e. cultural, geographical, and occupational influences. These influences cannot be overlooked and the macro systems must be tailored to overcome these differences, otherwise the macro systems will never become fully accepted and, therefore, fully efficient. If those who set the parameters of the macro systems do not consider these influences, some of their decisions may have damaging effects on the users of these macro systems.

Furthermore, if we do not look carefully at the social implications of the macro systems, organizations like the *International Society for the Abolition of Data Processing Machines* will become increasingly powerful. The Society's objective is to question man's reliance upon the computer by damaging input information, e.g. punching extra holes into keypunch cards, etc.

SUMMARY

The most extensive use of computers has been, and is, for routine data processing and computations. Only recently, has some progress been made in using the computer to supply information to aid management decision-making.

There is a virtual avalanche of data and information generated in our economy. Every manager can attest to the difficulty of keeping abreast of the facts, opinions, reports, inquiries, literature, and other communications that affect his job. In addition, each manager, knowingly or unknowingly, misses data and information that could be vital to his responsibilities. The growing complexity of our world and the pressures for rapid response to stimuli, add to the manager's burden.

In recent years, there has been a considerable shift in managerial talent. This is evidenced by the rapid growth of graduate schools of business which are molding potential managers to work with modern management technologies and the behavioral sciences.

Both the pressures of the information explosion and the capabilities of the new managers are inexorably leading to the need for MIS that will support decision-making in the rapidly changing business world and government. A responsive MIS will be highly dependent on the power and speed of computer-communications systems.

However, it is abundantly clear that there are formidable barriers before such computer-based MIS are commonplace. These barriers include: high cost of designing, installing, and operating MIS; shortages of systems people capable of developing workable MIS; and difficulties in gaining acceptance of MIS by those affected, the men who will have to use such systems productively.

The next chapter provides a survey of the computer field.

KEY CONCEPTS OF THE CHAPTER

1. Up to this time, most computer resources have been devoted to routine data processing.

2. The information explosion is making the computer more indispensable as a way of life in organizations. Manual or mechanized methods cannot cope with the volume of data, the complexity of some of the processing, and the rapidity with which results are needed.

3. MIS has been relatively slow to develop because of the extensive technical and economic commitments that are required, and the lack of persons competent to plan and design such systems.

4. Management science is an important adjunct of MIS. It involves, in appropriate applications, the use of mathematical models which provide more elaborate analyses of problems.

5. There is a substantial human behavior challenge to gain acceptance of MIS, and to train employees to productively use such systems.

6. The formal MIS is one aid to management. The manager still must balance other sources of information with that derived from the computer; other sources include: oral briefings, the "grapevine," hearsay, as well as intuition and inspiration.

DISCUSSION QUESTIONS

General Background (Seminar/Classroom Discussion)

1. Describe management information systems, as distinguished from data processing.
2. Describe the characteristics of an MIS with which you are familiar.
3. Why is the computer an important part of many management information systems?
4. Why hasn't there been greater progress in implementing MIS?

Operational and Technical

1. Identify a computer data processing application in your organization. How might

that application be upgraded so that it generates management information? Why haven't such improvements been made?
2. Is your organization's computer being used primarily to process routine data? What barriers deter broader use of the computer for MIS?

Policy

1. Does your organization have a formal MIS plan? Of what value is such a plan? What are the difficulties in formalizing MIS?
2. What do you think are managers' attitudes about the computer as an aid to their decision-making? What can be done to make the computer more responsive to decision-makers?

Areas for Research

1. Determine which application in your organization most closely adheres to the characteristics of a good MIS. Try to identify the reasons why it is so effective. How can the success factors be applied to other applications?
2. Interview several executives to determine their chief sources of information for decision-making. How important is computer-generated information versus other sources (e.g., manually prepared studies, oral briefings, external sources such as journals and intelligence)? How can your organization's computer supply improved information to executives?
3. Ask several managers what procedures they use in making their vital decisions. Can you develop a general pattern or model which describes their decision-making process? Why is such a paradigm important in MIS planning and design?
4. Suggest a method for evaluating whether computer-generated information and reports have a real value—or whether they can be classified as "paperwork pollution." How can we distinguish between vital information and wasteful information?

BIBLIOGRAPHY

Ackoff, Russell L. and Patrick Rivett. *A Manager's Guide to Operations Research*. New York: John Wiley & Sons, Inc., 1966.

Beer, Stafford. *Decision and Control*. New York: John Wiley & Sons, Inc., 1966.

Blumenthal, Sherman C. *Management Information Systems*. Englewood Cliffs, New Jersey: Prentice-Hall, Inc., 1969.

Burch and Strater. *Information Systems*. Philadelphia, Hamilton Publishing Co., 1974.

Davis, Gorden. *MIS: Conceptual Foundations*. New York: McGraw-Hill Book Co., 1974.

Hartman, W., et al. *Management Information Systems Handbook*. New York: McGraw-Hill Book Co., 1968.

Hertz, David B. *New Power for Management*. New York: McGraw-Hill Book Co., 1969.

Lucas, Henry. *A Casebook for Management Information Systems*. New York: McGraw-Hill Book Co., 1976.

Murdick, Robert G. and Ross, Joel E. *Information Systems for Modern Management.* Englewood Cliffs, New Jersey: Prentice-Hall, Inc., 1971.

Rappaport, Alfred, ed. *Information for Decision-Making.* Englewood Cliffs, New Jersey: Prentice-Hall, Inc., 1970.

Steiner, George A. *Top Management Planning.* New York: The Macmillan Co., 1969.

Tomeski, Edward A. *The Computer Revolution.* New York: The Macmillan Co., 1970.

Tomeski, Edward A. "Management Information Systems, in Computers in Business." San Francisco: Holden-Day, Inc., 1979, pp. 426-449.

Wagner, Harvey M. *Principles of Management Science.* Englewood Cliffs, New Jersey: Prentice-Hall, Inc., 1970.

Whisler, Thomas L. *Information Technology and Organizational Change.* Belmont, California: Wadsworth Publishing Company, Inc., 1970.

FOOTNOTES

[1] Peter F. Drucker, *Technology, Management, & Society* (New York: Harper & Row Publishers, Inc., 1970), p. 172.

[2] Gaylord A. Freeman, Jr., "The Role Top Management Must Play in MIS Planning and Implementation," *Founder's Conference,* Society for Management Information Systems, September 8-9, 1969, unnumbered pages.

[3] John Gardner, *Self Renewal* (New York: Harper & Row, Publishers, Inc., 1965), pp.

[4] Robert O. Groover, *PERSYM* (Washington, D.C.: Office of the Assistant Secretary of Defense, Manpower and Reserve Affairs, September 1969).

[5] PRL-TR65-6, 6570th Personnel Research Laboratory, Aerospace Medical Division, Air Force Systems Command, Lackland Air Force Base, Texas, March 1965.

[6] Russell L. Ackoff, "Management Misinformation Systems," *Management Science,* December 1967, pp. 147-156.

[7] Anthony Downs, *Inside Bureaucracy* (Boston: Little, Brown & Co., Inc., 1967), pp. 262-269.

[8] James Schlesinger, "Systems and the Political Process," *Journal of Law and Economics,* October 1968, pp.281-298.

[9] G.W. Dickson and John K. Simmons, "The Behavioral Side of MIS," *Business Horizons,* August 1970, pp. 59-71.

[10] John B. Bentar, "Electronic Fund Transfer," *Harvard Business Review,* July-August 1977.

[11] "The Impact of Corporate EFT," *EDP Analyzer,* December 1977.

[12] "POS Systems," *Datamation,* December 1977.

[13] Lawrence Moule, "National EDP Network Will Computerize Canada's Trade Procedures," *Canadian Datasystems,* August 1976.

[14] ————, "Trade Network Will Monitor Canadian Shipping," *Canadian Datasystems,* September 1976.

[15] Milan Zeleny, "Intuition and Probability," *The Wharton Magazine,* Summer 1977, pp. 63-68.

[16] Joseph Anthony Svestka, "A System Model for Controlling the Operations of Check Processing in a Branch Bank Network," *Interface,* November 1976, p. 69.

[17] K.W. Shepperd, "Applying Simulation Techniques to Legislative Analysis," *Interface,* November, 1976; Dwight Crane and Knopp and Pettigrew, "An Application of Management Science to Bank Borrowing Strategies," *Interface,* November 1977.

[18] Joe B. Wyatt, "Computer Systems Simulation," *The Information Systems Handbook* (Homewood, Illinois; Dow Jones-Irwin, 1975) pp. 378-382.

[19] R.H. Osborn and J.G. Hunt, "Design Implications for Mechanistically Structural Systems in Complex Environments," *The Management of Organization Design* (New York: North-Holland, 1976), p. 1172.

7

The Computer in Perspective

We are now faced with a new ultimate weapon. This is the computer whose potential impact may surpass that of all of man's earlier devices. Many deplore the computer and some even fear it as more monster than machine. Whatever we think of it, however, we must adjust to it. This does not imply resignation, but rather that we must understand the true nature of this latest of man's inventions and learn how its powers can be combined with our own abilities to be used to the best advantage of humanity.

Ashley Montagu and Samuel S. Snyder

OBJECTIVES OF THE CHAPTER

A broad survey of the computer is presented in this chapter, including the people who work with computers and anticipated trends in the technology. Certain areas of social responsibility are indicated where the computer industry and users could improve their performances and public image.

THE "AGE OF COMPUTERS"

The computer is certainly one of the century's most important and pervasive technological developments. It is, today, almost indispensible to the functioning of large organizations, and is becoming increasingly so to medium-sized and smaller organizations—and is thus affecting the daily lives of all of us, if not as employees, then as consumers and citizens.

Kahn and Wiener state, in *The Year 2000*, that:

. . . by the year 2000, computers are likely to match, simulate, or surpass some of man's most human-like intellectual abilities, including perhaps some of his aesthetic and creative capabilities, in addition to having some new kinds of capabilities that human beings do not have . . . the last third of the twentieth century may well be known as the age of computers . . .[1]

TYPES OF PROCESSING SYSTEMS

Man supplements his work by using a variety of tools and machines. The computer is one of the most powerful of these aids. These processing tools and machines can be classified as: manual systems, mechanical systems, or automatic systems.

Manual Systems

These consist of hand tools and other machines controlled by the human being, who uses his own physical energy as power source. The individual typically operates at his own speed, and exploits his ability to act in a flexible manner as a situation requires.

Mechanical Systems

These systems consist of various powered machines and tools. They are generally designed so as to perform their functions with little variation. The power is largely provided by the machine, and the operator's function is essentially one of control.

Automated Systems

When a system is highly automated it performs its functions largely without human intervention. Such a system needs to be fully programmed in order to take appropriate action for all possible contingencies. When deviations from some programmed norm takes place, feedback and correction can be automatic. Human functions in such systems are those of prescribing the program for the equipment to follow, monitoring, maintenance, and handling exceptions not covered in the program.

The modern electronic computer, of course, is an automated system. As factories and offices have moved from manual and mechanical systems to automated systems, revised allocation of work between employees and machines become necessary.

All data processing, whether done by manual methods or the latest electronic automated methods, consists of one or more of the following steps: originating-recording, classifying, sorting, calculating, summarizing, storing, retrieving, reproducing, and communicating. The means of performing the steps vary according to whether manual, mechanical, or automated systems are employed. Figure 7-1 summarizes how these steps are accomplished under varying processing methods.

PROCESSING METHODS	Originating-Recording	Classifying	Sorting	Calculating	Summarization	Storing	Retrieving	Reproducing	Communicating
Manual Methods	Human observation; hand-written records; pegboards	Hand posting; pegboards	Hand posting; pegboards; edge-notched cards	Human brain	Pegboards; hand calculations	Paper in files, journals, ledgers, etc.	File clerk; bookkeeper	Clerical; carbon paper	Written reports; hand-carried messages; telephone
Manual with Machine Assistance	Typewriter; cash register; manual	Cash register; bookkeeping machine	Mechanical collators	Adding machines; calculators; cash registers	Accounting machines; adding machines; cash registers	Motorized rotary files; microfilm		Xerox machines; duplicators; addressing machines	Documents prepared by machines; message conveyors
Electromechanical Punched Card Methods	Prepunched cards; keypunched cards; mark-sensed cards; manual	Determined by card field design; sorter; collator	Card sorter	Accounting machines (tabulators); calculating punch		Trays of cards	Manual tray movement	Reproducing punch	Printed documents; interpreter
Electronic Methods	Magnetic tape encoder; magnetic and optical character readers; card and tape punches; on-line terminals; manual	Determined by systems design; computer	Off-line card sorter; computer sorting	Computer		Magnetizable media and devices; punched media; computer	On-line inquiry with direct access devices; manual movement of storage media to computer	Multiple copies from printers	On-line data transmission; printed output; visual display; voice output

Figure 7-1 Methods and steps in data processing.

There are no clear-cut guidelines that indicate the degree to which work should be automated or computerized. In general, the economics of the situation is that everything possible should be done to improve the speed and accuracy, and lower the cost of work—and this almost literally can mean "automate or computerize everything possible consistent with obtaining cost advantages and other benefits to justify the investment."

However, the strategy should also be one that, to the fullest extent possible, results in a structure of work and an environment that is interesting, motivating, and challenging to human beings. Computer manufacturers, when they design equipment and supporting programs, and users, when they design applications, give too little attention to the best balance of assignments between workers and computers. The general criterion that appears to have been used is: whenever possible computerize all of the work. Work that

Assignments to People	*Assignments to Machines*
• Recognize patterns of complex stimuli which may vary from situation to situation	• Sense stimuli that are outside man's normal range of sensitivity
• Sense unusual and unexpected events in the environment	• Apply deductive reasoning, such as recognizing stimuli belonging to a general class
• Remember principles and strategies rather than masses of detailed information	• Monitor pre-specified events
• Draw upon varied experience in making decisions to situational requirements	• Store coded information quickly and in substantial quantity
• Select alternative mode of operation, if certain modes fail	• Retrieve coded information quickly and accurately when specifically requested
• Reason inductively, generalizing from observations	• Process quantitative information following specified programs
• Apply principles to solutions of varied problems	• Make rapid and consistent responses to input signals
• Make subjective estimates and evaluations	• Perform repetitive activities reliably
• Develop unique new solutions	• Exert considerable physical force in a highly controlled manner
• Concentrate on most important activities, when overload conditions require	• Maintain performance over extended periods of time
• Adapt response to variations in operational requirements	• Count or measure physical quantities
	• Perform several programmed activities simultaneously
	• Maintain efficient operations under conditions of heavy load
	• Maintain efficient operations under distractions

Figure 7-2   Allocating assignments to people and machines.

possibly should remain under human control is turned over to the computer; this can reduce employees' satisfaction and incentive. On the other hand, work may be assigned to workers which should be computerized; such work may be onerous and boring to humans, and reduce their morale. Figure 7-2 depicts one schematic for allocating work to people and to machines. *From their experience and research, the authors think that systems should be built around people and not computers.* This simple caveat is, unfortunately, not frequently followed in practice. Chapter 11 deals in more detail with this subject.

HISTORY OF THE COMPUTER

The concept of computing by aids goes back as far as the Chinese abacus (circa 450 B.C.). More recent landmarks include Pascal's and Leibnitz's mechanical calculators (17th century), Babbage's concept of an analytical engine (19th century), and Hollerith's mechanical punched card equipment used in the census of 1890.

The modern era of computers can be traced by the following developments: Vannevar Bush's analogue computer at the Massachusetts Institute of Technology (1925-1935); Aiken's work at Harvard (1939-1944) which resulted in the Mark I, considered to be the world's first fully automatic computer; J. V. Atanasoff who, in the late 1930's developed a computing machine; Mauchley's and Eckert's work (in the 1940's) at the Moore School of the University of Pennsylvania which resulted in the first electronic computer, ENIAC; and Princeton University's von Neumann's theories of stored programs and the application of the binary number system to computers. The first commercial stored-program computer, UNIVAC, was sold to the U.S. Bureau of Census in 1951.

The computer field has been distinguished by extremely rapid growth, since the first commercial application of 25 years ago, and by dramatic technological breakthroughs. In general, four successive computer "generations" are identified. The period of 1946 to 1954 is considered to be one of emergence and experimentation and so precedes the first generation.

First Generation, 1954 to 1959

These early computers employed vacuum tube circuitry, had limited storage capacity, and were generally rated in speeds of seconds or milliseconds (1/1,000 of a second). They were programmed in machine-level, detailed, numeric programming languages.

Second Generation, 1959 to 1964

In this period, the transistor largely replaced vacuum tubes in computers. Magnetic cores were used for internal storage, while the secondary storage capacity of the computer was considerably increased. Second generation computers were generally rated in terms of speeds of milliseconds or microseconds (1/1,000,000 of a second). Higher-level, general programming languages were introduced, replacing some of the arduous detailed machine-level programming.

Third Generation, 1964 to 1970's

Monolithic, integrated semi-conductor circuits were introduced, with the benefits of reliable solid-state electronics. Mass storage devices, and improved input and output devices received attention in order to keep pace with the very fast speeds of the computer's main memory. Computer internal speeds of nanoseconds (1/1,000,000,000 of a second) were attained in some computers. Data transmission to and from a remote central computer, and computer time-sharing, reached a level of effectiveness in some organizations. Useful extensions to the higher level programming languages were introduced.

Fourth Generation, 1970's to 1980's

Since the introduction of the third generation computers, there have been many new products and technical developments. However, none of them has been significantly major to identify clearly a "fourth generation" computer period. While the first and second generations of computers each lasted about five years, the third generation has lasted almost a decade. In view of this, it would be reasonable to assume that the computer manufacturers will, in the near future, continue product obsolescence by introducing a truly fourth generation computer.

A super-computer, specially built for the National Aeronautics and Space Administration at a cost of $30 million, may be the prototype for the new generation. Some of its features: faster than existing super-computers by 10 to 20 times, parallel computer processing (several computers working as a team), storage that ranges up to trillions of characters, and memory based on laser technology.

The computer's rate of technological advance has been nothing short of fantastic. Compared to manually operated desk calculators, modern computers offer an increase in speed by a factor of about 100 million. Computer speeds have about doubled each year over the past twenty-five years. The human mind can scarcely grasp the meaning of such a vast increase in speed. Some appreciation can be gained, however, by comparing the advance in computers with that of another well-known form of technology, transportation.

The private automobile provides perhaps a tenfold increase in speed over the horse and buggy; nevertheless, this increase in private transportation has been enough to bring about profound changes in our society and economy (not all of them for the good, unfortunately). The speed of a subsonic jet aircraft is about ten times that of the passenger train, an increase enough to add greatly to personal mobility and usher in the age of the jet set. The supersonic jet doubles the speed of commercial aircraft; nevertheless, it still travels only 400 times faster than a man walking.

In other fields of technology, an order of magnitude advance (an increase by a factor of ten) has very often rung in a new era. And yet in the field of computers we see a change of eight orders of magnitude compressed into but a single generation. Not surprisingly, we have not learned to cope with our new-found superabundance of computation.[2]

One of the most pervasive trends is that towards relatively smaller, less costly computers (micro- and mini-computers); this trend allows the placement of computer power where needed. Because of technological breakthroughs these inexpensive computers are sometimes as powerful as the large, expensive computers of a few years ago! It also opens the personnel computer market for home use in family budgeting, games, homework, menu planning, etc. It is expected such personal computers will cost as little as a television set.

THE COMPUTER INDUSTRY*

In about thirty years, this relatively new industry has had tremendous growth. The annual increase in revenues of the United States' computer industry has been in excess of 20 per cent during the period of 1961 to 1980. If any semblance of this growth continues in future years, it is likely that the office, computing, and accounting machines industry (as classified by the federal government) could become the largest single industry in the United States, surpassing the petroleum and automotive industries.

Economic growth of the country as a whole in terms of real GNP between 1965 and 1980 is projected at 4.3 per cent, and the office, computing, and accounting machines industry forms the most rapidly growing industry (Figure 7-3). For this period, the industry is forecasted to have more than a 10 per cent average annual growth rate.

*Data about computer industry obtained from: Bruce Gilchrist and Richard E. Weber, eds., *The State of the Computer Industry in the United States* (Montvale, New Jersey: American Federation of Information Processing Societies, Inc., 1973); Philip S. Nyborg, Pender M. McCarter, & William Erickson (Eds.), *Information Processing in the United States* (Montvale, New Jersey: American Federation of Information Processing Societies, Inc., 1977).

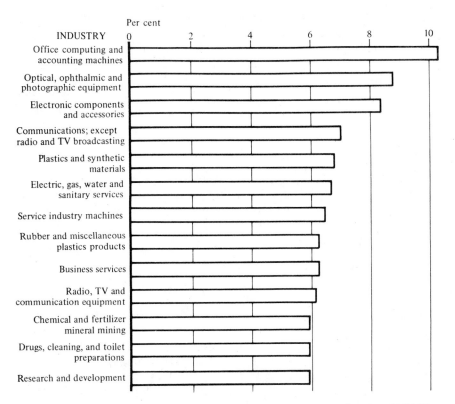

Figure 7-3 Average annual growth rates of fastest growing industries, 1965–80. (*Patterns of U.S. Economic Growth*, **Washington, D.C.: U.S. Department of Labor, 1970, p. 33.**)

Computer production now dominates the office, computing, and accounting machines industry, as a result of having multiplied its output several times over during the last decade. In some recent years, computer output has grown at the staggering rate of nearly 40 per cent a year. Based on past performance, together with an expected growth of computer use in communications and data transmission—and even a possible introduction into the consumer market— the projected growth rate of this industry will undoubtedly remain high through the 1980's.

The size of the computer industry is indicated in Figure 7-4. In 1971, it is estimated that U.S. firms generated total revenues in excess of $14 billion by providing the market with computers and related devices, supplies, and services. More than 70 per cent of that total revenue was derived from the domestic market, and about 30 per cent from exports overseas. The forecast for 1980 is that, for the world market, revenue will be about $50,000 million with about 50% of revenue from overseas.

	1971 Estimate			1980 Estimates
	U.S.	Overseas	World	World Total
Computers and Related Equipment	6,885	3,810	10,695	48,300
Services and Supplies	3,460	240	3,700	15,700
Total	10,345	4,050	14,395	64,000

Figure 7.4   Revenue of U.S. firms in computer industry (in millions of dollars).

In 1971, there were about 89,000 computers installed in the U.S. Of these computers, 55,000 were in the general purpose category while about 34,000 were special purpose or mini-computers. These 89,000 computers were estimated to have a value of $31 billion. Outside of the United States, there were more than 36,000 computers installed as of 1971. By 1980, there were about 1,000,000 installed computers having a value of over $150 billion.

Figure 7-5 shows that the United States' computer industry has supplied in excess of 70 per cent of the computers that are installed throughout the world. The United States has had a world-wide dominating position in the computer market since the early days of the industry. Figure 7-5 also shows that the U.S. is the largest user of computers, having in excess of 50 per cent of the installed general-purpose computers in the world.

While it is difficult to pinpoint the number of people involved, it is estimated that about 600,000 workers are engaged in the engineering, production and marketing of hardware, services, and supplies for the U.S. computer industry.

The computer industry is frequently pictured in terms of several companies that manufacture and market general-purpose computers: Burroughs Corporation, Control Data Corporation, Honeywell Corporation, International Business Machines Corporation (IBM), National Cash Register Company (NCR), and Sperry Rand Corporation (UNIVAC Division). A number of additional organizations have entered the field including Digital Equipment Corporation, Tandy Corporation, and Apple Computer Inc. However, there are thousands of other organizations in the industry; one estimate indicates that there are about 5,000 firms which contribute hardware, components, supplies, and services directly related to the computer industry.

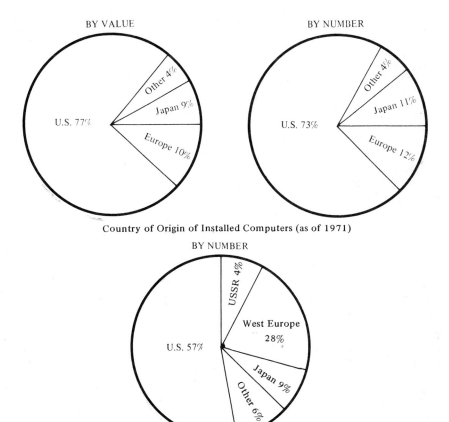

Country of Origin of Installed Computers (as of 1971)

Country of Location of Installed Computers (as of 1976)

Figure 7-5   Worldwide computer statistics.

COMPUTER USERS*

The computing industry can be viewed from the standpoint of users' expenditures as opposed to the computer industry's performance. Users' expenditures are for computer hardware, supplies, and services, as well as internal salaries and

---

* Data about computer users obtained from: Bruce Gilchrist and Richard E. Weber, eds., *The State of the Computer Industry in the United States* (Montvale, New Jersey: American Federation of Information Processing Societies, Inc., 1973); Philip S. Nyborg, Pender M. McCarter, and William Erickson (eds.). *Information Processing in the United States* (Montvale, New Jersey: American Federation of Information Processing Societies, Inc., 1977).

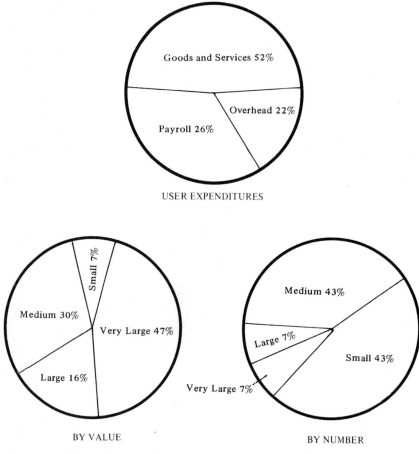

Figure 7-6 Distribution of U.S. installed computer systems. *

overhead. Approximately $38.4 billion, or about 3 per cent of the GNP, was spent for computing services by United States' organizations in 1976. Figure 7-6 indicates that about 52 per cent of the total expenditure for computers goes for outlays for goods and services from the manufacturers and suppliers. Another 26 per cent is expended for internal payrolls related to the computer function. Various overhead expenditures account for the remaining 22 per cent in expenditures.

Data processing is becoming a sizable cost of an organization. One study has estimated that organizations spend somewhere in the range of .5 to 4 per cent of revenue or gross sales for their data processing.[3]

It is estimated that about several hundreds-of-thousand organizations in the

*These figures do not reflect the growing impact of personal computers.

United States had one or more computers installed by the end of 1980. Since there were 1,000,000 computers installed, it is obvious that a number of organizations had more than one computer. The largest single user of computers, the federal government, had reported almost 10,000 computers in use at the end of 1980.

Some industries have been particularly intensive users of computers; these include: banking, insurance, aerospace, education, utilities, and airlines. Other industries have been relatively sparing in their use of computers; these include: retailers, local governments, metal manufacturers, wholesalers, food products manufacturers, and others.

Figure 7-6 shows that 86 per cent of installed computers (in the U.S.) are of small or medium size. Small computers are those with monthly rental less than $2,500; medium computers rent between $2,500 and $10,000. Slightly more than 30 per cent of installed computers are considered large (rental $10,000 to $40,000) and a few super computers may rent for upward of hundreds-of-thousands of dollars a month. The ratio of purchase price to monthly rental varies by machine, but it is usually in the vicinity of 45 to 1. The relative dollar value of large and very large computers is much greater than would be suggested by their number alone; while accounting for only about 14 per cent of the computers, these systems account for about 63 per cent of the value of installed systems.

While the percentage of gross national product (GNP) spent on computer usage in the United States is increasing dramatically, the amount spent per capita is increasing at even faster rate. In 1970, about 2% of the GNP could be attributed to computer usage; by 1980 the figure was over 5%; and by 1990 it is likely to be about 9%. The per capita spending on computer usage was about $100 in 1970, $350 in 1980, and is likely to be around $700 by 1990.

Employment Patterns

It is estimated that as of 1980, over 1 million persons were employed in computer-related occupations with computer-using organizations. The following occupational distribution is estimated for users' staffs:

Occupation	Number
Programmer	300,000
Systems Analyst	150,000
Computer Operator	300,000
Keypunch Operator	200,000
Equipment Maintainers	100,000
	1,050,000

As previously indicated, there are also about 600,000 persons employed by computer manufacturers and suppliers. In addition, computer installations call for various administrative and clerical employees. Also, in many organizations there are employees who are peripherally involved in data processing as adjuncts of their primary occupation. For example: engineers and scientists who use the computer for numerical analysis of research problems, teachers who use the computer as an aid in instructing students, and stockbrokers who use a computerized quotation system to obtain latest prices. Thus, several million workers directly use computers on-the-job.

There is increasing demand for virtually all computer skills except that of key punch operator. Direct entry by employees, who are not computer specialists, is reducing the need for key punch operators. It is predicted that the computer industry will offer more new career opportunities than almost any other professional field in the future.[4]

Education and Training Patterns

In the early years of computers, most employees obtained their training from the computer manufacturers or through on-the-job training. As computer installations grew in number during the 1960's, private computer schools, the public school system, and colleges and universities embarked on training and educational programs to answer the growing demand for computer-oriented workers.

Since 1965, the number of college students awarded degrees in computer-related programs has increased significantly.

Year	Associate Degree	BA/BS Degree	MA/MS Degree	PhD Degree
1964-65	–	67	112	6
1969-70	6,478	1,544	1,459	107
1974-75	8,000	5,039	2,299	213

Of course, it is likely virtually all college students, whatever their major, will receive some training in computer use. Similarly, computer education is spreading in high schools and grade schools according to the National Center for Education Statistics. In 1974-1975 women received 19% of all undergraduate degrees in computer and information sciences and 14.7% of masters' degrees. By 1978-1979, the figures were 28% and 19% respectively. It is evident that women will play an increasing, meaningful role in the computer field. This indicates the growing interest, demand, and acceptance of the computer field as a distinctive occupation. The U.S. Department of Labor has indicated that,

Among the most rapidly growing occupations will be those directly related to work with computers; for example, systems analyst and computer programmer, in which employment may double or triple by 1980.[5]

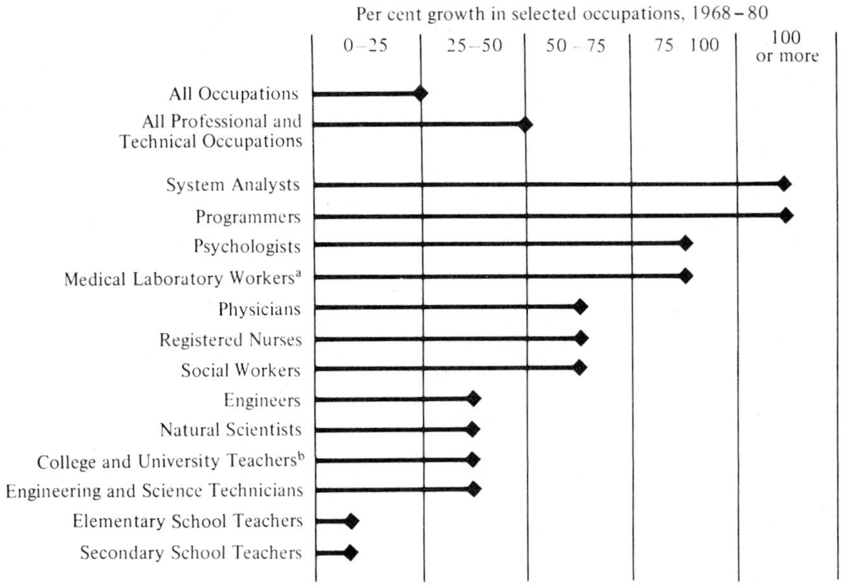
Per cent growth in selected occupations, 1968–80
0–25
25–50
50–75
75–100
100 or more
All Occupations
All Professional and Technical Occupations
System Analysts
Programmers
Psychologists
Medical Laboratory Workers[a]
Physicians
Registered Nurses
Social Workers
Engineers
Natural Scientists
College and University Teachers[b]
Engineering and Science Technicians
Elementary School Teachers
Secondary School Teachers

[a]Includes technologists, technicians, and aides.

[b]Full-time, holding rank of instructor or above.

Figure 7-7 Employment requirements will rise much faster in some professions than in others. (*Manpower Demand and Supply in Professional Occupations,* Washington, D.C.: U.S. Department of Labor, 1970, p. 163.)

Figure 7-7 elaborates on this forecast. It would appear that the demand for higher-level computer employees will tax the capacity of educational and training organizations and staffs to produce a sufficient supply of such persons.

It is interesting to note that computer technicians are very vulnerable to obsolescence. Probably in no other field is there such a pressing need for continuing education and training. This is due to the never ending stream of new computer products, services, and techniques. The following examples illustrate this condition:

- A professor of computer sciences remarked, "About four years ago I was a skilled programmer. Since that time I have concentrated on systems theory. With the many changes in programming techniques, I don't think I could really qualify any longer as a top level computer programmer."
- In order to broaden his background, a systems analyst-computer technician asked for a transfer to the personnel department. He worked in the personnel department, as a senior personnel interviewer, for three years. When he looked into the matter of transferring back to his old job, he realized that it would be an almost impossible task to catch up on developments.

- Two ex-computer technicians recently met on the street. They had not seen each other for about five years. John said, "I couldn't keep up with the ridiculously fast pace in the computer field. I am now a real estate agent in a small office." Vincent replied, "Sounds great. I opened an art shop to get away from the pressure in the computer rat race."

HIGHLIGHTS OF THE COMPUTER

A computer consists of a central processing unit (CPU), and input, output (I/O) equipment for getting instructions and data in, and processed results back out of the CPU. The CPU has a memory component, with retentive capability, for storing instructions and data. The arithmetic and logic component performs calculations and logical comparisons on data, while the control component monitors all parts of the computer. Figure 7-8 is a schematic of the major components of a computer and the flow of data and control that takes place in the computer.

Some of the reasons that the computer has merited such great promise, include:

- It is a general purpose equipment capable of handling virtually any imaginable problem that can be defined.

- Its vast speed and storage capacity permit it to process work that would take large numbers of humans to perform. Further, some of the work (because of both magnitude and complexity) would be beyond the practical capability of human.

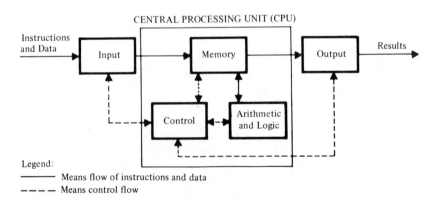

Figure 7-8   Schematic of a computer system.

- Before the computer can process work, people must carefully state what it is the computer is to do. This can result in better human understanding of of the nature of their work, and can be a basis for improvement of it.

Wide Variety of Computers

The user has a wide variety of alternative ways of gaining access to computers. The user can, of course, lease or purchase a computer. A group of users can lease or purchase a computer and share the facility. Also, there are computer service bureaus which will provide as much computer time as is needed, and the user pays only for the time used.

As indicated previously, the range of computers is considerable. There are small computers available which can be leased for under $1,000 a month; at the other extreme there are very large computers that can lease for hundreds-of-thousands of dollars a month. And now there are micro- and mini-computers which sell for as little as several hundred dollars!

A detailed feasibility study is needed—which analyzes the user's applications, economics, technology, and human factors—before a decision is made about the appropriate computer for an organization.

Input and Output (I/O)

There is a growing variety of input and output devices that communicate directly with the computer. Besides the conventional I/O devices (punched card devices and magnetic tape drives) which have long been used, there are more recent developments: scanning and character recognition devices that can read patterns of print and handwriting, plotters that can draw graphs and maps, cathode ray tubes which display information on television screens, voice response units, microfilm storage and retrieval, etc.

Data terminals are available which allow people to communicate directly on-line with the computer, in much the same fashion as one uses the telephone instrument to obtain a connection anywhere in the world. The data terminal permits the user to obtain a "connection" with any data stored in the computer system. The data terminal gives the user the opportunity to employ the computer on an interactive basis.

There still remains, generally, a lack of balance between input and output speeds and the internal speeds of computers. In most systems, I/O remains a bottleneck; it is difficult to feed data to the computer and get the computer to generate output as rapidly as the computer can do its internal computations and logic.

Remote Access

Today, remote data terminals can be connected, via communication lines, to a central computer. A number of data terminals can use the computer in a time-sharing mode; because the speed of the central computer is so great, each user appears to be receiving the complete attention of the computer. Thus, even a small size user, employing a relatively inexpensive data terminal, can gain access to a powerful computer when such access is required.

Data transmission also makes possible computer-to-computer communication. Such a possibility suggests inter-organization systems (one organization's output is another organization's input).

Computer Programming

To activate the computer to do a job, a list of instructions in proper sequence (the computer program) must be fed into the computer. These instructions must be written in computer languages that are still sufficiently complicated to require a specialist for most program development. Some progress has been made to simplify programming, primarily by development of higher-level programming languages which have similarities to normal English and mathematical expressions. However, the programming languages are still highly stylized and somewhat difficult to apply without considerable training and experience. The ultimate objective is to permit a user who knows very little about computers to be able to give instructions to the machine in solving specific problems—i.e., to "write his own program."

Operating Systems

The operating system is a special kind of program: it is usually supplied by the computer manufacturer and handles the automatic management of a computer system. It handles the allocation of computer hardware (processing time, storage, etc.), the sequencing of jobs, and various record-keeping tasks. The operating system is an integral part of the overall computer system, since all other programs obtain access to hardware resources only through the operating system. The operating system also allows the computer to work in various programming languages [e.g., COBOL (Common Business Oriented Language), FORTRAN (Formula Translation System), etc.].

Software Packages

The number of standardized computer programs, written by users, computer manufacturers, consultants, universities, the governments, etc. is growing. It is thus possible that a user need not completely develop a computer program; a suitable program may be available that will suit the organization's needs.

Some of these standardized programs (called software packages) perform a generalized function such as sorting or standard mathematical operations (e.g., regression, correlation). Other packages deal with tasks specific to a given application such as payroll, accounting, or inventory control. Often such programs require that the organizations wishing to adopt them for use, adjust to the standards of the program—or considerably modify the package.

Data Base

The availability of large storage devices and supporting programs have been developed to answer the demand for large files of on-line data. A data base permits more efficient storage of data and non-redundancy of data items, and promotes a more efficient processing and accessing of information. Where it is not used, there are usually separate files with no interrelationship established between the files (even though there is a logical relationship and interdependency). The data base is built on the concept of integrated data files and, consequently, it is a basic building block of management information systems.

Man-Machine Interface

There are two interfaces in the computerization process: a man-to-man interface between the user and the programmer, and a man-to-machine interface between the programmer and the computer (Figure 7-9). If a computer is to be more accessible to its users, we need to improve these two interfaces. One possibility is to teach the person with the problem some programming language. Another answer is to formulate a language that is

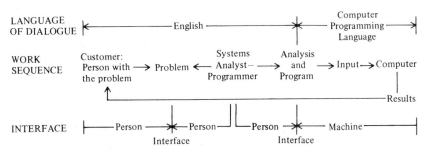

Figure 7-9 Person-machine interface.

natural for the user, and then make it convenient for him or her to have access to the computer. In effect, the overall programming process is thus collapsed, bringing the person with the problem directly to the computer with which he can communicate in a language not requiring special training. Some limited accomplishments have been made in this area. However, the programming languages remain somewhat difficult for the average layman— or if they are very simple, they lack the power to handle problems of any complexity.

Computer Applications

When organizations first installed computers, they tended to isolate a single activity, such as payroll or accounts payable, and developed a computer program for some part of it. Frequently, a series of computer programs evolved over time which pertained to any one application area. Usually, this effort simply computerized previously manual procedures or mechanical punched card procedures, which view the organization as fragmented processes rather than as an interlocking, integrated entity. Many organizations have accumulated an extensive number of such narrow computer programs, which process routinized jobs; these programs have limited applicability to management-level problems.

The computer has the capability of being used on higher-level problems and can be integral to management information systems which are supportive of managerial decision-making. Chapter 6 discussed management information systems. Chapter 9 will survey a series of computer applications in the personnel function.

COMPUTER TRENDS °

Some of the more significant trends in computer technology are briefly indicated as follows:

1. Computers are becoming faster, smaller, and less expensive. Increased speed will enable computers to further expand the scope of computerized applications. Miniaturized computer equipment and data terminals provide for increased mobility. Reduced cost of computer processing will broaden the availability and use of this technology; very small organizations, neighborhood businesses, and even individuals are potential new markets for computers.

2. Computer power will become available in much the same way as

° For an excellent source of this material, refer to Paul Armer, *Computer Aspects of Technical Change, Automation, and Economic Progress* (Santa Monica, California: Rand Corp., undated).

electricity and telephone services are today. A very large-scale central computer, servicing numerous unaffiliated users, can potentially make available extensive data banks that are not feasible for any individual organization to maintain. Reliable and low cost computer service, to many smaller users, can be made available via such a "computer utility."

3. Information itself will become inexpensive and readily available. Increased demand for computerized information will result in establishment of data banks that were heretofore too expensive to collect.

4. Computers will become continually easier to use. Programming languages will become more generalized and more similar to every day English. The computer equipment, itself, will be simplified for human operators and the equipment will attain higher levels of reliability.

5. Organizations already utilizing computers will expand from record-keeping and accounting applications into management science and decision-making. Improvements in computer technology, availability of more qualified computer technicians, and growing sophistication of management will result in shifts to computer applications of a higher order.

6. Computer manufacturers and others will assume more of the burden of providing packages of pre-tested programs for specific applications and industries. The availability of packaged programs will make computer use more appealing for the many organizations that cannot afford to design, develop, and test complicated programs.

7. Computers will be used to control complete systems. Such highly automated systems will become economical to use in process organizations, production lines, materials handling, testing and quality control, laboratory research and tests, etc.

8. Computers will be used to process pictorial images and graphic information. The computer's capability to process images and drawings, together with its ability to calculate, will revolutionize the designer's work by making design more rapid and less expensive.

9. Input and output devices will become more varied, more flexible, and less expensive. As computer use spreads to smaller users, and utility-type computer services become more prevalent, input and output devices will become even more important.

Armer has depicted some of the dramatic technological improvements in computers (Figure 7-10). Basically, the graphs stress that the computer's speed and processing power are increasing at astonishing rates; on the other hand, computer size and cost are diminishing.

Future Uses of Computers

Notwithstanding some disappointments and limitations (often attributable to humans rather than to the computer) of experiences with the computer to

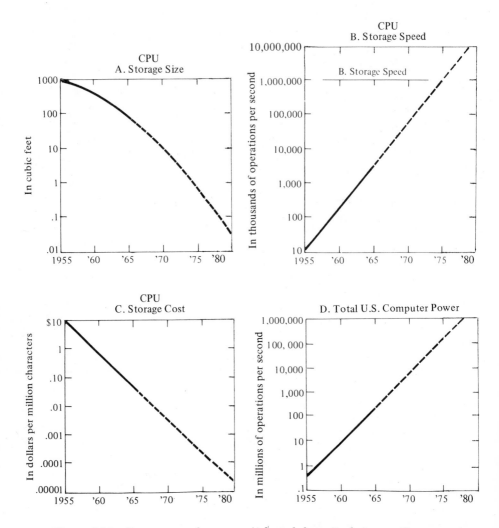

Figure 7-10 Computer performance. (Adapted from Paul Armer, *Computer Aspects of Technological Change, Automation, and Economic Progress*, Santa Monica, California: Rand Corporation, undated, pp. 211, 212, 229.)

date, a great deal of optimism still abounds among computer people. The optimism is reflected in their predictions of future uses of computers:

1. The data terminal connected to a computer and information storage will permit most work, education, and buying to be done at home. Instead of people going from various locations to central offices, schools, and stores,

these institutions will send their messages to the individual's home. Will this portend a return to the strong family unit, since members of the family will have less reason to leave their domicile?

2. The money and check transactions of our society will be replaced by the electronic transmission of financial transactions between banks, organizations, and the individual. The emergence of the so-called "checkless and cashless society" would make possible almost instantaneous transfers of debits and credits. It would also have other social implications; for instance, what would happen to crime statistics, as robbery for cash becomes impossible?

3. Instantaneous communication, computation, and information will permit governments to function in a more democratic fashion. The citizens can, collectively and individually, make their opinions known and more directly influence government decision-making. The town hall concept of total citizen participation becomes feasible again, and the need for remote, representative government diminishes.

The significance of these predictions, even if only partially accurate, will be considerable for our economy and society.

2001: A COMPUTER SPACE ODYSSEY*

HAL, a computer, was one of the principal characters in the classic science fiction motion picture "2001: A Space Odyssey." HAL stands for *H*euristically-programmed *Al*gorithmic-computer, which simply means that HAL can teach himself how to do new things, just as humans do. As HAL learns, he grows new neural networks to cope with his new functions; thus, he is more adaptable than the human specimens around him.

Most of the things HAL did in the film are already within the capabilities of existing computer technology; among these are:

- Guide space vehicles.
- Monitor assemblages of humans and equipment.
- Alert for emergencies which are beyond human capacities to understand or sense.
- Interact with humans in intellectual diversions such as chess.

So the year 2001 can be said to be here today as far as computer capabilities are concerned. However, there is one important exception. What made HAL unique, in contrast with today's computers, is the way it interacted with humans. Rather than using pushbuttons, manual devices, and media (e.g., magnetic tape, punched cards) to communicate with the computer, the astronauts in "2001"

* Adapted from the author's article "2001: A Computer Space Odyssey," which appeared in Journal of Systems Management, April 1978.

interacted with HAL in humanlike terms. HAL conversed orally in normal English, and understood the spoken words of humans.

While a communicating computer, such as HAL, may be science fiction today, there is growing awareness that the science fiction of today presages the reality of tomorrow. In less than two decades we will be in the year 2001. Will society have its human-like HAL by then?

Communicating in Society

Communication is one of the fundamental characteristics of a society. Most managers, professional and technical personnel will readily agree that the volume of communications, in their respective area of expertise, has become almost unmanageable. And probably the worst has yet to come!

Some of our communication systems appear to be at the point of technical and economic collapse. The postal system is handling approximately 100 billion pieces of mail per year. Service seems to deteriorate and costs rise as volume increases; thus, the economic dictum of the larger the scale-of-operation the more efficient the operation does not seem to apply in the case of the Post Office.

Facts about telephone communication, almost exclusively concerned with the transmission of oral messages, are even more impressive. It is estimated that an average of about 500 million telephone calls are made each day in the United States. If this figure is translated to yearly figures, it is beyond ordinary comprehension.

A study[6], at Bell Telephone Laboratories, indicated that about two-thirds of the time of employees is spent in some form of communication. Other studies[7] support the conclusion that managers, office workers, professional people, and technicians spend a considerable amount of time in the communication activity. Further, face-to-face oral communication tends to be the most prevalent mode of employees.

The Need for a HAL-like Computer

The volume of communication is unlikely to decrease. It is suggested that, in coping with the problems of communication, society needs to make better use of the enormous information handling capacities of computers.

Most people are interested primarily in what the computer can do for them, and not in how the computer does it. The interaction between people and computers can be thought of as conversation. The interaction is characterized by commands, statements, queries, answers to queries, and other messages between people and the computer.

Currently, the human being has to learn a "foreign" language (that of the computer) in order to instruct the computer what to do. It is granted that computer programming languages are continually being improved in attempts to develop those easiest for the user and most efficient for the computer. For some programmers, particularly those with mathematical aptitudes, the computer languages (e.g., ALGOL, APL, FORTRAN, BASIC) are reasonably similar to normal mathematical language. However, it is suggested that a much simpler method of communicating with the computer is necessary if the masses of people are to use them as easily as they use the telephone.

Today, most messages between the human and the computer require recording on some type of keyboard device. The so-called conversational mode, which exists today, between people and computers, is relatively stilted, esoteric, and often frustrating. Perhaps even more important, communication with computers requires thought processes that are unfamiliar and unnatural for most people.

In order to develop a HAL-type computer, which can accept human conversation and respond similarly, there is need to know first how people naturally communicate with each other. Apparently there are still considerable gaps in applied research related to understanding human communication. Yet, such understanding would be required to develop the general principles required for a truly conversational computer.

Generally, if a phenomenon can be defined in precise, quantitative terms, engineers can build a machine to simulate it. It is the current inability to describe how we hear and recognize speech that stands in the way of designing functional conversational computers.

A Beginning: Primitive HAL's

There are already some modest advances in limited voice recognition systems. In most computer installations the input and output functions done by voice could be handled by more conventional methods, such as punched card devices. However, sometimes the computer user is too occupied to concentrate on a terminal. For instance, aircraft pilots are not in a position to divert their attention to operate a computer terminal or monitor its output among the maze of instruments they must monitor during flight but they can speak to a computer, and listen for its response. Existing voice response systems, such as those used by the telephone company to tell the time of day, contain pre-recorded words spoken by a human. The computer finds the words it wants from a file stored on magnetic tape or disks, and strings them together as needed. To date, however, these systems have only limited capability.

Voice recognition equipment is beginning to do simple jobs in data entry. Most of the applications require discrete or isolated word recognition systems. That is, the speaker must pause between each word. The user must orient the system to recognize his/her enunciation of the words in the vocabulary to be used. This is done through repetitive utterances of those words to produce a sound reference pattern that can be stored in some machine retentive components of the computer. After this is done, the system can be programmed to respond to the user's spoken command with an appropriate action.

- In one such system, disabled programmers can now send input into the computer by merely saying them, and a CRT (cathode ray tube) display provides visual verification that the correct input has been communicated to computer storage.
- In many clerical operations, the clerk's hands are busy handling documents. Consequently, in such instances it would frequently be more efficient to speak the input data rather than to wait until the hands are free to depress keys on an input keyboard. A number of organizations are already using such voice recognition data entry.

While these are very modest beginnings, they are positive movements toward a HAL-like computer.

The Value of HAL-type Conversational Computers

Studies[8] indicate that most people prefer to deal with other people. There is some evidence that human, or human-like, interaction in computer systems would create a more favorable attitude of people toward computers, and would alleviate the alienation that many humans have for computers.

Human communication can, of course, be of many kinds ranging from the very personal, between two people, to that which is very impersonal. The very large, impersonal purpose of communication—and the primary general purpose for which computers are designed—is the transmission of factual information.

Perhaps the most obvious function served by factual communication is the transmission of very specific information in response to inquiries. Computers can do a good job at this kind of communication because they can search through enormous files of data for exactly the information that is wanted. It is suggested that in many cases it would be more natural and efficient if such interaction was oral and auditory—rather than keyed-in or visual as is now the case.

Spoken requests are easier to make than any type of keying-in process. Similarly, spoken replies would probably be easier to assimilate unless the reply was so complex as to exceed the memory span of the listener.

Free browsing is at the other end of the continuum from simply inquiry and communication of facts, for browsing means that the individual is not looking for anything in particular. Little research has been done on the nature of such browsing. Yet, it is probably a widely used technique and may be important for providing unexpected sources of stimulation and creativity. Thus, although most browsing is now done visually (e.g., browsing through a journal), it might be interesting to study the problems and possibilities of using the auditory channel for browsing.

Research has indicated that oral communication to be, in fact, a more rapid mode of communication than any keying-in process or handwriting. Of course, the challenge is in formulating the rules of human oral communication—so those rules can be passed on to a real-life HAL computer. The challenge is great since, as we know, few humans follow immaculate prose that are grammatically correct. Often human communication is quite idiomatic, and does not follow closely the grammatical, syntactical, or semantical rules.

One of the greatest difficulties with communication is the emotion (or meaning) behind the communication. We are aware that the tone of a voice or gesticulation can convey a variety of messages for a common set of words. Can HAL computers cope with these types of challenges?

Science Fiction or Reality?

Carl Hammer, director of computer sciences for Sperry Rand Corporation, has indicated that 1M chips will permit artificial intelligence including computer voice input, and chips with 10M capacities will permit language translations— from print to print. Chips with 100M capacities will allow voice-to-voice language translation which could put most human translators out of jobs!

Since extrapolation shows that computers, if they keep improving, will exceed the human brain in raw data processing capacities in several . . . it seems in the cards that humans and machines will eventually communicate in ordinary human language. Computers will become more able to do more and more of the things that the human nervous system can do. They will become, in fact, more and more human.

Although the difficulties undoubtedly are formidable, one of the great technical and humanistic breakthroughs in computers would be a HAL-like computer that could communicate freely on human terms with people. There are two decades until the year 2001, more than enough years for the computer industry to translate science fiction into functional reality!

PROBLEMS OF THE COMPUTER FIELD

The computer industry has had a hyperactive existence, during its short twenty-five years of existence, investing heavily in research and development. Undoubtedly, part of the reason for this dynamic product situation is related to competitive factors. It is also related to the manufacturers' planned obsolescence of products with the expectation that users will periodically upgrade computer installations. Some of the more highly articulated problems and dissatisfactions of the computer industry may be highlighted as follows:

1. In a recent survey, several hundred users of IBM computers expressed serious concern about the reliability, availability, and serviceability of their

systems. Almost half of the users expressed dissatisfaction with their computer systems, including the equipment and programs supplied by the vendor.[6]

2. The engineering of computer equipment leaves something to be desired in a number of areas: noisiness, security and privacy protection, complexity of operations, difficulty to program, inadequate standardization and inter-equipment compatability, etc. Also, there is a plethora of computer-related equipment and services that border on the chaotic.

3. The American National Standards Institute (ANSI) is an organization that has tried to promote desirable standardization within the computer industry. However, because of the extensive membership and tedious procedures for developing and gaining approval for standards, progress has been very slow. Further, the equipment manufacturers have a dominant voice on many of the committees of ANSI and, consequently, their viewpoints tend to prevail over the dissipated views of users.

4. New computer products, which obsolete older equipment, frequently require that the user redesign computer applications to a considerable extent.

5. Modern computer equipment has sometimes resulted in more complex devices for humans to use—rather than bringing simplification.

6. The marketing people in the computer industry have a tendency to greatly oversell their products, creating over-expectations from users. Too often these marketing people are reluctant realistically to apprise users of problems likely to arise from the use of their products (e.g., conversion requirements, staffing and training needs).

7. It is not rare that customers, in effect, are testing and debugging the computer industry's products. The industry has an apparent habit of introducing and marketing goods and services that are not thoroughly checked-out for flaws.

8. One computer manufacturer, International Business Machines Corporation (IBM), has a dominant share of the market (about 70 per cent). The federal government and various court cases are attempting to determine whether IBM's position is monopolistic and tends to have undesirable results for users and smaller computer firms. It is well known that IBM products tend to set a *de facto* standard for much of the computer industry.

9. As previously discussed at length, there has been a continued shortage of well-educated computer personnel—particularly higher-level analysts and programmers.

What have the above conditions meant to the computer user? The user has been faced with an almost continual surge of computer equipment and services; the user frequently feels helpless in coping with the situation. The shortcomings of the computer industry's products have, of course, reflected badly on the image of computer departments and computer staffs. *The managements of using organizations are becoming hardened to the computer, as they see frequently unfulfilled promises on the part of the vendors and their internal staffs. The net effect is a diminished esteem and an increased scepticism about the potential of the computer.*

Computer Errors

Computer errors plague management, consumers, and employees. A few examples are provided:

- A young Arizona pneumonia patient received a bill from a hospital computer charging him not only for his chest ailment but also for delivery room and nursery costs—alleging that he had given birth to a baby girl.

- An employee who had a weekly salary of $150 was issued a check for $1,500—and he cashed it.

- The stockholders of one company were paid a dividend of $1.20 a share rather than 12 cents a share as declared by the board of directors.

- One man gave twenty magazine subscriptions to friends as gifts, but the donor got all the magazines while his friends got all the bills.

- A woman was repeatedly billed for a balance of $0.00. After her repeated failure to pay her account, the matter was turned over to a collection agency. She finally solved the matter—by sending a check for $0.00.

- One of the largest stockholders of a billion dollar industrial organization had the name of Alfred A. Smit. One of his dividend checks was misprinted by the computer; his last name was printed in such a way as to form an obscene word.

It is difficult to attribute such errors to a particular cause; each occurrence requires a careful audit before fixing blame. It is quite obvious that many of them can be traced to poorly designed computer applications, and inadequate audit trails and controls. Other errors can be caused by malfunctioning computer equipment and programs, supplied by the vendors, that have not been debugged or properly maintained.

The kinds of errors identified above are of a nuisance value and create considerable inconvenience, cost, and ill will. In addition, if such nuisance errors occur in relatively simple processing, the manager must be rightfully concerned that the computer may supply him with faulty information which is used for more vital purposes (e.g., deciding the location of a new plant, selecting between alternative investment opportunities, etc.).

Corrective Measures

There would appear to be need for the following:

1. An orderly approach to product research and development, and a more responsible posture in marketing computer goods and services.

2. *Increased research and study of the adequacy of human engineering of computer products and, where necessary, the application of psychological and sociological insights so that the products fit the capacities of people.*

3. Acceleration of desirable standards in the computer industry to ease the confusing differences that exist and to simplify computer equipment and programming.

Well!—Back to the old drawing board."

Drawing by Porges. From *The American Legion Magazine*. (Reproduced with permission)

4. More effective joint-user action that will offer practical and definitive guidance to the computer industry, rather than user groups being dominated by the industry as they tend to be.

5. Increased resource commitment to educating and training the quantity and quality of individuals needed to cope with computer technology.

Chapter 13 explores some ways users can design systems which minimize error-prone computer applications.

Both computer vendors and users should have an alertness to their joint social responsibility for controlling the problem of ecological pollution that has been attributed to the computer and related machines.

SUMMARY

The computer is one of our most important technological developments. It has very great significance for society now and in the future.

The modern computer has evolved over the last thirty years. In that time, the computer industry has grown to be one of the largest in our economy, and it is growing at a faster rate than any other industry. The United States has a leadership position in both the manufacture and use of computer systems. The computer field is making available a large number of job opportunities; for instance, systems analysis and computer programming are two of the fastest growing occupations. Higher education is having difficulty in training enough persons to fill the demand for highly qualified individuals.

The computer industry's products and services have been very dynamic, but there are indications that the problems of vendors and computer users have outpaced the industry's technological progress. As a result, users and individuals have had some adverse experiences with computers—which dampens enthusiasm for it. With the probability that the computer will have an increasing impact on society, there is need for both the computer industry and users to give adequate attention to the social and human factors related to computer systems.

Chapter 8, which follows, takes an overview of the impact of the computer on the managerial process and organizational structural patterns.

KEY CONCEPTS OF THE CHAPTER

1. Computers are important tools and are used, by organizations, in combination with manual and mechanical systems.

2. An important consideration, which is too often not given adequate attention, is the best balance of work for people and machines. Too frequently, technicians attempt to turn over as much work as possible to

machines and they do not take into account workers' feelings and motivations.

3. The computer industry is one of the largest, and is rapidly growing. The new goods and services of the industry have appeared on the market in staggering numbers and with bewildering frequency.

4. The computer field offers one of the fastest growing employment areas. In particular, the occupations of systems analyst and computer programmer are attractive career opportunities.

5. The impact of the computer on society and people requires greater social responsibility on the part of the computer industry and using organizations. Up to now, the young industry has experienced the euphoria of fast growth, but concurrently there have been dramatic cases of over-selling and over-expectations which have reduced confidence in computer systems.

DISCUSSION QUESTIONS

General Background (Seminar/Classroom Discussion)

1. What is a computer? What functions does it perform?
2. Why have computers become so important to society in such a short span of time?
3. What is the relationship of automation and computerization?
4. What is computer programming?

Operational and Technical

1. What changes and disruptions occurred during your organization's last conversion to a new computer? How might the conversion have been made smoother?
2. To what extent do computer equipment and vendor-provided programs cause major problems in the operations of the computer department? How might an organization influence vendors in the computer industry to supply more reliable and useful products?
3. How can a computer technician keep abreast of the many new computer goods and services that are available? How does one evaluate the relative worth of such goods and services?

Policy

1. Does your organization have a long-range plan for its computer systems? Why is planning particularly necessary for computer resources?
2. Does your organization give as much attention to the people affected by computers, as it does to the physical computer and its uses? Why is the people factor prone to be overlooked?
3. Is the computer department's performance evaluated as rigorously as that of other operating departments? Why have some computer efforts evaded close scrutiny?
4. It is not unusual for a large organization to spend hundreds-of-thousands or

millions of dollars on its computer effort. Have your organization's policy makers adequately studied and evaluated the goods and services supplied by the computer industry? Is your organization getting good value for its expenditures?

Areas for Research

1. What are your organization's total expenditures per annum for computers? Of this amount, what percentage is for computer goods and services, computer staff, overhead? How do these figures compare with those of other organizations in your industry? Explain any significant differences.
2. Study any major computer application. What determined which specific tasks would be computerized and which would be retained for manual processing? Might job enrichment studies suggest that some work, put on the computer, should be turned back to people?
3. What are the educational backgrounds of systems analysts and programmers working in your organization? What percentage are college graduates? Have any majored in computer-related areas? How do these figures compare with those of past years? Explain the reasons for differences and changes.
4. Interview several thought leaders. What have been their experiences with computers as it affects their life? Ask them whether and how they think the computer industry can become more socially responsible.

BIBLIOGRAPHY

Armer, Paul. *Computer Aspects of Technical Change, Automation, and Economic Progress*. Santa Monica, California: Rand Corp., undated.

Awad, Elias, *Computers in Business*. Englewood Cliffs, New Jersey: Prentice-Hall, Inc., 1977.

Clarke, A.C., *2001; A Space Odyssey*. New York: The New American Library, 1968.

Gilchrist, Bruce and Richard E. Weber, eds. *The State of the Computer Industry in the United States*. Montvale, New Jersey: American Federation of Information Processing Societies, Inc., 1973.

Heyel, Carl. *Computers, Office Machines, and the New Information Technology*. New York: The Macmillan Company, 1969.

Martin, James and Norman, Adrian R. D. *The Computerized Society*. Englewood Cliffs, New Jersey: Prentice-Hall, Inc., 1970.

Nyborg, Philip, and McCarter and Erickson. *Information Processing in the United States*. Montvale, New Jersey: American Federation of Information Processing, 1977.

Orlicky, Joseph. *The Successful Computer System*. New York: McGraw-Hill Book Co., 1969.

Sackman, Harold. *Computers, System Science, and Evolving Society*. New York: John Wiley & Sons, Inc., 1967.

Shank, R. C. and K. M. Colby (eds.) *Computer Models of Thought and Language*. San Francisco: W. H. Freeman and Company, 1973.

Taviss, Irene, ed. *The Computer Impact*. Englewood Cliffs, New Jersey: Prentice-Hall, Inc., 1970.

Tomeski, Edward A. *The Computer Revolution*. New York: The Macmillan Co., 1970.

Tomeski, Edward A. *Computers in Business*. San Francisco: Holden-Day, Inc., 1979.

U.S. Department of Labor. *Patterns of U.S. Economic Growth*. Washington, D.C., 1970.

_____, *Manpower Demand and Supply in Professional Occupations*. Washington, D.C., 1970.

Wiener, Norbert. *The Human Use of Human Beings: Cybernetics and Society*. Boston: Houghton Mifflin, 1950.

FOOTNOTES

[1] Herman Kahn and Anthony J. Wiener, *The Year 2000* (New York: The Macmillan Co., 1967), pp. 86-89.

[2] James C. Emery, "An Overview of Management Information Systems," *Special Report,* Society for Management Information Systems, September 1972, p. 25.

[3] C. Robert Hollinger, "Managing the Computer for Competitive Advantage," *Business Horizons,* December 1970, p. 17.

[4] G. Truman Hunter, "Manpower Resources for Management Information Systems," *Founders' Conference,* Society for Management Information Systems, September 8-9, 1969, unnumbered pages.

[5] U.S. Department of Labor, *Manpower Demand and Supply in Professional Occupations* (Washington, D.C.: U.S. Government Printing Office, 1970), pp. 162-163.

[6] Alphonse Chapanis, "Explorations in Human Communication," *American Psychologist,* November 1972, p. 952.

[7] R. Stewart , "How Managers Spend Their Time," *Management Today,* 1967, pp. 92-160; J. R. Hinrichs, "Communications Activity of Industrial Research Personnel," *Personnel Psychology,* 1964, 17, pp. 193-204.

[8] R. G. Kinkage, E. W. Bedarf, and H. P. Van Cott, "Science Information Requirements of Scientists," American Institutes for Research Tech. Reps. 2 and 3, 1967.

[9] Alphonse Chapanis, "The Communication of Factual Information Through Various Channels," *Information Storage and Retrieval,* Vol. 9, 1973, pp. 215-231.

[10] "Papers Reveal IBM User Dissatisfaction in, '69," *Computerworld,* June 27, 1973, p. 6.

Part II Cases

SOUTHEAST RESEARCH CO.

MASTERS INC.

STUART UNIVERSITY

HAMMERNTONG CORPORATION

MIDDLE CITY

PYRAMID

SOUTHEAST RESEARCH CO.

Mr. J. T. Runner, president of Southeast Research Co. (known as SRC), was educated at Columbia University and Harvard University, and his management philosophy focussed on the participative methods in a democratic organization. He believed in having employees practice management-by-objectives. Each employee was expected to set down in writing a description of what he wished to accomplish and the standards by which his performance should be measured at specific intervals of time.

Recently, Mr. Runner was wondering about the effectiveness of the information system that had been installed in SRC several years ago. Because of his concerns, Mr. Runner had a systems study made of the information system. The study revealed the following:

1. The system contains redundancies and inconsistencies. A number of employees and units seem to be working on similar projects, although they may be approaching the problems in somewhat different ways.

2. The system tends to be very elaborate and rigid. It requires considerable time for the employee to make up the periodic reports for the system, and the rigidity sometimes interferes with the flexibility and responsiveness desired by employees to make a change to capitalize on new opportunities which may arise.

3. Some managers keep separate records over-and-above the formal information systems. There is some definite duplication of records because of this. In other cases, the managers appear to think that the formal information system cannot provide some information that they need.

4. If one department is out-of-phase in progressing toward its goals, it may upset the schedules of other departments that are working on interdependent projects.

5. The system does not take into account uncontrollable events such as strikes, an energy crisis, etc. If progress is retarded due to such events, the manager must bargain about the matter with the president.

QUESTIONS

1. What do you think of Mr. Runner's method of management?
2. How can Mr. Runner check on the validity of the systems study's findings?
3. If the findings are valid, what changes might be considered by Mr. Runner?

MASTERS INC.

Mr. James Walters, president of Masters Inc., was invited to make a presentation to a business policy class of the local university. Mr. Waters decided to talk about management information systems. His main thesis was that many organizations had installed expensive computers and that they were not needed. He used his own company to illustrate the point. Mr. Walters said:

We are a relatively small firm with 200 employees. Our sales have been steadily growing, our profit is satisfactory, and our surplus excellent. Our products are considered to be of the best quality in the field and, consequently, we can charge a higher price for them. We are not unionized, have low employee turnover, and our wages are higher than our competitors.

We have just a couple of people in our accounting office, and they do all of the bookkeeping and financial analysis. Our payroll is done by an outside service bureau.

Why should we consider computers and sophisticated management information systems, since we are so successful without them?

QUESTIONS

1. Do you agree with Mr. Walters' views about his small, successful firm not needing to consider the use of computers and a MIS?
2. What questions would you have for Mr. Walters if you were a student in the business policy class?
3. If you were a computer vendor's representative, how might you try to convince Mr. Walters that a computer might be beneficial to his organization?

STUART UNIVERSITY

Stuart University was founded in the 1890's and has an enrollment of more than 10,000 full-time equivalent students and about 500 faculty members.

Administratively, the university consists of the board of trustees, the president, and vice presidents of academic affairs, research, financial affairs, student affairs, public relations, and planning. The various academic units are administered by deans and their assistants. Administration has historically been relatively centralized and informal. Recently, there has been a gradual movement toward some decentralized decision making as well as formalizing of policy and procedure.

The data processing center began operating in the late 1950's, mostly for academic uses in the mathematics and science areas. At that time, the center was administered on a part-time basis by a faculty member. In the 1960's, the data processing center was placed under a director reporting to the vice president of planning. After a few years, the major use of the computer was for administrative applications rather than for academic work. In the early 1970's, a university computer committee was established; it recommended the establishment of an integrated information system for the university. A systems task force was designated to design and develop such a system; the head of the task force reported to the vice president of planning. The task force was assigned two goals:

1. The design and development of two data bases: a student file and a faculty file. These would constitute the beginning of an integrated information system.

2. An attempt to develop a university simulation model to be used as an aid in predictive planning for the university.

Recently, the use of the computer has been increasing in the academic areas for educational and research purposes. The data processing center, however, is concentrating most of its time on administrative areas. Consequently, there have been growing complaints from faculty that educational technology is being neglected, and that such neglect harms the quality of the university education and research effort.

QUESTIONS

1. Do you think the faculty complaints appear justified? What can the faculty do to alleviate the problem?
2. What is your assessment of the university computer committee and its role related to the data processing center? Reconcile the responsibilities of the vice president of planning, director of the data processing center, director of the systems task force, and that of the committee.
3. What is the best way of balancing the center's service to the administrative and academic users of the university?
4. What actions would you take if you were the vice president of planning?

HAMMERNTONG CORPORATION

The computer policy committee was a top management advisory committee which met once a month to review the progress of the computer task force, which was conducting studies on the feasibility of installing a new powerful computer at the corporate headquarters of Hammerntong Corporation.

At the critical meeting in which a decision was to be made, Alec Wacker (head of the computer task force) made his presentation covering the task force's report, "Application of the Zeus 2000 Computer to the Problems of the Hammerntong

Corporation." As was the case in most of the meetings, Alec Wacker dominated the meeting with his technical know-how. Although O. U. Foote was the chairman of the computer policy committee, his largely financial background limited his ability to judge Wacker's technical expertise.

At the end of Wacker's presentation, Foote summarized the meeting and its conclusions as follows:

1. It is recognized that changes in management philosophy are required and the computer policy committee accepts the recommendations that Hammerntong will employ an integrated systems approach to computers.

2. Based on the recommendations of the computer task force, the policy committee agrees that a Zeus 2000 computer should be ordered for the company. Wacker should contact the president to arrange for a review of the proposed plan with the board of directors of the company.

The computer policy committee members voted to approve the resolutions, and the meeting ended.

QUESTIONS

1. What concerns do you have about the adequacy of the proposal by the computer task force?
2. Did the computer policy committee competently execute its responsibilities?
3. How would you strengthen Hammerntong's handling of computer plans and decisions?

MIDDLE CITY

Middle City has a population of about 500,000. It has a mixed population of well-to-do families, the middle class, and a segment of the poor.

Up until 1969, there were a number of data processing installations in the city government. There were installations in the city hospital, highway department, board of elections, welfare department, and finance department.

In 1969, it was decided to consolidate all data processing into a central data processing department to be responsible to the commissioner of finance. The officials in the hospital, elections board, and highway and welfare departments were not enthusiastic about the decision of the mayor and the city council. The decision was the outcome of a feasibility study conducted by the city's outside auditors, who indicated that considerable savings could accrue from data processing consolidation.

The manager of the data processing department was instructed to convert all existing applications to the new computer. This was done with a very limited staff of seven systems analysts-programmers. There was no time for any significant redesign of systems; the conversion was done in the most expeditious method. During this period, the welfare case load "exploded" and the new computer was devoted increasingly to the handling of the vast volume of welfare records, claims, and checks.

The manager of the data processing department said:

"We just do not have the manpower to do our job properly. We merely dumped poor applications onto the new computer.

Also, the administrators aren't really interested in developing better administrative systems. For instance, except for payroll, we hardly do any personnel work on the computer. It is still done manually. We don't know what manpower planning is."

The commissioner of welfare was heard to state:

"That central data processing department is fouling up our welfare records. It was better when we had direct control over our own computer. Now we have to fight to get our work processed. We are competing with half a dozen departments for computer time. And the center, where the new computer is, has a staff that doesn't really understand welfare work. There are literally hundreds of corrections each week! I am going to politic to get our own data processing facility. It is better that way."

QUESTIONS

1. Why do you think the consolidation of Middle City's computer facilities has caused major difficulties?
2. If you were the manager of the central data processing department, what actions would you take to try to improve the situation?
3. Do you agree with the position of the commissioner of welfare?

PYRAMID

In seventy-five years, Pyramid has grown from a small organization to one which in 1974 should do approximately $5 billion worth of sales. Its diversified product line includes: lighting equipment and fixtures, appliances, communications equipment, medical equipment, and others.

Basically, the company is organized by product line; each product line is headed by a managing director and reporting to the director are a financial manager and an operations manager. Each of these product line divisions has worldwide responsibility for profits. The managing director reports directly to the president's office.

Over the past ten years, computers have made a very strong impact on the company. At present, 125 computers are installed in Pyramid's 70 locations. The annual computer equipment expenditures are about $15 million. These computer facilities are not bound together in any formal way. They report either to their local national organization or to a product division and, in some cases, to both. Their staffs are drawn almost exclusively from the country in which they are located.

The central office of Pyramid has a computer department. It contains a group of experts whose services are available on a charge-out basis to the divisions. Its objectives are:

1. Provide superior technical know-how to the rest of the organization.
2. Offer central coordination of computer matters.
3. Assist with training people where appropriate.
4. Issue formal procedures, on a general level, throughout the organization.
5. Service the information and data processing needs of the central office.

QUESTIONS

1. What are the advantages of decentralizing control, over computers, to the local organizations or product division? What are the weaknesses?
2. What are some of the managerial problems, related to computers, in an organization the size and complexity of Pyramid?
3. Is a single integrated management information system possible in an organization such as Pyramid?
4. How can an organization assure itself that it is obtaining full value from such a vast network of computers as exists in Pyramid?
5. Do you have any suggestions about the objectives of Pyramid's central computer department?

PART 3
COMPUTER SYSTEMS SERVING SOCIAL SYSTEMS

This part of the book considers the impact and use of computer systems in the social systems of organizations.

Chapter 8. *Impact of Computers on Management and Organizations* reviews the positive and negative effects of computers on managers and organizations and forecasts the ways in which computer systems may change institutions and their administration.

Chapter 9. *Use of the Computer in the Personnel Process* analyzes the current status of computer use in personnel departments. A model of a modern personnel system is described, and a series of specific computer applications identified. In addition, the authors present guidelines for improving existing computer efforts in personnel departments.

Chapter 10. *Use of the Computer for Training and Development* discusses the potential of computers for training and educational purposes, and details the application in two areas: management games and computer-assisted instruction.

Chapter 11. *Social Issues and the Computer* explores dehumanization, unemployment, privacy, and crime as they interrelate with computer use.

Chapter 12. *Organizing and Staffing the Computer Department* surveys the organization and staffing needs and challenges in a computer department.

Chapter 13. *Designing the Personnel Information System* outlines some of the specific requirements of an integrated employee information system.

Chapter 14 Case Examples: Integrated Personnal Information Systems presents in some detail three actual applications.

In sum, Part III *describes some of the major interfaces between the human system* (explored in Part I of the book) *and the computer system* (discussed in Part II of the book). In doing this, *the authors have identified how a computer system should serve the social system of an organization—and not vice versa.*

8

Impact of Computers on Management and Organizations

The future manager will find the computer as much a fact of life as children today find the telephone . . .

The computer is a tool of liberation if used correctly. Otherwise, you become its servant. It should liberate you from being chained to operations and to your desk and enable you to have time for people and for the outside, where the results are.

Peter F. Drucker

OBJECTIVES OF THE CHAPTER

The broad implications of the computer for organizations and managers are surveyed. The authors look at both the positive and negative aspects of computer use. Particular attention is devoted to the ways the computer may alter organization patterns and managerial decision-making. Both personnel administrators and computer planners should have keen interests in such changes.

THE PROS AND CONS OF COMPUTERS

The Promise

The positive view of the computer is that it aids man by extending his scope and reach. Man, freed from repetitive jobs and aided in the doing of complex tasks, can now, to use Drucker's phrase, use his time "for tasks that require perception, imagination, human relations, and creativity." [1] On the other hand, a *Fortune* article, critically appraising the overly glamorized aspects of computers, concluded that,

Electronic computers have been long touted as the certain cure for the problems and ills of top management . . . But now . . . businessmen are less and less able to state with assurance that it's all worth it.[2]

171

Even the well known computer expert and widely quoted champion of automation, Diebold, has observed that,

> . . . in most government areas . . . information technology is grossly under-utilized. We have largely converted old data collection and control systems to computerized operation rather than designing new systems to utilize the potential of the new technology.[3]

The potentials of the computer were publicized to such an extent that it was almost inevitable that the results would be somewhat short of the aroused expectations. On the other hand, examples of solid achievements of the computer do exist and there is the promise of more solid attainments in the future.

The well over 1,000,000 computers installed in the United States are testimony to the fact that despite specific disappointments, the acceptance of computers—by organizations and individuals—is widespread.

Disillusionment

One problem has been that the early emphasis in computer installations was on savings in administrative costs—which meant a reduction in clerical payroll, despite circumlocutions such as "freed for other duties." Later, much publicized disillusionment resulted when, in the climate of business recession, controllers found that despite large-scale computerization, administrative costs had not been reduced or, in some cases, had increased. However, with the continuing increase in administrative complexity (larger scale of operations, more paperwork called for by increasing governmental regulation, international as well as domestic operations, etc.) the computer has become indispensable, not to reduce the administrative payroll, but rather to handle an increase in workload that would otherwise be intolerable. The Federal Social Security Administration, for example, has indicated that the computer has enabled it to absorb a more than 100 per cent increase in workload with only a 35 per cent increase in staff.[4] Experience has shown that few persons are actually terminated when a computer is introduced, although there is "invisible disemployment" in terms of absorbing added workload and constraining staffing needs in a growing organization.

Poor preliminary estimating of the costs of computerization has also been a problem. Commitment to computerization can involve substantial costs, both of a one-time start-up variety (equipment, suitable facilities, air conditioning, etc.) and the continuing costs of computer operations. Too frequently, these costs prove to be greater than those forecasted in computer manufacturers' proposals and organizations' feasibility studies. Recent surveys indicate that as many as 50 per cent of computers may cost more than their attributable savings.[5]

Problems of Computer Personnel

There have been substantial problems in recruiting, developing, and retaining a sufficient number of competent people for the computer field. In particular, there has been a shortage of the talented systems analysts and computer programmers needed to work on sophisticated applications. Too frequently, systems are designed that bring discredit to the computer field. For example, there is often inadequate provision for editing, controls, and audit trails needed to prevent entry of incorrect data and generation of faulty output. Chapter 12 discusses staffing in more detail.

The Need for a Broader Vision

Computer professionals have, in recent years, increasingly emphasized that the true justification for a computer installation today is actually not in specific, attributable savings in administrative costs. They emphasize that in addition to the sheer handling of workloads that would be unmanageable by manual or other mechanized means, a computerized management information system (discussed in Chapter 6) is called for, making use of data banks, time-sharing, communications technology, and remote interactive linkages of the user and the computer. Such a broadened vision opens up totally new dimensions of management decision-making, real-time feedback, information retrieval and dissemination, and control. Unfortunately, it appears that most computers are used essentially for speeded-up routinized work previously done by manual or mechanical means. There has been a simple transference of that work to the computer, with little real attempt at achieving a truly integrated management information system. In fact, old manual and mechanical procedures are often duplicated in the new computerized systems. As previously cited, a study by a billion dollar organization of its numerous computers revealed that a very small proportion of the computer-generated output (about 4 per cent) could be classified as of interest to top management; the remaining 96 per cent were of a routine nature.[6]

Other Problems

There are also organizational problems. The relative newness and technical nature of the computer field have tended to make adjustment within the organization difficult. Not infrequently, the computer department is viewed as a "foreign service" outside of the mainstream of the organization.

An organization may become too dependent on computers (e.g., all records of the company stored in the computer center). This situation can make the organization vulnerable to major problems if the computer facility should experience such things as loss of power for extended periods, fire, flood, sabotage, etc. This calls for a whole host of measures that are still widely neglected: contingency plans in case of disaster, backup power facilities, provision for reconstruction of vital records, security precautions, etc.

MANAGEMENT RESPONSIBILITIES

Management Involvement

Several managerial improvements will strengthen the computer function. Perhaps most important is the need for high-level management involvement in the planning for, and the auditing of the performance of the computer function. The lack of such involvement has been a prime reason for the widespread underemployment of computers.

There is now a trend toward having the manager of the computer department report directly to a top executive. Chapter 12 discusses this in more depth. Such an organizational arrangement serves to make the computer activity more sensitive to the needs of the organization as a whole, and to make managers of line divisions and departments aware of the potentials of the computer for their operations. In the past, most computer departments were placed far down in the organizational structure, frequently reporting to a middle-manager of a specialized function (e.g., Assistant Controller).

Management Know-How About Computers

The top managers in an organization should have an understanding of broad computer concepts, the effect of the newer management information systems on traditional concepts of organization, the impact of computer systems on employees, and the implications of large-scale systems for society as a whole. This background should permit them to provide general leadership to the computer professionals who plan for and design systems. Only with such participation will the top managers be sure that the human and social implications of proposed systems are consistent with organizational creeds and policies.

In turn, computer managers and their staffs should be more sensitive to the specific needs of the using departments, and how departmental systems can be made to fit in with the organizational needs of the company as a whole. They should develop greater sensitivity to human needs, so that they are better able to serve individuals, groups, as well as the organization.

Planning for Computers

As computer technology has advanced and as applications have multiplied in size and complexity, the job of managing an organization's computer activities has become more intricate and difficult. To keep on top of this problem, there is need for formal planning for computer resources and applications. Only through such planning (which may have a horizon of from two to ten years) can an orderly and professional approach to computers be achieved. It must address problems such as:

- Technological change in equipment and programming options, and an appraisal of cost and performance.

- Improvement in existing computer applications, and identification of new applications.

- Manpower needs and training requirements to achieve the goals of the computer department.

- Implications of the plans where scarce resources must be prudently allocated.

Management Audit of Computers

The computer department should be subject to effective management control techniques. The mystique of the computer has sometimes permitted managers of computer departments to evade the rigors of appraisal applied to other units of an organization. However, the very nature of the computer's operation, characterized by rapid technological developments and high turnover of staff, and its influence as a change agent affecting other parts of the organization, make periodic and continuing management audits essential.

A continuing or periodic management audit requires that the computer department's performance be evaluated by objective criteria: plans versus actual, chargeouts to using departments, user satisfaction, competency and performance of computer staff, employee turnover, comparison of indexes with other computer facilities, effective utilization and efficiency of computer systems and computer programs, etc.

HUMANISTS' ROLES IN COMPUTER SYSTEMS

It is interesting to note that a considerable number of the problems discussed thus far are closely related to the human resources of the organization and, consequently, should be of interest to the personnel function and social scientists. *Experience has shown that the problems of communicating and motivating—and not the technical ones—are the most important in computer efforts.* Rico, in an interesting study of the people problems related to computers, concluded:

> The advancing level of office technology has serious manpower implications for the firm . . . The electronic computer produces a significant change in firms' work methods, resulting in important qualitative changes in the process by which human resources are utilized.

> The personnel department plays a sterile and inconsequential role in the management of change in most firms. The personnel department was not consulted, and generally had little or no idea of the organizational and manpower problems associated with computerization.[7]

There are, of course, far-reaching changes when a computer is installed or an existing activity is computerized—changes that affect operating procedures, document content and format, reporting practices, etc. People will respond to these changes with attitudes which range from quiet acceptance, through passive indifference, to hostile rejection. If an atmosphere of cooperative acceptance is to be established and maintained, management must play an active role as both motivator and monitor. A conference on personnel research concluded that:

> . . . if computer science is to become socially responsive, it needs to become thoroughly humanized—which means the scientific study of the human use of computers—an orientation . . . that is nowhere on the computer horizon today.[8]

Unfortunately, such a humanistic approach to computerization is all too rare. A study of some seventy organizations indicated that there are serious shortcomings in dealing with the human problems related to computers in many instances. The study suggests that this is a significant cause of computer shortcomings.[9] *Properly oriented, trained, and motivated people are essential in making computerization a success.*

COMPUTERS AND DECISION-MAKING

While most computer time is still assigned to routine data processing work, the computer is increasingly being planned for higher-level assignments.

However, the computer has potential for being of considerably more aid to management than presently attained in most organizations. Simon takes a strong stand on this matter:

> The electronic computer is bringing about, with unexpected speed, a high level of automation in the routine, programmed decision-making . . . The area of programmed decision-making is being rapidly extended as we find ways to apply the tools of operations research to the type of decisions that have up to now been regarded as judgmental . . . The computer has extended the capability of the mathematical technique to problems far too large to be handled by less automatic computing devices, and has further extended the range of programmable decisions by contributing the new technique of simulation.[10]

While the authors believe that Simon's stated views are somewhat optimistic when contrasted with the limited achievements in MIS, it is instructive to be aware of the computer's potential.

Figure 8-1 is an adaptation of a chart which depicts some of Simon's ideas about decision-making. Programmed decisions, which are routine and repetitive, are those most frequently handled by existing computer applications. Decisions that are referred to as being non-programmed are difficult to structure and standardize; most of such decisions must ultimately be made by humans. Simon has been conducting research into the possibility of using a general problem-solving program (GPS) that, in essence, would enable the computer to respond effectively to this latter classification of decisions. This approach involves a type of "artificial intelligence," since the computer would perform functions that are normally considered as being human (e.g., learning, adapting, reasoning, self-correction, improvement). Artificial intelli-

TYPES OF DECISIONS	DECISION-MAKING TECHNIQUES	
	Traditional	Modern
Programmed Routine, repetitive decisions.	Habit. Clerical routine. Organization structure.	Computers. Management science.
Non-programmed One-shot, ill structured, novel, policy decisions.	Judgment. Intuition. Creativity. Rules-of-thumb.	Heuristics. Interactive computers. Artificial intelligence.

Figure 8-1   Decision-making paradigm.

gence requires a heuristic program which attacks a problem by a trial and error approach. Most conventional programs are deterministic in that they simply execute a pre-set series of routines; this is obviously inadequate for higher-level decisions that are not subject to precise definition in advance.

An example of a programmed decision would be the determination if an employee earned more than the maximum amount for which social security deductions are to be taken; all of the factors are defined and they form a precise algorithm. A non-programmed decision might involve unexpected events (e.g., a war, natural disaster) or a unique activity (e.g., embarking on a new venture or a new product line).

While the computer is likely to absorb an increasing amount of the current decision-making, managers will be motivated to seek new challenges in uncharted areas that, at least for some time, will not be susceptible to computerization. This will tend to bring new complexity to management and require better qualified managers. Jay Forrester's simple chart (Figure 8-2) depicts this tendency of the constantly expanding frontier of knowledge moving from the precisely defined routines, which can be automated, to the newly identified problems or those which have not yet been identified or imagined. Forrester places this forecast in succinct perspective:

> Just as the pace of technological change has quickened, so is the pace of managerial change accelerating. As present policy-guided decisions become automatic, and as

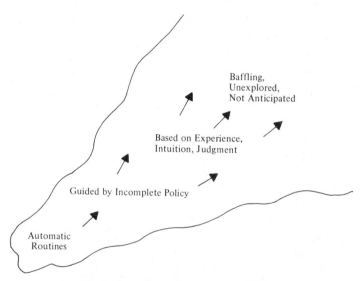

Figure 8-2   Beyond computerization.

today's judgment decisions are prescribed by policy, the creative manager will be faced by new problems and opportunities.

HOW THE COMPUTER AFFECTS MANAGEMENT AND ORGANIZATION STRUCTURE

Figure 8-3 displays a comparison of four authors' (Dearden, Hertz, Simon, Whisler) views about the computer's impact on organization and management. All four of the authors see the computer as a tool that will tend to bring about some degree of centralization and programmed decision-making. These authors appear to differ as to the degree of intensity of centralization and programmed decision-making that will take place, and what these trends mean in terms of the dynamics of organizational and human functions.

Figure 8-4 indicates some of the major kinds of changes that are induced by computer technology. Such changes involve new patterns for executives and organizations. As indicated in the chart, the limitations of human beings are supplanted or supplemented by the computer.

While the computer will contribute to managerial decision-making, it will not replace the human being. Many problems that face management are not primarily of a quantifiable nature but, rather, deal with the unstructured world of people, politics, and policy. While even in these qualitative areas future computer applications may develop, it is likely that human judgment will prevail in the person-computer partnership. A study of decision-making in the Internal Revenue Service revealed that informed managers still rely much more on qualitative then quantitative criteria in appraising performance, even when quantitative measures are available and in use.[11]

Rather than being overly concerned about the computer replacing managers, the concern is whether managers will be able sufficiently to structure current decision-making so that it can be handled by the computer. Moreover, the manager must be able to adapt to a greater fluidity in his work, for he will be a seeker of new problems. When the problems are sufficiently structured it is likely that many can be best handled by the computer. This moves the point of managerial decisions ahead in time, for the manager must define decision rules rather than make the actual decisions. Kast and Rosenzweig have made a relevant point about this idea:

> As more decision-making becomes susceptible to programming, the basic management functions may be altered. Top management will have to deal with longer-range planning and will need a better perception of how the business system interacts with the competitive and environmental systems. By programming his more routine, mechanical decisions, the manager will have more time available to deal with the highly variable factors of human motivation and participation.[12]

Computer's Affect on Organization

. . . the computer will result in some limited centralization. Where, in the past, authority to make decisions was decentralized because it was not practicable to obtain sufficient timely information centrally, there will be a tendency to centralize—in those instances where better decisions can be made centrally.[13]

Information technology has changed the economics of control; increased centralization becomes almost irresistable as more computers are used by more organizations. It is doubtful that centralization will continue to the degree that is technically possible—but it is likely that we will continue to move toward increased centralization of organizational control.[15]

Computer technology permits the creation of an information network which, like the human central nervous system, is not merely a network of communicating cells, but essentially a unifying mechanism for the organization of experience. This means increasing coordination of operations, revising the historical tendency toward progressive fragmentation and subdivision of the organization . . .[17]

Computer's Affect on Management

The job of the operating manager will be no easier in the future, although some decisions now made at the operating level will be made higher up. The increase in the complexity of most operating jobs will more than offset the fact that the operating manager has been relieved of some decisions.

At the higher management levels, the jobs will become more demanding. Because better information will be available, a more capable type of management will be required to utilize this information effectively.[14]

. . . in the highly developed manager-machine systems of the future, computer systems will perform most of the computation function and much of the communication task. The manager's time will be increasingly dominated by goal setting and pattern perception, and with the kinds of communication that can stimulate an emotional response in other humans in the organization.[16]

Scientific, nonintuitive methods can gradually change the structure of decisions at the executive level, making some routine and eliminating them from successive higher management levels, and substituting for them entirely new and potentially more creative decisions. Thus the executive is freed to devote himself to decisions of more significance and scope . . .

Figure 8-3 Views on computer-induced change.

Computer's Affect on Organization	*Computer's Affect on Management*
	Management science techniques, coupled with effective computer systems, provide today's managers with timely, accurate, and relevant information that permits them to cut through the complexities and uncertainties of business situations and thereby to select strategies and tactical courses of action and to exercise control with greater confidence in the outcome than ever before.[18]
The automation of important parts of business data processing and decision-making activity and the trend toward a much higher degree of structuring and programming of even the non-automated part will radically alter the balance of advantage between centralization and decentralization . . .	. . . the task of middle managers today is very much taken up with pace setting, with work pushing, and with expediting. As the automation and rationalization of the decision-making process progress, these aspects of the managerial job are likely to recede in importance.
. . . we can summarize . . . by saying that the new developments in decision-making will tend to induce more centralization in decision-making activities at middle-management levels.[19]	. . . In terms of subjective feel, the manager will find himself dealing more than in the past with a well structured system whose problems have to be diagnosed and corrected objectively and analytically and less with unpredictable and sometimes recalcitrant people who have to be persuaded, prodded, rewarded and cajoled. . . . Man does not generally work well with his fellow man in relations saturated with authority and dependence, with control and subordination even though these have been the predominant human relations in the past. He works much better when he is teamed with his fellow man in coping with an objective, understanding, external environment. That will be more and more his situation as the new techniques of decision-making come into wide use.[20]

Figure 8-3 **(Continued)**

Non-Computer Era	*Computer Era*
• Human memory and files	• Data banks
• Manual search and human recall	• Information storage and retrieval
• Specialization and simplification to cope with volume, complexity, distances	• Integration via general systems in order to consider all vital factors
• Written policies and procedures, habits and traditions, executive interpretation	• Automated systems with feedback and correction
• Executive review	• Pre-programmed selection of exceptions for attention or disposition
• Executive judgment and intuition about complex and creative matters	• Testing via models and simulation
• Human forecasting and best estimates	• Quantification via econometrics, mathematical programming, network analysis
• Rule-of-thumb and subjective evaluation and discontinuous control	• Augmented standards and continuous control

Figure 8-4   Computer's increased role in organizations.

Man-Machine Systems

The future generation of managers, having been educated with the computer as a normal tool, will use the computer much more extensively than present managers. Wider use will be made of interactive computer systems. In such systems, the managers employ a data terminal connected to a computer to explore alternatives and to obtain information in response to queries. The strengths of man (recognition of subtle patterns, association, learning, originality, inductive reasoning, etc.) are combined with the strengths of the computer (handling mass data, speed, reliability, accuracy, etc.). Such an approach can increase the manager's ability to explore rapidly and efficiently numerous opportunities, a process which is clumsy and slow today when implemented by man alone.

Figure 8-5 is a schematic of a model of an interactive man-machine decision-making system. A manager can raise a host of "what if" questions about his or her organization, and get back quick answers showing the impact of the proposed change on the financial condition, work schedule, manpower planning, and other aspects of performance. The program calls on specified logic from the software for the problem at hand, using pertinent information

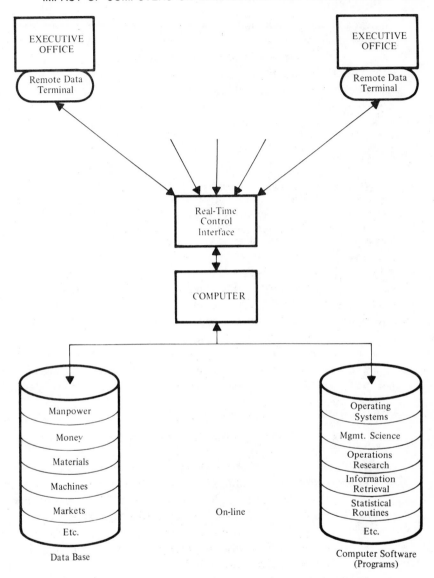

Figure 8-5 Interactive decision-making.

from a bank of general and specific data. The program utilizes rapid computations from the time-shared computer. In a few moments the effects of the proposed change are displayed for the manager's inspection. The new information may lead then to a decision by the manager or to further questions concerning additional alternatives.

Terrance Hanold, the chairman of Pillsbury Company (an organization that has exhibited leadership in computerized MIS), provides some pragmatic substantiation of these views. In discussing his firm's working MIS, he has indicated that,

> Modern information systems have multiplied the data relevant to management decisions, as well as the tools for putting it to work in the decisional process. Data reflecting the living present is opportunity. Its vast increase as we reach into real-time systems has opened the way to the involvement of many more brains and talents, of many more disciplines and technologies, to mine the profits it enfolds.[21]

Through the use of management science models and computers, many factors can be considered at the same time; systems of several hundred variables are not infeasible. It is difficult for humans to handle problems where as many as five factors are considered simultaneously. Moreover, the computer's calculations can be made so quickly, that scores of computer runs can be carried out testing various alternatives. Therefore, tremendously complex problems, which could only be solved by the manager using judgment, estimates, and intuition can now be examined, to some extent, in a quantitative manner.

Centralization/Decentralization

The tremendous capacity of the computer encourages centralization of computer processing and preparation of information, which draws to it many functions once performed by other departments. There is an obvious requirement to achieve some degree of standardization and coordination in computerized MIS. This is difficult to attain without centralization. While, generally, increased centralization of information *processing* is probably a trend, the same does not necessarily hold true for *decision-making*. In fact, one study indicates that the computer can abet decentralization of decision-making, since the computer can free lower-level managers of many day-to-day problems that formerly took much of their time.[22] With more time, such managers can make relevant decisions and not, as previously, channel the problems to higher-levels for decisions. McLuhan supports this view, when he writes, "Cybernation in effect means a new world of autonomy and decentralism in all human affairs . . ."[23]

Computerized information systems usually involve a power struggle, since such systems tend to shift the locus of physical location and control over vital information, thereby causing disruptions in the balance of political power among various groups. As a result, it may be difficult to attain optimal MIS; it is more likely that compromise will be necessary in such systems. Reasons why computerized information systems are retarded in many organizations are the following: lack of computer familiarity by managers, shortage of competent analysts and programmers, policies and procedures which impede the integration of data, lack of coordination among units of the organization, and others. Until such barriers are satisfactorily resolved, it will be difficult to notably advance MIS. Diebold forecasts the attainment of integrated information systems in the 1980's:

> In the two-decade span from 1965 to 1985, computer systems applications will evolve from the unrelated elementary uses which were typical of the 1950's and early 1960's to the highly integrated and interdependent systems projected for 1985.

SUMMARY

There are pro and con views about the net benefit derived, to date, from computers. While perhaps the expectations have been greater than the fulfillment, there is little question about the wide acceptance of computers as integral tools in organizations.

Management should take a stronger hand in the computer effort in such areas as: goal-setting for the computer department, gaining personal familiarization about the broad aspects of computers, encouraging longer-range planning for computer resources, and management audits of computer use.

The computer can extend the reach of the manager, free him from routine decisions, and allow him time to tackle more unique and unstructured problems (including those related to human relations). *It is likely that many managers of tomorrow will be interacting closely with the computer, and will combine the rational, scientific-humanist facets of joint man-machine decision-making.*

While there appears to be a trend toward some degree of centralization of information in the computer operation, decision-making can be either centralized or decentralized, depending on organizational needs. There are indications that the computer has and will be impacting the organization structure. Many of these specific changes have not been adequately researched, and only tentative interpretations of trends can be made.

The next chapter presents some specific material about computer uses in personnel departments.

KEY CONCEPTS OF THE CHAPTER

1. It is important to balance the positive and negative results of computerization. Part of some of the expressed disillusionment is due to the over-glamorized nature of the computer field, and the over-expectations of users.

2. The real justification of computers is often based on intangible benefits, rather than on tangible benefits (e.g.. reduced payroll costs). Notwithstanding considerable public controversy, the computer has become an almost indispensable component in many organizations and in our society.

3. Some keys to successful computer use appear to be greater managerial participation in the effort and increased involvement of humanists (e.g., social scientists, personnel professionals, psychologists).

4. As the computer is used for higher-level problems, managers will be confronted by newer, novel challenges. Managers will be freed of routines and will be able to devote time to exploring new opportunities.

5. While the computer is undoubtedly influencing such variables as organization structures and centralization/decentralization, there is a lack of clarity about the general nature of the patterns evolving. Continued study and research are needed in these areas.

DISCUSSION QUESTIONS

General Background (Seminar/Classroom Discussion)

1. Identify some of the benefits that are generally anticipated from computerization?
2. What have been some of the negative experiences with computers?
3. What features of computers have enabled these devices to have such a substantial impact on management and organizations?

Operational and Technical

1. In planning for computer applications, to what degree does your organization compare the anticipated costs and benefits of such projects? How are intangible benefits considered in the analysis?
2. Contrast, for one or more projects, the anticipated costs/benefits with the actual costs/benefits. Why might actual costs/benefits vary considerably from original estimates? How can cost/benefit estimates be made more realistic?
3. Select one significant computer application which generates information for decision-making. How has this computerization induced change in decision-making by administrators? Can it be established that decision-making is improved through computer-based information systems?

Policy

1. From a managerial standpoint, what have been the major benefits derived from computers?
2. How involved is management in major decisions regarding computers? Does management defer decisions on technical matters to technicians? How are such decisions appraised?
3. Does your organization conduct a periodic and formal management audit of its computer systems? What kinds of improvement can stem from such audits?
4. Has your organization tried to anticipate how the computer will change managers' responsibilities and functions? What plans might be formulated to cope with such change?

Areas for Research

1. Discuss with several managers how the computer has affected their areas of responsibility. Do the managers have real insight about the capability and limitation of a computer? Do the managers' perceptions of improvements (or lack of them) agree with the computer department's views? Try to reconcile the differences in perception, of managers and the computer department's staff, regarding improvements attributable to the computer.
2. Solicit the comments of several older managers and several younger managers about the implications of computerization for the management function. Contrast the managers' apparent attitudes (e.g., hostility, enthusiasm, disinterest) about computer trends. Explain any differences in attitude of older and younger managers.
3. What special problems are involved in the use of interactive computer terminals? Do computer technicians face a decline in importance as interactive terminals become more widely used?

BIBLIOGRAPHY

Diebold, John. *Business Decisions and Technological Change.* New York: Frederick A. Praeger, Inc., 1970.

Drucker, Peter F. *Technology, Management & Society.* New York: Harper & Row Publishers, Inc., 1970.

——. *The Age of Discontinuity.* New York: Harper & Row Publishers, Inc., 1969.

Forrester, Jay W. *Industrial Dynamics.* Cambridge, Massachusetts: MIT Press, 1961.

Heyel, Carl, ed. *The Encyclopedia of Management.* New York: Van Nostrand Reinhold Company, 1973.

Lazarus, Harold, E. Kirby Warren and Jerome E. Schnee, eds. *The Progress of Management.* Englewood Cliffs, New Jersey: Prentice-Hall, Inc., 1972.

Mailick, Sidney and Edward H. VanNess, eds. *Concepts and Issues in Administrative Behavior* (Englewood Cliffs, New Jersey: Prentice-Hall, Inc., 1962).

Martin, James and Adrian R. D. Norman. *The Computerized Society.* Englewood Cliffs, New Jersey: Prentice-Hall, Inc., 1970.

Myers, Charles A., ed. *The Impact of Computers on Management.* Cambridge, Massachusetts: M.I.T. Press, 1967.

Rico, Leonard. *The Advance Against Paperwork.* Ann Arbor, Michigan: University of Michigan, 1967.

Simon, Herbert A. *The Shape of Automation.* New York: Harper & Row Publishers, Inc., 1965.

Taviss, Irene, ed. *The Computer Impact.* Englewood Cliffs, New Jersey: Prentice-Hall, Inc., 1970.

Thompson, Howard. *Joint Man/Machine Decisions.* Cleveland, Ohio: Systems & Procedures Association, 1965.

Tomeski, Edward A. *The Computer Revolution.* New York: The Macmillan Co., 1970.

Tomeski, Edward A. *Computers in Business.* San Francisco: Holden-Day, Inc., 1979.

Whisler, Thomas L. *Information Technology and Organizational Change.* Belmont, California: Wadsorth Publishing Company, Inc., 1970.

FOOTNOTES

[1] Peter F. Drucker, *The Age of Discontinuity* (New York: Harper & Row Publishers, Inc., 1969), p. 259.

[2] Tom Alexander, "Computers Can't Solve Everything," *Fortune,* October 1969, p. 126.

[3] John Diebold, *Business Decisions and Technological Change* (New York: Frederick A. Praeger, Inc., 1970), p. 257.

[4] Society for Personnel Administration. *Proceedings—Automation Today and Tomorrow* (Washington, D.C., May 13, 1966), p. 11.

[5] George J. Berkwitt, "Recession Explodes the New Myths of Management," *Management Review,* November 1970, p. 15.

[6] Society for Management Information Systems. *Proceedings of Second Annual Conference* (Chicago, 1971), unnumbered pages.

[7] Leonard Rico, *The Advance Against Paperwork* (Ann Arbor, Michigan: University of Michigan, 1967), pp. 8, 304–305.

[8] "Conference on Personnel Research," *Datamation,* August 1968, p. 76.

[9] Bernard Baum and Elmer Burack, "Information Technology, Manpower Development and Organizational Performance," *Academy of Management Journal,* September 1969, pp. 279–291.

[10] Herbert A. Simon, *The Shape of Automation* (New York: Harper & Row Publishers, Inc., 1965), p. 75.

[11] Larry E. Greiner, Paul D. Leitch, and Louis B. Barnes, "Putting Judgement Back Into Decisions," *Harvard Business Review,* March-April 1970, p. 60.

[12] Fremont E. Kast and James E. Rosenzweig, *Organization and Management: A Systems Approach* (New York: McGraw-Hill Book Co., 1970), p. 164.

[13] John Dearden, *Computers in Business Management* (Homewood, Illinois: Richard D. Irwin, Inc., 1966), p. 287.

[14] Ibid., p. 285.

[15] Thomas L. Whisler, *Information Technology and Organizational Change* (Belmont, California: Wadsworth Publishing Company, Inc., 1970), p. 62.

[16] Ibid., p. 182.

[17] David B. Hertz, *New Power for Management* (New York: McGraw-Hill Book Co., 1969), p. 184.

[18] Ibid., pp. 16, 29.

[19] Herbert A. Simon, *The Shape of Automation* (New York: Harper & Row Publishers, Inc., 1965), pp. 104, 107.

[20] Ibid., pp. 108–109.

[21] Society for Management Information Systems. *Proceedings of Founders' Conference,* unnumbered pages; Terrance Hanold, "A President's View of MIS," *Datamation,* November 1968, pp. 60–62.

[22] S. R. Klatzky, "Automation, Size, and the Locus of Decision Making: The Cascade Effect," *The Journal of Business,* April 1969, pp. 148–149.

[23] Marshall McLuhan, *Understanding Media* (New York: The New American Library, Inc., 1966), pp. 104–107.

9

Use of the Computer in the Personnel Process

. . . 'human relations' is becoming a scientifically rooted field, as evidenced by the increasing use of the behavioral sciences . . .

The effectiveness in dealing with organizational interdependency requires quick feedback of valid information to the parts in order to maintain a delicate balance. Quick feedback and valid information, in turn, require participants who feel free to tell the truth and confront conflict openly and constructively. Here again, our modern institutions leave much to be desired.

Chris Argyris

OBJECTIVES OF THE CHAPTER

The authors identify some reasons why personnel systems have not been particularly progressive, and discuss the attitudes and expectations of personnel administrators. Dichotomous approaches to computerization are presented—a fragmented approach and a systems approach—together with a number of specific computer applications. The authors indicate the organizational characteristics required to attain effective personnel systems.

STATUS OF COMPUTERIZATION IN PERSONNEL

The authors' experience with and research in scores of organizations (businesses, federal government departments, states, local governments, agencies) reveal that the personnel function has not been generally progressive in the use of computers. A not atypical example of the low priority given to personnel systems is presented below:

- The personnel director of a large electronics firm discussed with the computer manager the possibility of computerizing various personnel statistics. There was need for such information as: turnover rate by department and job classification, number of minorities and females employed compared to total employment, schedule of retirements by department and job classification, etc.

The computer manager discussed the matter with his boss, the controller. The controller said, "The hell with the personnel department. They don't have any leverage. The big decisions are in production, finance, and marketing; that's where the money is. We can't waste our time developing computer programs for counting bodies."

Lagging Use of Computers

The use of the computer to process personnel work, by and large, lags behind the introduction of the computer in other parts of the organizations. Although many organizations began using computers prior to 1960, in numerous instances the personnel applications were not, to any extent, computerized until well after 1960. While all of the organizations analyzed by the authors have computers, some are still not using the devices for any personnel application whatsoever.

Basic Applications Computerized

The most extensive computerized applications in the personnel area are those which can be considered routine and related to financial systems: payroll, employee benefits, personnel budgets, and various statistics (e.g., pay, personnel, positions). The areas which have been less subject to standardization and which contain higher-order decisions are largely uncomputerized (e.g., manpower planning, collective bargaining). While the personnel function has obtained some relief from its paperwork burdens through use of the computer, it has obtained comparatively little aid from it in the area of planning and decision-making.

Lack of Planning

Generally, there is weak coordination between computer staffs and personnel staffs. One result of this is the lack of common plans about objectives concerning personnel systems. In fact, in many organizations, there is a dearth of planning about computerizing personnel systems. Activities are computerized on an incremental, disjointed basis.

Limited Generation of Management Information

There were mixed results to the question, "Does the computer provide information for decision-making that might otherwise not be available?"

Some organizations (e.g., federal government departments) answered very affirmatively. Other organizations (including many businesses and local governments) responded without consistency, as many responding negatively as positively. However, the breadth of such computer-generated information, in any organization, appears to leave much to be desired. The authors found, for instance, that very few organizations of any type are using computers for sophisticated modelling of such areas as manpower planning and collective bargaining strategies. Thus, the use of the computer as an information generator has only touched the top of the iceberg.

Low Status of Personnel Systems

Typically, the computerized personnel systems are relatively poorly designed compared to other application areas. In businesses the financial, marketing, and manufacturing functions tend to have more sophisticated computer application designs. In government the financial, law enforcement, health, utilities, motor vehicle, and welfare functions have better designed systems than do the personnel departments. These findings reinforce the conclusion that the personnel function has been given low priority in computer planning and development.

Fragmentation of Personnel Applications

One of the key indications of a well-designed computer application is the degree to which related work is integrated. (The importance of systems integration was stressed in Chapter 5.) However, the fact is that very few organizations have highly integrated personnel systems. A large number of organizations are operating with extensively fragmented computer applications, a practice which results in duplication of files and processing, and inconsistencies between data, files, and output.

Dependence on Computer Technicians

The personnel function is highly dependent on computer technicians for any computer work. First, few personnel departments have control over the computer being used to process its work or the computer applications being processed by computer departments. Second, most personnel departments have little or no staff competency in systems analysis or computer applications. Third, personnel administrators have limited awareness of the potentials of the computer as applied to their departments. Fourth, as a result of the foregoing, it was determined that very few personnel departments make any use of interactive data terminals which permit the user to directly access the computer without intervention of computer specialists.

It would appear that personnel departments must develop increased competency in modern personnel systems in order to promote and facilitate the design and installation of such systems. Such know-how will encourage a more effective team effort between personnel departments and computer departments. In essence, the authors think that computer staffs should become more "personnel systems" oriented—and personnel department staffs should become more "computer systems" oriented—without usurping each other's primary specialty.

Absence of Cost Indexes

Many organizations lack reliable figures about the cost of computerized applications. However, where cost allocations are made, the personnel department should be aware of the cost of each job or report processed for it by the computer department. Such cost figures should be available to equate with the usefulness and benefits of computer processing. Without such cost control, the computer can be used to spew out all kinds of marginal and useless reports which collect dust on desks, window sills, or bloat file cabinets.

Certain cost indexes will be useful for purposes of comparing the personnel department's overall computer utilization. For instance, the percentage of the personnel department's budget that is expended for computer processing can be compared to other units of the organization, or to other personnel departments.

PERSONNEL DEPARTMENT ATTITUDES ABOUT COMPUTERS

The authors interviewed scores of personnel administrators. A summary of the administrators' views about the computer are presented below.

Value and Impact of Computer

The administrators most frequently identified the following as the value/impact of computers:

- Faster availability of reports.
- Absorbs increasing workload without comparable increases in staff.
- Some reduction in clerical costs.
- Improved accuracy of reports.

- Frees staff of routine work and makes them available for more important duties.

- Generates information not before available.

Most Valuable Output

There is no agreement about the computer applications and reports that are of most value to the personnel administrators. It appears that the utility of computer outputs varies with the organization, its goals, and the style of the administrator. Among the computerized applications that are most often cited as being useful are:

- Analyses of positions, employees, retirement, minorities, and turnover.

- Studies of salary and cost data to determine the impact of alternative proposals on budgets.

- Provision of a reliable tickler system which triggers appropriate actions (e.g., performance review, salary increase, training required, etc.).

- Searches for qualified personnel for particular positions.

Difficulties with Computers

Administrators most often report the following difficulties with computers:

- The long period of time it takes to develop systems, produce operational computer programs, and modify existing computer programs.

- The low priority given to personnel applications, both for developing new computer applications and for obtaining work processed of existing applications.

- Output reports that are sometimes unreliable because input data are inaccurate or systems design is faulty.

- Communications barriers between computer technicians and personnel staff.

- The high cost of computerization.

Some of these difficulties (e.g., difficulty in maintaining accuracy) appear to contradict the previously cited value of the computer (e.g., improved accuracy of reports). This indicates the mixed experiences and attitudes of administrators and organizations.

APPROACHES TO COMPUTERIZATION
OF THE PERSONNEL PROCESS

Fragmented Approach

An approach often taken is to computerize particular existing phases of the personnel process in relative isolation from the rest of the process. Figure 9-1 illustrates such compartmentalization. Unfortunately, this approach impedes coordination and the achievement of commonality of objectives. Moreover, it necessitates considerable searching and analysis by the personnel staff. Data are scattered through many files (e.g., employee records, recruitment, education and training, payroll, medical, benefits, etc.). Further, there is frequently both a considerable overlap and duplication of data and, perhaps more important, a not infrequent disparity between data which should coincide or relate. Finally, the files are frequently not up-to-date. Studies have indicated that organizations may have hundreds of separate and distinct personnel documents, and may record hundreds or thousands of different items of data on documents; some of the items of data are reported time and time again on different documents. As a result, the personnel staff has difficulty in accurately and quickly searching for data to provide answers, and it neglects important personnel activities, including human contacts, due to the pressures of handling clerical work.

Inasmuch as the human factors, as previously indicated, have been the major retardants of computerization (rather than the technical problems of computers), it is even more interesting that the personnel function is perhaps the single area of organizations in which most remains to be done in applying the computer.

- Even in the Department of Defense (DoD), where a unification of the three services has been a major goal for some years, there are significant dissimilarities between the personnel systems of the Army, Navy, and

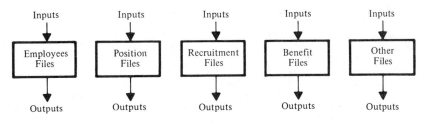

Figure 9-1 Personnel data processing.

Air Force. There is a lack of integration between the three services' personnel systems—and even considerable segmentation within any one service (e.g., lack of coordination between military and civilian records). It is interesting that even in the DoD—which is the largest user of computers and where much sophisticated work has been done with computers—that fragmented personnel applications still exist. Of course, the magnitude of the DoD's data processing—involving millions of active and inactive military personnel and civilians—may be one reason for the lack of integration of the personnel applications.

Systems Approach

The opposite approach to computerization is to develop an overall plan for a personnel MIS. As it proves economically and technically feasible, particular phases of the MIS can be computerized in a planned sequence.

A model of a personnel information system is presented in Figure 9-2. The

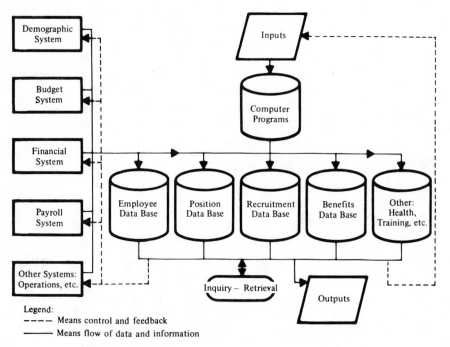

Figure 9-2 Personnel integrated information system.

system is designed within an overall plan; consequently, there is a high degree of coordination and commonality of goals. It is to be noted that there is a single stream of input data, through an array of appropriate programs. The several data bases are linked together for coordinated processing. Also, other related systems (such as the budget and financial systems) have clearly defined communication paths to and from the personnel system. Outputs from the system are available to administrators, personnel staff, and authorized employees. Provision is available for authorized personnel to directly interrogate and use the system via a remote data terminal.

There is need to view personnel within a total system, interrelated and interacting with the other systems—the financial and various operational systems. This approach entails integrating, by use of the systems approach, the multiple files (including employee records, recruitment, positions, benefits, etc.). It also aims at maintaining the records up-to-date, so that inquiries are answered with timely and accurate information. Such an approach should result in elimination of a great deal of duplication and inconsistencies in existing files.

If an effective computerized data system for personnel is to be developed, certain minimum essentials must be met. A personnel data base must be established which includes all data needs for making decisions, and for fulfilling legal and other report requirements. The data include facts about employees, such as: skills, personal history, employment record, benefits, etc. In addition, data about positions, the personnel budget (appropriations, authorizations, commitments, expenditures), as well as other relevant data can be included. Before inclusion in the data base, the data must be edited to assure accuracy, non-redundancy, and consistency. Provision must be made for updating the data, so that they reflect a status that is current and useful to the user. In addition, there must be adequate assurance that the data in the data base are available only to authorized individuals.

Since the data base usually entails consolidation and integration of formerly scattered and segmented files, it should provide information that is more pertinent and reliable than that previously used. Provision must be made to give those who formerly accessed the unintegrated files access to the integrated data base. The same data base can be tapped by all interested and authorized individuals, to serve their particular requirements. In addition, management can use the data base to monitor the personnel effort.

For the personnel manager, management-by-exception can be programmed for such on-going problems as determining those employees for whom salary increases are overdue, determining which recommended pay changes are in excess of or below specified criteria, determining those employees whose pay levels are inconsistent with their performance appraisals, identifying personnel or organizational units that have excessive lost time, and indicating manpower requisitions that have remained unfilled for excessive periods of time, etc. In addition, management is in the position to make studies that were difficult, if not impossible, to make previously. Employee bargaining groups might want to know the specific costs if vacation allowances are extended an additional week for certain employees. It might be desirable to identify all jobs that will be open, in the next several years, due to retirements. Identification of recruiting sources that will lead to reduced costs and an increased quality and quantity of candidates could be facilitated.

Eventually, an organization's computerized data bank might be supplemented by having it interconnected with external data banks. For example, it would be possible to have computer communications with a cooperative industry-wide data bank, a network of public and private employment offices, or government entities.

Such a broad computer network provides a basis for such operations as: a rapid job-man matching system, consolidation of manpower data, comprehensive salary surveys, etc.

- The federal Civil Service Commission (CSC) has made a study of the feasibility of developing a government-wide personnel system. The basic concept involves a central data bank for all federal employees, doing away with the conventional personnel file folders in decentralized offices, and the use of remote data terminals for inquiry and answer purposes to personnel offices in the many federal departments and agencies. The magnitude of such an effort is made clear by the Commission's estimate that it would take more than $50 million and five years' effort to implement such a comprehensive system. Of course, the system must provide for the millions of federal civil servants, active and retired, as well as having provision for handling the thousands of job applicants. It was estimated that the current annual cost of about $75 million, for doing paperwork and preparing reports by current methods, would be reduced under the proposed new system to about $25 million per fiscal year. Thus, savings resulting from elimination of duplication and efficiencies in scale-of-operation were projected, which would recoup the implementation cost in the first year that the system was operative. To date, only limited progress has been made in moving towards such a grand-design system.

SELECTED EXAMPLES OF COMPUTERIZED PERSONNEL APPLICATIONS

Manpower Planning

Computerized information systems are a basis for improving and extending manpower planning in organizations. (Chapters 3 and 4 discussed the macro and micro aspects of manpower planning.) Manpower planning requires use of extensive data about supply and demand factors; management science techniques may be useful for certain analytical and modeling purposes.

A simulator can be built which contains personnel policy assumptions and profiles on current employees. This depicts the situation as it is. Next, the simulator can identify what the impact of retirements and normal attrition will be on the work force. Finally, the anticipated workload requirements is provided to the simulator, and it determines what positions and how many will have to be filled by dates under the stated policies. There is now indication of the practicality of a simulation model of business careers that can give coherence and relevance to the various phases of the selection, training, motivating, and promotion processes.

At present, local governments often lack basic data needed for manpower planning. Generally, basic employment data are available such as: total numbers employed, employment by occupation, and employment by agency. However, other data are not readily available: occupation by agency, occupation by function, personal characteristics (age, sex, education) by occupation. Other problems include lack of adequate job descriptions, lack of standardized occupational definition, and no central personnel office responsible for vital personnel matters.

The state of Minnesota has recently begun development of a conceptual model for a state manpower planning system.[1] This includes the design of a computerized manpower information system to make the plan a reality. The model will relate data on employment histories and occupational structures to programs in agencies, and changes in population growth, personal income, and economic activity and growth. The model will also be used to determine the adequacy, in terms of quantity, of the state's work force to meet the current and anticipated programs and goals.

The state of Pennsylvania has linked together its computerized inventory of manpower (claimed to be the first comprehensive one in a state) with the state's planning-programming-budgeting system (PPBS). The two systems particularly merge in the preparation of the manpower statements for program revision requests. Bauer makes the following comments about the system:

. . . increased computerization, implementation of PPBS, quantification of outputs, and a professionalization of the personnel system have produced rapid advancements in our forecasting capabilities.

Manpower planning and development is the foundation of an effective personnel system . . .[2]

Personnel Statistics

An example of a personnel statistics application is IBM's approach for its 150,000 employees in the U.S. This approach, using computerized data banks and communication links, has a selective bank of data in the organization's corporate headquarters and more extensive data banks in the divisional offices. However, the entire system is interconnected and standardized to allow for communication and interchange of data. An interesting feature of the system is a matrix program which permits retrieval, formatting, and manipulation of information in up to a six-dimensional matrix; the average response for a matrix is a half-hour. Liebtag indicates:

A one-dimensional matrix might list number of employees by age; a second dimension would add service; a third would add salary; and a four-dimensional matrix would list number of employees by age and service, within salary, within educational level. Up to 50 ranges or breakdowns can be handled for each variable . . . And within these variables and ranges, entire divisions or specific locations can be excluded, as well as employees hired after a specified date.[3]

Skills Inventory and Job-Man Matching

A skills inventory involves having the characteristics of personnel available in computerized storage. By computerized searches, individuals with particular skills and attributes can be quickly identified.

A carefully designed skills inventory can be used for a number of purposes:

- Special research studies, such as skills having highest turnover rates, apparent salary inequities, or low productivity.

- Deriving the best mix of skills for project teams.

- Facilitating manpower plans by analysis of available skills.

- Making more equitable promotion decisions on the basis of merit ratings and critical skill requirements.

Computer-based job-man matching is intended for the rapid searching through the qualifications of large numbers of persons to locate those who most closely match the requirements of a position that has to be filled. The government of Canada has developed one of the most comprehensive job-man matching systems. The U. S. Employment Service has been promoting and testing various computerized systems (a basic one is operative in Baltimore, a more sophisticated system is being tested in Utah, among other governmental units). These government systems will be discussed at more length in Chapter 11.

The Civil Service Commission of the federal government has perhaps the most comprehensive computerized data bank (for a single organization) of actual and potential talent. It contains information on the work experience, educational backgrounds, and special qualifications of approximately 30,000 key government executives. This data bank is a help to the Commission in fulfilling its responsibilities to agencies in staffing for immediate and future needs. Personnel research, by use of the computer and the data bank, is taking place to determine such things as: why people come into government, why they leave, how top jobs are filled, mobility between agencies, relationship between education and career success—in short, specific information about career patterns and progressions. Such a system is vital in light of the possibility that, in the foreseeable future, as high as 40 per cent of all the nation's professionals will be working for local, state, or federal governments.

Recruitment

The computer can be used for notifying applicants of examinations, and for providing them with feedback of their test scores. Grading of tests and selection of questions for tests can be done by computer. Rather than taking weeks to advise applicants of their status, they could be notified of their examination results and possibly even of their appointments to positions right after the completion of their examination.

By a continuous analysis of turnover and the profiles of the employees affected, it is possible to develop an indication of high-risk candidates and low-risk candidates. This can reduce both recruitment and other costs connected with employee turnover.

Large organizations can use the computer to aid in determining recruitment requirements; this includes allocation of time at colleges, related costs of transportation and moving, and evaluating the effectiveness of recruiting.

Selection

Increasing research is being devoted to developing computerized simulations of human thought processes. Such studies, referred to as heuristic programs, are based on the following assumptions:

- Humans, in making decisions, break complex problems into numerous simpler but interrelated sub-problems.

- Individuals also develop and follow with some consistency decision rules, which can be identified and isolated to handle such sub-problems.

- Complex thought processes can be represented by networks of simple decision branches, reflecting these rules.

Figure 9-3 illustrates how computerized interpretive simulations might be used as prescriptive models for personnel selection.

Education and Training

Computerized educational situations can be used for management training and development purposes; for example, computerized management games can be employed to help improve the analytic and decision-making skills of managers. Computers can be used in aiding instruction of personnel, especially in jobs which require a large number of workers to do similar work. The computer can be a most useful tool for tailoring an individual's training program to his level of knowledge and his speed of learning.

The use of the computer, for training and education, is covered in greater detail in Chapter 10.

Inquiries

The executive can access the computer, via a television-like screen data terminal on his desk, and make remote inquiries. By simple manipulation of buttons, for instance, the executive can obtain a display of all personnel with certain qualifications. Or if he wished to review the record of a specific employee, that record will be displayed.

One of the major problems confronted by managerial and professional personnel is that of attempting to keep up with the rapidly increasing amount of information being made available in their areas of interest. As one means of helping to overcome this problem, attempts have been made to develop what are called computerized selective dissemination of information systems.

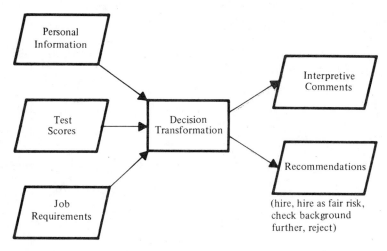

Figure 9-3   Decision process in personnel selection.

While such systems vary one from another, they usually provide for abstracts of articles, books or reports which are stored in some computer mass storage. The materials are so coded that different individuals can have retrieved from the system those items of specific interest to them.

Performance Evaluation

Quantification of performance appraisal data can help to overcome the manager's difficulties in dealing with numerous variables. Of course, the use of mathematical models for appraisal purposes is only one facet of total performance appraisal and should supplement, not replace, the manager's judgment.

Easton presents a model which permits comparison of an individual's performance with that of an ideal person for each of multiple performance criteria, and provides for combining multiple criterion scores into an overall evaluation of merit.[4]

Colvin develops a quantitative technique for the appraisal of personnel.[5] His approach involves relating performance of all employees under a supervisor to the supervisor's average performance ratings. This permits better comparisons of appraisals in different departments, since some supervisors' ratings are likely to be more (or less) favorable than others. The technique also requires performance data to be compared over successive rating periods since an individual's performance, as compared with the average of his group, may change over time.

Medical and Safety

Computerized accident analysis can provide clues and insights about where accidents are prone to occur, with which kinds of work, under what conditions, and the cost of such events.

Collective Bargaining

The computer can help in the preparation of profiles of the work force composition, profiles of union election histories, and can be used for costing out alternative settlements during negotiations, etc.

An integrated personnel system is being developed in the Port Authority of New York and New Jersey. One area that stimulated management's interest in such a system was the need for better information for labor negotiations. The Port Authority has been faced with increasing unionization and related demands. The computer is viewed as a tool that can provide various analysis that would have been difficult, or impossible, to obtain by conventional methods.

Psychology

The computer has pertinence in the field concerned with the human mind and motivation. As previously mentioned, Herbert Simon has been developing a computer problem-solving program called General Problem Solver (GPS) designed to model some of the main features of human problem-solving.[6] It searches selectively through an environment in order to discover and assemble sequences of actions that will lead from a given situation to a desired situation.

Another study involves the development of a computer simulation model of a firm and incorporates the behavior of management and work groups.[7] It analyzes the behavior of the model within an experimental design and emphasizes the effects of the work groups on the performance of the firm.

At a meeting of the American Psychiatric Association, the feasibility of computer-generated psychiatric diagnoses was explored. One research group cited the following advantages of using the computer:

. . . there is the value of necessarily perfect reliability in the sense that given the same data, the computer will always yield the same diagnosis.

. . . the computer program can utilize rules developed from a large and more diverse sample of actual patients than any single clinician can command.

. . . the rules by which a computer assigns a diagnosis are explicit and public.

. . . empirically based rules constitute at least potential advances in our scientific understanding of the complex relationship between symptom characteristics and diagnoses . . .[8]

EFFECTIVENESS OF PERSONNEL SYSTEMS

The authors have established a measure of effectiveness for personnel systems. A highly effective personnel system was considered to be one that contained the following characteristics:

- Information useful to management's decision-making.
- A broad range of personnel applications.
- Integration of data files, processing, and outputs.

A weak personnel system is, conversely, one that has the following characteristics:

- Routine data processing having little or no information for decision-making.
- A limited number of personnel applications.
- Unintegrated data files, processing, and outputs.

On a scale of 100, the authors found the following in a study of 90 organizations:

- Federal government departments are the most consistently effective users of personnel systems, with an average effectiveness index of 77.

- Private sector organizations (industry, banks, insurance companies, transportation, retailing) and state governments had approximately the same effectiveness index, 60.

- County and city governments have the weakest personnel systems. The research indicated an average effectiveness of about 40 for each of these types of organizations.

ATTAINING AN EFFECTIVE PERSONNEL SYSTEM

The authors' research sought out those variables which appear to be present in organizations with effective and ineffective personnel systems.

Effective Personnel Systems

1. *Personnel Function*

- Concentrates on professional personnel activities.
- Is involved in organization-wide manpower planning.
- Coordinates with organization-wide planning effort.
- Devotes considerable attention to manpower development.
- Activates programs to encourage high productivity.
- Is involved in computer plans and design of computer applications.
- Acts as change agent.

2. *Computer Function*

- There is an active research program in advanced computer techniques.
- There is broad use of the computer for many personnel applications.
- Personnel systems are integrated.
- It seeks, with the personnel function, identification of information for planning and decision-making.
- Makes considerable use of management science.
- Emphasizes the systems approach and MIS.
- Personnel systems have high priority in the computer department.

- The costs and benefits of all computer applications are itemized and available to the users.

Ineffective Personnel Systems

1. *Personnel Function*

- Is absorbed with routine paperwork.
- Lacks organization-wide manpower planning.
- Is not involved in organization-wide planning effort.
- Is viewed as a supplier of "bodies" to fill jobs.
- Absence of definite programs to attain high productivity.
- Lacks involvement in computer plans and projects related to personnel applications.
- Takes narrow view of personnel function and takes conservative stance regarding change.

2. *Computer Function*

- Exerts little effort on computer research and use of advanced computer techniques.
- Makes narrow use of the computer for the personnel area.
- Personnel data files and programs are fragmented.
- Computer output consists mainly of routine reports.
- Little use made of management science.
- Absence of overall systems planning and MIS design.
- Personnel systems have low priority in the computer department.
- Inadequate cost figures regarding computer applications.

The mere existence of a powerful computer does not assure that an organization will make highly effective use of it. *As suggested by the above, an organization's effectiveness in computer use will largely be determined by the progressiveness of the organization in providing modern leadership and an environment conducive to high performance by motivated employees. It is not so much the computer that counts in attaining effective systems, but rather it is the way the computer is applied by people.*

SUMMARY

There is ample indication that the personnel function has been lagging behind other areas in the use of computers. It appears that a great many organizations that use the computer for the personnel activities apply it for routinized clerical work. Limited use is made in the area of MIS. *More imaginative use of computers for personnel work would likely result in better use of human resources.*

One approach is to computerize existing personnel work; this usually results in a fragmented design. In such an approach only modest benefits are attained and, indeed, current problems may be accentuated. The preferred approach is to use the systems concept to develop an MIS for the personnel area. The benefits of such an integrated system range from providing more accurate information to providing a data base that can service top administration's strategic planning needs in the area of manpower.

Before maximum benefits can be obtained from computerized personnel systems, organizations may have to make more fundamental adjustments (e.g., improve the quality of their personnel and computer staffs, strengthen planning in the computer and personnel functions, provide for more modern leadership).

Chapter 10, which follows, expands on how the computer can be used for training and development purposes.

Chapters 13 and 14 present more comprehensive illustrations of personnel applications.

KEY CONCEPTS OF THE CHAPTER

1. The personnel function has not, generally, been an effective user of computer systems.

2. Personnel administrators have mixed reactions about the benefits derived from computerization in their departments.

3. The prevalent approach to computerizing personnel applications is a fragmented one. Generally, such an approach involves few applications, lacks integration, and does not provide information for management purposes.

4. A systems approach to personnel applications entails the integration of a broad array of personnel work, and generation of information useful for management decision-making. There are few systems such as this in operation.

5. There are many potential computer applications in the personnel area. Each organization should use cost/benefit approaches to determine which uses best serve their needs.

6. There is a series of characteristics which are related to effective use of computers for personnel activities. An organization may have to make more

fundamental changes before it can attain satisfactory personnel systems. Computer equipment alone is not the answer.

DISCUSSION QUESTIONS

General Background (Seminar/Classroom Discussion)

1. Why has the personnel function lagged behind other organizational functions in computerizing its activities?
2. Comment on the following statement: "Since the personnel function is human relations-oriented, it should not use the computer, which is often considered dehumanizing."

Operational and Technical

1. What level of priority does personnel work receive in your organization's computer department? Is that priority consistent with the dictum that "Our most important asset is our human resource"?
2. Identify several jobs involving personnel work that could profitably be computerized. What prevents such improvements from being implemented?

Policy

1. Comment on the following statement: "The personnel administrator has, at best, an unenthusiastic view of computers. The personnel administrator views these modern machines as technical tools of interest to engineers and mathematicians— but not to social scientists and people-oriented managers."
2. Assess the status of your organization's personnel system. Has it been extensively computerized? Is it responsive to top management's needs for human resource information and decisions?
3. Identify several specific types of personnel information, not currently available, that would be helpful to management. What are the barriers to obtaining the information?

Areas for Research

1. Rate your organization's personnel system by the following criteria: breadth of applications, extent of integration of the applications, and the volume of information for decision-making. Compare your organization's personnel system with that in one or more similar organizations. How might your organization's personnel system be improved?
2. Arrange for a "free-for-all" symposium between the personnel department's staff and the computer department's staff. Have an open agenda on the general topic of "How the two departments can be mutually supportive in building a computer system which does not sacrifice human values while improving operational efficiency." After the symposium, list the ideas and suggestions generated at the meeting and distribute them to the attendees. How can some programs be instituted to implement the positive results of the meeting?

BIBLIOGRAPHY

Bricker, John J. *The Personnel Systems Concept.* New York: American Management Association, 1965.

Bueschel, Richard T. *EDP and Personnel.* New York: American Management Association, 1966.

Dukes, Carlton W. *Computerizing Personnel Resource Data.* New York: American Management Association, 1971.

Flippo, Edwin F. *Principles of Personnel Management.* New York: McGraw-Hill Book Co., 1971.

Geisler, Edwin B. *Manpower Planning: An Emerging Staff Function.* New York: American Management Association, 1967.

Martino, R. L. *Personnel Management Systems.* Wayne, Pennsylvania: Management Development Institute, 1969.

Morrison, Edward J. *Developing Computer-Based Employee Information Systems.* New York: American Management Association, 1969.

Rico, Leonard. *The Advance Against Paperwork: Computers, Systems, and Personnel.* Ann Arbor, Michigan: University of Michigan, 1967.

Siegel, Abraham J., ed. *Impact of Computers on Collective Bargaining.* Cambridge, Massachusetts: MIT Press, 1969.

Smith, A. R., ed. *Models of Manpower Systems.* New York: American Elsevier Publ. Co., Inc., 1971.

Tomeski, Edward A. *Effects from Computerization in Public Personnel Administration.* Unpublished DPA dissertation, New York University, 1972.

Wasmuth, William J., et al. *Human Resources Administration.* Boston: Houghton Mifflin Co., 1970.

Weatherbee, Harvard Y. and Gleen A. Bassett. *Personnel Systems and Data Management.* New York: American Management Association, 1971.

Zungoli, Serafino Salvatore. *A Critical Evaluation of Computer Applications in Support of Personnel Management.* Unpublished Ph.D. dissertation, American University, 1967.

FOOTNOTES

[1] Paul A. Roberts, "Problems and Prospects of Manpower Planning: An Example," *Public Personnel Review,* April 1970, p. 128.

[2] William J. Bauer, "Pennsylvania's Manpower Mandate," *Public Personnel Review,* April 1971, p. 113.

[3] Wesley R. Liebtag, "How An EDP Personnel Data System Works for Corporate Growth," *Personnel,* July-August 1970, pp. 15–21.

[4] Allan Easton, "A Forward Step in Performance Evaluation," *Journal of Marketing,* July 1966, pp. 26–32.

[5] C. O. Colvin, "A Mathematical Exercise in Salaried Performance Evaluation Theory," *Personnel Journal,* June 1965, pp. 307–313.

[6] Herbert A. Simon, *The Sciences of the Artificial* (Cambridge, Massachusetts: M.I.T. Press, 1969), pp. 66–68.

[7] Eugene E. Kaczka and Roy V. Kirk, "Managerial Climate, Work Groups, and Organizational Performance," *Computer Simulation of Human Behavior*, John M. Dutton and William H. Starbuck, eds. (New York: John Wiley & Sons, Inc., 1971), pp. 286–298.

[8] "Computers 'Outpsyche' Psychiatrists," *Computerworld*, June 20, 1973, p. 23.

10

Use of the Computer for Training and Development

What passes for education today, even in our 'best' schools and colleges, is a hopeless anachronism.

In the technological systems of tomorrow—fast fluid and self-regulating-machines will deal with the flow of information and insight. Machines will increasingly perform the routine tasks; men the intellectual and creative tasks.

The technology of tomorrow requires . . . men who can make critical judgments, who can weave their way through novel environments, who are quick to spot new relationships in the rapidly changing reality. It requires men who, in C. P. Snow's compelling term, "have the future in their bones."

Alvin Toffler

OBJECTIVES OF THE CHAPTER

The role of the computer in training and development is discussed. Two training techniques are explored in some detail: computerized management games and computer-assisted instruction.

NEW CHALLENGES FOR TRAINING AND DEVELOPMENT

Talented manpower resources are scarce and need to be husbanded and utilized carefully.

The continuous change in programs, applicable technology, and administrative forms that characterize any viable enterprise creates a concomitant need for training and retraining executives and employees.

An integrated training and development program has both an organizational and an individual focus. Organizationally, it aims to provide a basis for rational and effective manpower planning and utilization. In its individual focus, it endeavors to provide appropriate growth opportunities so that each person can cope with change.

In today's dynamic society, it is imperative that managements recognize the need for developing their employees to enable them to keep abreast of new information and to develop new skills. This is particularly true at management levels, where computerization has brought profound changes in the availability and dissemination of information, in the decision-making processes, in organizational hierarchies and alignments—all over and above the new behavioral skills called for by social and political change. Greenlaw has drawn attention to problems in this area:

> . . . it would appear that in the design of many off-the-job training programs, inadequate consideration is given to the other systems elements which have an important bearing on the outputs of those managers whom the organization is attempting to develop—i.e., organizational memory, input, control, and feedback . . . certain kinds of human relations problems in the business firm seem to occur more because of the existence of stress situations which are largely a function of organizational design—work flow inputs on the job, types of interaction patterns required, etc.—than because of any major inadequacies in the human skills of the organizational members so involved . . . Yet in designing, and in deciding on which managers are to participate in many so-called 'human relations' courses in industry today, concern is given only to the modification of the human skill (transformational abilities) of the manager, without consideration of the impact that such other organizational system elements may be having on his performance output.[1]

Greenlaw suggests a broader role for the training director, and presents a model of a systems view of management development (Figure 10-1).

Organization training appears likely to move from traditional skill and knowledge training toward broader organization development and change. To understand and deal with the behavior of people, it is useful to view the organization as a social system, rather than as a mechanical system of technical skills directed by rational rules. Figure 10-2 contrasts traditional training with an organization-change approach.

Bennis points to the new challenges facing the training director brought about by these developments:

> I have suggested that the training and development director of the future has in store at least six new and different functions: (1) training for change, (2) systems counseling, (3) developing new incentives, (4) socializing adults, (5) building collaborative, problem-solving teams, and (6) developing supra-organizational goals and commitments . . . It is clear that they signify a fundamentally different role for personnel management from 'putting out fires' and narrow maintenance functions. If training and development is to realize its true promise, its role and image must change from maintenance to innovation.[2]

TRADITIONAL TRAINING TECHNIQUES

A host of traditional training techniques are used. Some of the more widely used traditional training techniques are recapitulated briefly below. All have their appropriate place in a training program.

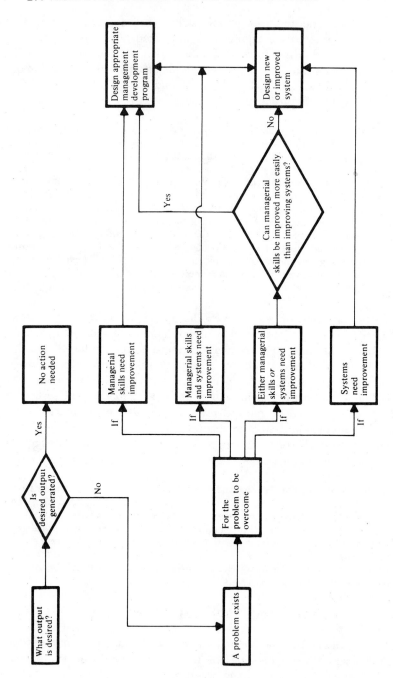

Figure 10-1 A systems view of management development. (Adapted from Paul S. Greenlaw, "Management Development: A Systems View," *Personnel Journal,* April 1964, pp. 205–211.)

Dimension	Traditional Training	The Organization Change Process
Unit of Focus	Individual.	Interpersonal relationship teams, work units, intergroup relations, superior-subordinate relations.
Content of Training	Technical and administrative skills.	Interpersonal and group membership skills—communication, problem-solving conflict management, helping.
Target Subjects	Primarily first line employees and supervisors. Managers trained outside organization.	All levels. Usually initial intervention with upper management in-house.
Conception of Learning Process	Cognitive and rational.	Cognitive, rational, emotional-motivational.
Teaching Style	Subject matter and teacher centered.	Participant, immediate experience, problem-solving and subject matter centered.
Learning Goals	Rationality and efficiency.	Awareness, adaptation and change.
View of Organization	Discrete functional skill units.	Social system.

Figure 10-2 Comparison of traditional training and the organization change process. (William B. Eddy, "From Training to Organization Change," *Personnel Administration*, January-February 1971, p. 39.)

The Lecture Method

The trainer delivers, primarily orally, material that has been prepared in advance. There may, or may not, be discussions between the lecturer and trainees to supplement the lecture.

The Conference

The conference involves the training group in a problem-solving or knowledge-acquisition situation in which trainees contribute ideas and make suggestions. The central concept is that participants learn from each other rather than through formal instruction. The conference leader asks questions to stimulate further discussion, but seldom answers them himself. His or her skill lies in eliciting participation by all members of the group, in guiding them (in structured conferences) to agreement on an indicated conclusion, and in summarizing salient points.

The Case Study

A case study is a written description of a situation that includes one or more problems requiring decisions or solutions. Detailed surrounding information is given and, as in real life, not all of the information is necessarily relevant. After studying a case, trainees discuss it together in an attempt to discover the main issues and to suggest ways to solve them. There is not necessarily one "best" solution. Learning is promoted by individual participation and group discussion.

Brainstorming

Brainstorming is a formal activity in which a group of persons uninhibitedly present ideas as to how to solve a selected problem. Certain general rules apply: criticism of an idea is barred, modification or combination with another idea is encouraged, a large quantity of ideas is sought, and novel ideas are encouraged. The entire process is intended to encourage creativity and to remove the constraints to which people frequently are habituated.

The effectiveness of any training technique is, of course, dependent on factors such as the objectives of the training, quality of the trainer, acceptance of the technique by the trainee, trainee's motivational level, organizational climate and, importantly, the opportunity which the trainee may have to apply what he learns.

CONTEMPORARY TRAINING TECHNIQUES

Some of the newer training techniques include the following:

In-Basket Assignments

The in-basket is a simulation of the executive's in and out desk trays containing reports, memoranda, mail, and other typical items. The trainee is required to read these items, analyze the problems they present, perceive their interconnectedness, and determine a course of action much as he or she would in carrying out work in an organization. This technique is often part of the Assessment Center approach to qualification appraisal.

Problem-Solving Techniques

A widely used program originated by Kepner and Tregoe helps participants to develop skills in problem analysis and decision-making.[3] The program presents new ideas, new skills, or new ways of approaching old ideas and skills; an opportunity to put these innovations into practical action; and feedback as to (1) the results of the actions taken, and (2) the relationship between what was done at each step of the way and the end result. Participants are given a chance to learn concepts, use them, and get an evaluation of how well they performed. In the process they learn much about their communications skills, ability to devise creative solutions to problems, and their collaborative skills in interpersonal relations.

Managerial Grid

The managerial grid, developed by Blake and Mouton, postulates two universal dimensions of management—a concern for people and a concern for production.[4] Five major styles of management are identified:

- A 1,1 represents minimum concern for production and minimum concern for people.

- A 9,1 style represents a high concern for production and a low concern for people in the sense that human elements are not allowed to interfere to any great degree with production.

- Similarly, a 1,9 management style represents a high concern for people, coupled with a low concern for production.

- A 5,5 style represents a balanced position between people and production.

- The ideal style is 9,9, in which concern for people is integrated with the goals of the organization.

During the training, there is assessment of each member's style by the other members of the group, and suggestions for self-improvement.

Sensitivity Training

Sensitivity training is also referred to as "laboratory training," or "T-Group" training. It is an intensive experience, usually residential and extending over a number of days, in which the content for learning how to behave more effectively in interpersonal situations is not outside the learners, but is their own behavior, the transactions among them as they struggle to create a productive work group and as they learn to help one another to learn and to change. Broadly, the goal of sensitivity training can be defined as helping trainees improve the quality of their membership and participation in human affairs.

Role Playing

The action goal of role playing is accomplished by people playing parts or roles (their own or someone else's) in a hypothetical drama or real situation. The basic process is interaction between people. The enactment of situations, spontaneity, experimentation, practice, feedback, and analysis are key ingredients of the technique.

Gaming

In the typical game, executives or students playing executive roles are grouped into teams representing the management of competing organizations and make the same type of operating and policy decisions that they might in real life. Using the set of mathematical relationships built into a model, the decisions are processed and result in a series of performance reports. These decisions and reports pertain to a specific time period (which may be a day, week, month, quarter, or year). Decisions are then made for the next period. They too are processed, and many years of operation can be covered in one short play, such as a few hours in a day.

Programmed Instruction

Programmed instruction is a sequential method of self-learning in which the learner is presented with material to learn and questions to answer. The material and questions start at a very simple level and graduate to more difficult levels. The trainee must answer correctly the immediate question— or go back to review the material which he or she has not understood. If the trainee answers the question correctly—he or she is requested to go on to the next set of material and related questions.

Concurrently with the development of these contemporary training techniques, there has been expanding use of devices to assist teaching and learning. These devices include films, slides, television, programmed teaching machines, and electronic computers.

The computer can be of significant aid in various teaching and educational

"I've had it explained to me, but I still don't understand it."

Drawing by Alan Dunn; Copyright 1957, The New Yorker Magazine, Inc. (Reproduced with permission)

areas. This is so because the computer has a vast storage capacity (for facts, alternatives, information, etc.), can be programmed for individual differences and logical patterns, and is rapid in processing data and responding to the user. The authors feel that there will be greatly increasing use of computers for educational and training purposes in government, businesses, and schools.

Two specific training areas—management games and computer-assisted instruction—are discussed below.

MANAGEMENT GAMES

A management game or simulation may be defined as a series of decision-making exercises structured around a model of an organization's operation, in which participants assume the roles of decision-makers. Thus, it involves the use of a model of reality comprising a bundle of interrelated variables, and the manipulation and/or observation of the behavior of the system over time.

The game is a dynamic training technique. Trainees, usually grouped in competing companies or teams, make decisions. Using a set of mathematical relationships built into a model, the decisions of the players are processed (frequently by computer) so as to produce performance reports.

Because of the complexity of the model, it is usually programmed for a computer, and the group decisions are entered on uniform data collection forms to facilitate computer input. Computer printouts show the results of decisions in the form of sales reports, cost reports, inventory and backorder status reports, profit and loss statements, cash-flows, balance sheets, etc. Decisions and reports pertain to a specific time period which, depending on the model, may be a day, week, month, quarter, or year. Decisions are made for the next time period; the decisions are processed, reports are generated and returned to players, and the game proceeds in this manner. Time is compressed and it is possible to simulate a year or several years of operations in a single day of game play.

The three basic components of a game are:

- A model which is a mathematical abstraction of an organization and its environment.

- A series of rules which govern the manipulation of the model.

- A set of rules which govern the activity of the participants in relationship to the game.

The competitive activity is governed by the model, which is a facsimile of the environment whose basic design the participants cannot control. The participants do influence the facsimile environment in the game by their decisions.

The rules which govern the participants' relation with the simulated environment prescribe the number, form, and timing of the decisions made by trainees.

Some of the uses made of games include:

- Teaching specific items, e.g., critical path method (CPM), linear programming, decision-making under uncertainty.

- Teaching the importance of behavioral patterns such as flexibility, team work, and transactional relations.

- Teaching the power of modeling and of mathematical approaches to problems.

- Generating a high degree of involvement as either an introduction or a conclusion to a broader training program.

Games may be extremely simple or of considerable depth and complexity. In some cases, computations are made manually, perhaps with the aid of desk calculators; in other cases the complexity of the model demands the power of a computer. Some games can meaningfully be played in their entirety in a few hours, while other games are played at intervals, over spans of several weeks. Some games are limited to a few participants while other games can accommodate numerous players. Figure 10-3 depicts a paradigm of a computerized management game.

In the matter of realism, there is nothing the best manually conducted

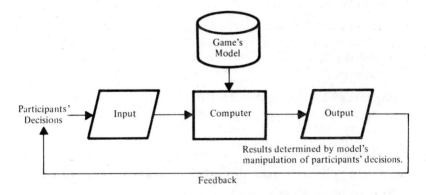

Figure 10-3   The management game.

game can do that the best computerized game cannot do, but there are many things a computerized game can do that a manual game cannot do.

A good computerized game allows for the use of a large number of judgmental factors, acts of God, and changes in the overall environment. It can incorporate scores of variables where the manual game has to stop at approximately a dozen. The computer variables are representable by mathematical functions which often are too complex for use in manual games.

During the game and at the end of the game, critique sessions are usually held. At such times the game administrator and the participants discuss the game and their performances. Participants may be competing against other participants and teams, or against their own prior performance.

Subsequent to a management development program, which had the management game as one of its prime training techniques, the following comments were volunteered by the attendees:

"It was the most exciting training program I have ever had."

"The best part of the entire program was the game."

"It was so realistic, because we had to make team decisions about almost real problems."

"I now have a better insight about the difficulty in making decisions and running a business."

Advantages and Disadvantages

Some of the advantages of games as a training tool are:

- The contraction of time. The participants can play the equivalent of several years in a day.

- A broad and integrated view of the problem area. The participants, to succeed, are required to set meaningful goals and plans, and to make logical decisions taking into account environmental, competitive, and internal factors.

- Experience in decision-making. Participants gain concentrated insight about decision-making under varying degrees of uncertainty. The relation of decisions and results becomes vivid.

- If the game involves team participation, the players learn the importance of coordination and cooperation in groups.

- The participants gain knowledge about competitiveness, and the difficulty in ascertaining the probable actions of the other players.

Some of the possible disadvantages of the game approach are:

- The cost of game training techniques may be higher than other teaching methods. This is particularly true when expensive computer time is involved.

- Intense personal rivalries may result from the competitive nature of games.

- The game model may overly simplify reality and thus not provide practical on-the-job benefits.

- Most games' models are series of equations that account for quantitative variables; they lack human-factor variables.

Examples of Games

Several games are briefly described below to indicate the scope and focus of such simulations.

1. *Harvard Business School Management Simulation.* This general business game allows teams of four or five participants to compete in a consumer goods market against as many as four other firms. Decisions are made in all the major functional areas of business. In manufacturing, teams must purchase and warehouse raw materials, schedule production, and determine labor utilization. Marketing decisions are made concerning number of products, prices, quality, advertising, and market research. Both short- and long-term loans are available. Companies can issue common stock, buy securities, and pay dividends.

This game is designed to reward consistent decision-making. Those teams which develop and follow through on coordinated strategies usually achieve adequate profits. They must utilize the past information about their firm, other firms, and industry trends.

This game was created to allow the players to coordinate their knowledge of the functional areas of business in a complex situation. It also allows the use of analytical techniques. Finally, the team nature of the game develops skills of communication and cooperation among players.[5]

2. *The Community Land Use Game (CLUG).* CLUG is an urban systems game that involves three to fifteen players in a sequence of highly interdependent decisions concerning real estate development, transportation, taxes, utilities construction, and building maintenance. The players' decisions result in foreseen as well as unforeseen consequences for community land use, economic base, level of employment, and financial position.

Aside from the fact that CLUG is one of the few games dealing systematically with urban factors, the game has advantages not found in many games: (1) no two plays of CLUG are the same, so it can be played repeatedly; (2) the outcome of play is determined by player decisions and is not predetermined or due simply to luck; (3) CLUG can be modified to meet a wide variety of needs.

The general purpose of CLUG is to provide intense experience with the growth, development, and resulting problems of urban growth—all in a very short period of time.[6]

3. *Staff Training Exercise for Programming Supervisors (STEPS)*. In this game, three-man teams are charged with effectively utilizing programmers to carry out a contract they have been awarded for the space-man missile control system. Each of the participants is the head of one of the three sections: control, processing, and input/output. Each player is assigned specific tasks which lead to completion of the programs for the contracted system. The objective of the team is to complete the programs by the specified date and within the $300,000 budget allocation.

Six personnel categories are provided with known costs and capabilities. All employees within a category are assumed to be of equal ability, with the exception that programmers who are transferred to jobs similar to others they have worked on are more efficient. Each programmer must be assigned to a specific phase of a particular program. During the twenty periods of the game, the three section heads are seated near each other to facilitate communication. They can hire, fire, transfer, or promote programmers to fit their specific needs. After a two-week period of simulated activity, four reports are prepared for the section heads to assist them in making future decisions.

STEPS was designed to train supervisors of a programming effort. The work environment seeks to simulate production and personnel problems and to develop decision-making competence.[7]

COMPUTER-ASSISTED INSTRUCTION (CAI)

Computer-assisted instruction is a type of programmed instruction. Each participant works individually on the programmed instruction materials at his or her own pace, and the instruction goes through the following steps:

1. A relatively small unit of information is presented to the participant. A statement to be completed or a question to be answered about this information is also included. This is known as the stimulus.

2. The participant is required to complete the statement or answer the question about the specific bit of information. He or she is said to be making a response to the stimulus.

3. The participant is then immediately informed whether the response is correct or not. If it is wrong, the person may also be told why. By this kind of feedback, the trainee is rewarded by providing the correct response; thus, a correct response is reinforced.

4. The participant is next presented with the second unit of information, and the cycle of presentation-answer-feedback (or more technically, stimulus-response-reinforcement of the correct answer) is repeated. The same cycle is repeated again and again as all of the necessary information is presented in logical sequence.

The program may be of several physical forms. It may be a book, film strips, auditory material used with a tape recorder and player, or it may be a combination of these devices and also an electronic computer.

Computer-aided instruction utilizes the capabilities of the computer to select, present, and evaluate responses to subject matter. The student interacts with the computer through a teaching terminal which may be a typewriter-like device, cathode ray tube, etc.

The computer's selective capacity operates so as to adapt instruction to the student's needs. This can be accomplished by displaying material of varying difficulty, providing remedial reviews or exercises when response indicates need, altering sequences and presentation modes, transferring control of the machine to the learner, and providing the learner opportunities to respond in different patterns. Data can be accumulated and stored by the computer, including data about the student's skill level, mathematical aptitude, vocabulary, reading comprehension level, etc. The data can influence the presentation and instructional sequences.

Many computer-aided instruction programs have been written to provide drill and practice and tutorial packages. In some respects these CAI packages are similar to the programmed instruction provided in programmed texts or non-computer teaching machines. However, as contrasted with the relatively static nature of texts and teaching machines, CAI permits rapid change and development. Further, the CAI approach provides vast information retrieval capabilities that can be employed in problem-solving. Additionally, CAI can be an invaluable source of data on students' performances. Since the computer can record in great detail the student's responses, errors, delays, and misinterpretations, the instructor can evaluate performances of both students and instructional material.

Some of the subjects that have been programmed for CAI include: mathematics, statistics, communication skills, accounting, economics, engineering, and computer programming. Figure 10-4 presents a simple example of how CAI interacts with a student.

It is also possible to use the computer for computer-assisted counseling.

PLEASE TYPE YOUR NAME

ROBERT VALENTINE

DRILL NUMBER 604032

L.C.M. MEANS LEAST COMMON MULTIPLE

___ IS THE L.C.M. OF 4 AND 9

TIME IS UP

 36 IS THE L.C.M. OF 4 AND 9

 23 IS THE L.C.M. OF 12 AND 8

WRONG

 24 IS THE L.C.M. OF 12 AND 8

 1 IS THE L.C.M. OF 15 AND 10

WRONG

___ IS THE L.C.M. OF 15 AND 10

TIME IS UP, ANSWER IS 30

 30 IS THE L.C.M. OF 15 AND 10

 60 IS THE L.C.M. OF 12 AND 30

 12 IS THE L.C.M. OF 2, 4, AND 6

_____

 40 IS THE L.C.M. OF 8, 10, AND 5

S. FOR SUMMARY S.

	NUMBER	PERCENT
CORRECT	14	70
WRONG	5	25
TIMEOUT	1	5

70% CORRECT IN BLOCK, 70% OVERALL TO DATE

GOOD BYE, O FEARLESS DRILL TESTER.

TEAR OFF ON DOTTED LINE

••

Figure 10-4 An example of computer-assisted instruction. (*Information*, San Francisco, California: W.H. Freeman and Company, 1966, p. 165.)

Drill-and-practice exercise, shown in abbreviated form, is typical of a simple computer-assisted instruction program that is designed to be responsive to the needs of individual students. The illustrated exercise is one of five that differ in their degree of difficulty; when the student types his name, the exercise best suited to him on the basis of computer-memory records of his previous performance is selected automatically. The first three questions and answers exemplify the ways in which the computer is programmed to deal with various shortcomings. The student fails to answer the first question within the allotted 10-second time limit; the computer therefore prints TIME IS UP *and repeats the question, which the student then answers correctly. A wrong answer to the next question causes the computer to announce the error and repeat the question automatically; a second chance again elicits a correct answer. A wrong answer to the third question is compounded by failure to respond to the reiterated question within the time limit. Because this question has now drawn two unsatisfactory responses the automatic* TIME IS UP *statement is followed by a printing of the correct answer. The question is now repeated for a third and last time. Whether or not the student elects to copy the correct answer (he does so in this instance), the computer automatically produces the next question. Only six of the 20 questions that compose the drill are shown in the example. After the student's last answer the computer proceeds to print a summary of the student's score for the drill as well as his combined average for this and earlier drills in the same series. The drill-and-practice exercise then concludes with a cheery farewell to the student and an instruction to tear off the teletype tape.*

Figure 10-4   (Continued)

Some portions of a counselor's daily activities can be assigned to a computer, such as the matching of student performance with schedule requests. Vocational and career opportunities can be correlated with the student's performance and interests. Relieving the counselor of some of his or her routine information disseminating tasks could provide more time for personal relationships between counselor and student.

Advantages and Disadvantages

The single most powerful advantage of CAI is that of individualized instruction and remedial capability. Most CAI packages, to date, have involved teaching basic facts. There is need to study pedagogical techniques to determine if CAI can be used to teach less structured material such as analysis of relationships, derivation of sets of abstract relations, group interaction, and judgments. It should be noted, however, that the cost of computer time, terminals, communication lines, and software packages (programs) can be considerable.

SUMMARY

In our complex and dynamic world, learning is a lifelong pursuit. Organizations have obligations to assist individuals and groups to develop their skills, attain personal growth, and thus assure that human resources are maintained at high levels of potential.

There is a broad series of conventional and more modern training techniques. Concurrently with these techniques there has been growing use made of computers, and other tools, for educational and training purposes. Schools, colleges and universities, the government and, increasingly, businesses will be employing the computer in conjunction with training and educational efforts.

Two major areas of computer use in training are: management games and computer-assisted instruction. In both of these areas some significant achievements and results have been attained; this should encourage personnel departments and computer departments to intensively explore their potentials in their organizations.

The next chapter probes the social issues related to computerization. The issues covered are dehumanization, unemployment, privacy, and crime as they relate to computers.

KEY CONCEPTS OF THE CHAPTER

1. Technological and other changes necessitate a lifelong approach to education and training. The alternative is personal and organizational

obsolescence.

2. There is particular need for employees to be trained in both systems skills and interpersonal relationships.

3. The computerized management game is a powerful training method that provides insight about problem-solving, decision-making, and competition.

4. Computer-assisted instruction is a technique that allows for individualized training and progress at one's own pace.

5. The computer will have an increasing role in the training and educational efforts of all kinds of organizations. The computer has capabilities (e.g., vast information storage, quick data processing, fast response) that are needed in a society which demands both broad and personalized education and training.

DISCUSSION QUESTIONS

General Background (Seminar/Classroom Discussion)

1. Why are training and development particularly important in the computer field?
2. In prior years, a high school or college education ended formal education for many people. Why is it now said that education is a lifelong process?

Operational and Technical

1. Are systems analysts and computer programmers in your organization trained in interpersonal skills? Is the personnel department staff trained in computer concepts? What is the value of such cross-disciplinary training?
2. Has your organization used the computer as a training tool? How can it be used for training administrators? How can it be used to train clerical personnel?

Policy

1. Does your organization have a formal training and development effort? Why is such a program necessary in today's environment?
2. What is your organization's policy about maintaining and improving employees' skills? What are the respective responsibilities (for maintaining skills) of the employer, employee, and government?

Areas for Research

1. Obtain a computerized management game and have some managers test its training effectiveness. Ask the managers how the game is helpful (e.g., encourages teamwork, encourages an analytical approach towards decisions).
2. Study the computer-assisted instruction technique. How might CAI be used to train members of the computer department and the personnel department? What other areas of your organization could make constructive use of CAI?

3. Conduct a survey of managers and employees in one or more organizations, about their attitudes concerning the adequacy of training and development programs in their companies. How can such training and development programs be made more effective and satisfying to managers and employees?

BIBLIOGRAPHY

Argyris, Chris. *Management and Organizational Development.* New York: McGraw-Hill Book Co., 1971.

Caffrey, John and Charles J. Mosmann. *Computers on Campus.* Washington, D.C.: American Council on Education, 1967.

Cohen, K. J., W. R. Dill, A. Kuehn, P. Winters. *The Carnegie Tech Management Game.* Homewood, Illinois: Richard D. Irwin, Inc., 1964.

Coulson, John E. *Programmed Learning and Computer-Based Instruction.* New York: John Wiley & Sons, Inc., 1962.

Craft, Clifford J., J. M. Kibbe, B. Nanus. *Management Games.* New York: Reinhold Publishing Corp., 1961.

Duke, Richard D. and Allen H. Schmidt. *Operational Gaming and Simulation in Urban Research—An Annotated Bibliography.* Michigan State University, 1965.

Goodlad, John I., et al. *Computers and Information Systems in Education.* New York: Harcourt, Brace & World, Inc., 1966.

Graham, Robert G. and Clifford F. Gray. *Business Games Handbook.* New York: American Management Association, 1969.

Greene, Jay R. and R. L. Sisson. *Dynamic Management Decision Games.* New York City: John Wiley & Sons, Inc., 1959.

Greenlaw, Paul S., L. W. Herron, R. H. Rawdon. *Business Simulation in Industrial and University Education.* Englewood Cliffs, N.J.: Prentice Hall, Inc., 1962.

Guetzkow H., et al. *Simulation in International Relations.* Englewood Cliffs, N.J.: Prentice Hall, Inc., 1963.

McClelland, David C. *The Achieving Society.* New York: The Free Press, 1961.

McKenney, J. L. *Simulation Gaming for Management Development.* Boston, Mass.: Harvard University Press, 1967.

Odiorne, George S. *Training by Objectives.* New York: The Macmillan Co., 1970.

Patten, Jr., Thomas H. *Manpower Planning and the Development of Human Resources.* New York: John Wiley & Sons, Inc., 1971.

Ricciardi, F. M. and C. J. Craft. *Top Management Decision Simulation.* New York: American Management Association, 1957.

Shubik, Martin. *A Business Game for Teaching & Research Purposes.* Yorktown Heights, N.Y.: International Business Machines Corp., 1963.

Taber, Julian I., et al. *Learning and Programmed Instruction.* Reading, Massachusetts: Addison-Wesley Pub. Co., 1965.

Thorelli, Hans B., Robert L. Graves, Lloyd T. Howells. *The International Operations Simulation.* New York: The Free Press, 1963.

FOOTNOTES

[1] Paul S. Greenlaw, "Management Development: A Systems View," *Personnel Journal,* April 1964, pp. 205–211.

[2] Warren Bennis, "Organizations of the Future," *Personnel Administration,* September-October 1967, p. 17.

[3] Charles H. Kepner and Benjamin B. Tregoe, *The Rational Manager* (New York: McGraw-Hill Book Co., 1965).

[4] Robert R. Blake and Jane S. Mouton, *The Managerial Grid* (Houston, Texas: Gulf Publishing Co., 1964).

[5] Robert G. Graham and Clifford F. Gray, *Business Games Handbook* (New York: American Management Association, 1969), pp. 210–211.

[6] Ibid., pp. 290–292.

[7] Ibid., pp. 387–388.

11

Social Issues and
the Computer

Computers should become a functional part of a life-oriented social system and not a cancer which begins to play havoc and eventually kills the system. Machines or computers must become means for ends which are determined by man's reason and will. The values which determine the selection of facts and which influence the programming of the computer must be gained on the basis of the knowledge of human nature, its various possible manifestations, its optimal forms of development, and the real needs conducive to this development. That is to say, man, not technique, must become the ultimate source of values; optimal human development and not maximal production the criterion for all planning.

Erich Fromm

OBJECTIVES OF THE CHAPTER

Often management and people are so absorbed in their day-to-day routines that they overlook the broader implications of activities and issues. The authors think this is true in the computer and personnel fields. The computer relates to a number of major social issues: dehumanization, unemployment, privacy, and crime. How these issues are handled could significantly affect the image of the computer in the view of society.

SCOPE OF THE SOCIAL CHALLENGE

A number of provocative social issues are entangled with the development and use of computers. As society becomes increasingly dependent on technology and machines, there are trends that can be considered dehumanizing. In the social system which is filled with cross-currents, there is evidence that such dehumanization stems from many causes. Family life is less stable

"You're born, you're processed and you die. That's life."

than in the past; mobility of individuals is increasing; loyalty to God, country, and home (by historical standards) is diminishing; large-scale, impersonal organizations control much of our lives. *The computer is frequently cited as a prime example of a dehumanizing tool; this is summarized in the oft-repeated parody of a computer saying: "do not bend, fold, staple, or mutlilate"—"I am a human being!"*

The introduction of tools, throughout history, has caused dislocation in employment and the nature of work. The spear and bow and arrow changed the hunters' techniques of pursuing game. The wheel considerably altered man's methods of transportation and hauling goods. The mechanical machines of the Industrial Revolution shifted a considerable part of the heavy workload from man to devices, and accelerated the rate-of-production in industry. The modern electronic computer introduces new patterns in man's handling of data and information, and even in man's use of his mental capabilities.

The computer's enormous data processing and retrieval capacities have created the potential of vast data banks containing information that has been heretofore largely unintegrated and, in many cases, not available before through conventional means. Concurrently with this development is the intensifying concern that such computerized data banks may be sources of danger to the individual's right to privacy, and that they may bring reality to the nightmare presented in Orwell's *1984*. Data banks contain seeds of centralized power over information which could be used for corrupt or unethical purposes.

The formidable power and mysterious features of the computer can, in the hands of persons or groups with evil intent, bring unexpected negative results to society. Might the computer be used by political leaders to manipulate the public by "tracking" opponents through computer analysis, and by directing variable messages that appeal to supporters and potential supporters? Might criminal elements use the computer to improve their gamesmanship in gambling activities, and to improve their planning and strategies in connection with major crimes (e.g., which banks to rob, at what time, etc.)? Will the computer increase the incidents of major white-collar crime in organizations —as companies turn over their records to the mysterious electronic beast that is controlled by esoteric technicians?

These social issues should be, of course, of deep concern to the humanist who desires that technological developments be used primarily for the benefit of society. The computer professionals must be sensitive to the social issues, in order to plan, design, develop, and implement computer systems that are responsive to the overriding needs of a moral and ethical society.

As the computer becomes more readily available and less expensive (as discussed in Chapter 7) it will have an enlarged impact on work and family life.

- Some substantial part of work may eventually be done at home with a computer console in a study, linked by communication lines to the employer's central data bank. It is not difficult to imagine many kinds of work that is adaptable to this return to working-at-home: managers, accountants, lawyers, secretaries, designers, market researchers, etc.

- The housewife may shop and order the family needs via a combination television catalog-computer data terminal which has communication links with the major retail warehouses. She will be able to select the category of merchandise she wishes displayed, in color, on a giant television screen. When ready to order, the depression of a few keys will immediately send a message to the retail outlet she prefers.

- The financial system of the nation will be processed by electronic computers and communication. Little if any conventional money or checks will be used. When a member of the family makes a purchase, the proper bank account will be instantaneously charged at the time of the transaction. Besides eliminating the need for current billing procedures, delays in collection will be eliminated.

- Children may receive much of their schooling at home, by the combination television-computer data terminal serving as a private tutor—as well as providing almost complete flexibility as far as curriculum selection is concerned.

If these predictions come to pass, the home and family life will regain much of its recently diminished importance. The extensive social problems related to transportation congestion, air pollution from automobile exhausts, the constantly increasing demands for vast public transportation facilities, and the great waste of time and money involved in going to and from work, shopping areas, and schools will be considerably reduced. Should the predictions develop, society would be faced with new dilemmas. What would happen to the mammoth office buildings in large cities when most administrative-type work can be performed at home? Do the multi-billion dollar shopping centers with their enormous parking areas become new "ghost" areas of a former way of life—as the housewife shops from the comfort of her home? Do banks become largely electronic services, as the bulk of cash transfers involve electronic payments and receipts; if so, are the numerous bank branches needed with their large clerical staffs? With the elimination of cash, what will happen to robbery statistics? If children can be better educated at home, what happens to our fantastic investment in schools' plant and equipment facilities, and the large number of teachers (since many lectures can be recorded on tape for re-use)? Kahn and Wiener have indicated:

> . . . the computer utility industry will become as fundamental as the power industry, and the computer will be viewed as the most basic tool of the last third of the twentieth century. Individual computers (or at least consoles or other remote input devices) will become essential equipment for home, business, and profession, and the ability to use a computer skillfully and flexibly may become more widespread than the ability to play bridge or drive a car (and presumably much easier).[1]

Certainly top management must be aware of these potential developments, for they are likely to change some of the very basic methods of conducting business. Planners in government and education must consider the enormous implications of the forecasts for the economy, cities, public programs, and education. More specifically, individuals engaged in personnel- and computer-related work will be facing significantly different challenges than now exist in their organizations. *Too little attention has been devoted to the potential use of computer-communications for the improvement of life and society.*

SOME DEHUMANIZING RESULTS OF COMPUTERIZATION

To a large number of people, the computer still remains a mysterious and threatening device. The computer is viewed as a composite of demonic and godly characteristics and capabilities, as can be seen from some of the terms used in referring to the computer: the giant brain, the monster, the black box. *Perhaps one of the fundamental reasons for the poor public image of the computer relates to the central role the computer has in many organizations. People and work must adjust to the computer, rather than vice versa.* While people have the capability of being adaptable, resentment is likely to occur if the adaptation is coerced and disturbs the preferred human system.

The computer, an inanimate device, creates a feeling of discomfort for many persons who prefer interacting with humans. The programmed computer is tireless, persistent, and rapid. As a result, the human can feel a sense of futility, fear, and harassment when interacting with a computer system. Computer-paced work, as currently designed, tends to be unsympathetic to individualistic human characteristics; it treats all persons with impersonal objectivity and uniformity.

Many people react negatively to the mechanistic requirements of computers. For instance, the advent of modern data processing has resulted in the diminished importance of an individual's name, and a growing importance of a whole series of number identifications: social security numbers, bank account numbers, employee numbers, credit card numbers, home and office phone numbers, insurance policy numbers, zip code numbers, license numbers, etc. Relatedly, some of the output (reports, bills, and even checks) of computers is unintelligible or unverifiable by the layman.

The very publicity about the power and potential of the computer as an indispensable tool can create a feeling of inadequacy on the part of individuals and groups that are affected by it. These negative reactions can be shared by such diverse elements as the middle manager who sees his routine decisions programmed, the older long-time employee who cannot adapt to the new technology, the relatively uneducated and unskilled worker whose background deters comprehension of abstract concepts, the customer who is plagued by computer communications, etc.

Interestingly, it is reported [2] that International Business Machines Corporation (IBM)—the largest computer manufacturer—is increasingly concerned about the dehumanizing aspects of the computers it uses for internal purposes. It appears that *IBM may be one of the most aware organizations that there is a social crisis with its own product.* As examples of this, IBM has:

- Instituted manufacturing facilities that are composed of small work groups (rather than impersonal assembly lines) and that employ job enlargement techniques (instead of monotonous minute tasks).

  In addition, because of dynamic computer technology, the work process is subject to planned change; thus the worker is frequently involved in training programs and adding new skills which prevents job boredom and provides for personal growth.

- Emphasized the individual rather than some abstraction of the person. For instance, IBM's records make prime reference to employees by name—and not by identification number.

  In addition, IBM has apparently been using its internal computers in an imaginative way for personnel-related applications (e.g., manpower planning).

- Encouraged company socializing by use of company-supported employee activities including country clubs, sports facilities, parties, and formal recognition of employees' accomplishments.

One probable by-product of IBM's active personnel posture is the fact that it is the nation's largest non-union employer.

IMPACT OF COMPUTERS/AUTOMATION ON MANPOWER

The National Commission on Technology, Automation, and Economic Progress concluded [3] that although technological change plays a major role in determining the particular persons who will be displaced, the rate of economic growth rather than technological change per se is the principal determinant of the general level of employment.

It is difficult to isolate and establish the impacts of computers and automation on such factors as unemployment, productivity, training and education. Other variables are also operating, e.g., changing social attitudes about work, shifts in organizational goals, the rise of new industries and products and the decline of others, and modification in life styles and consumer demands.

There is a close relationship between computers, as described in this book, and automation. Simply, automation means the processing of work by machines which, to a high degree, need very little human intervention. The major kinds of automation, all subject to control by computer, can be classified as follows:

- Office Automation: The handling of information and data involved in administrative processes by electronic data processors and related peripheral equipment.

- Production Automation: An assembly line in which machines doing many separate operations are linked together by automatic devices for transporting and transferring materials.

- Process Automation: The handling of continuous flow materials; this includes chemicals, oil, and power which are processed, transported, and stored automatically via a variety of instrumentation and machinery.

- Numerical-Control Machines: Precision equipment which can be made to perform a series of specific operations by means of instructions stored in a control device.

- Source Automation: Remote terminals which can send messages to and/or receive messages from a central processor. These include point-of-sales devices, data collectors in factories and offices, "dial-up" information banks, and other data terminals of various types.

- Robotics. The use of robots in place of human beings.

While in many cases automation in the factory is divorced from automation in the office, complete integration will eventually call for these two major components of a manufacturing organization to be linked. It is obvious that what is happening in the plant (e.g., use of materials and supplies, expending of labor, inspection for quality and flaws in products) have a direct relation to many administrative activities (e.g., inventory records, manpower planning, financial statements, customer complaints).

The promise of computerization and automation is that they will rid man of work that is toilsome and demeaning; that more and better products will become possible without an increase in the work force; and that with their aid, new forms of services, such as instant dial-up information retrieval, which would otherwise be visionary, can become everyday realities.

The threat of automation and computerization is, of course, layoffs and unemployment. However, there has been much controversy about the extent to which automation/computers do in fact imply a significant reduction in employment. Some observers believe that the threat of automation/computerization has been greatly exaggerated and that it is being introduced gradually and where introduced, does not appreciably decrease the need for workers, though it may change the nature of the jobs available for them. It seems clear that for a complex of reasons, prominently including automation and computerization—as well as the fact that in a competitive economy the more efficient survive—many, if not most, of our industries are able to increase production while holding relatively constant, or even decreasing, the size of their labor forces. What has happened thus far is that the net result has not been massive unemployment, but rather shifts in work (e.g., reductions in jobs for blue-collar and unskilled workers, and increases in jobs for service and skilled workers), and some general reduction in hours worked.

TECHNOLOGY AND WORK

Technology is creating accelerated change in all types of organizations (this was broadly explored in Chapter 2). This change affects work, positions, and the kinds of employees required (surveyed in Chapter 3).

Specific ways in which the computer is altering work and work relationships are highlighted in the following examples:

Displacement of People

Bank clerks once had the job of sorting and posting the massive numbers of checks processed in our national banking system. Now the process is largely automated; magnetic ink recording characters (MIRC) on checks are automatically read by computers which manipulate the checks and data speedily and accurately.

Change in Supervisory-Subordinate Relationships

Department store clerks previously had to obtain supervisory approval to sell items on credit. Point-of-sales devices, connected by communication lines to a computer, now perform a search of the credit status of the customer's account and informs the sales clerk whether to make the sale or not. In addition, the single entry at point-of-sales can simultaneously update sales records, customer records, and inventory records. In essence, the accounting records reflect the real-time condition of the organization; time lag is eliminated.

Relieving Shortages of Skilled Employees

Medical reports and analysis were often late, because of the need for accuracy as well as the shortage of trained health personnel. The computer is facilitating physical examinations (e.g., electrocardiogram, heart sounds, blood pressure, electroencephalogram) and providing analyses of laboratory tests. In theory, at least, the computer can handle every physiological signal used in disease detection or diagnosis. This helps relieve the shortage of staff in the medical field, makes medical care more widely available, and provides more rapid response where life may be at stake.

Custom Training

A continuing problem in teaching is the inability of a teacher to satisfy the needs of the many students that are usually in a class. Some students are bound to be neglected and their educational progress restricted. Computer-aided instruction (CAI) provides a data terminal for the student, who interacts with the computer (e.g., to learn algebra) and progresses at his or her own pace. This training technique was discussed in Chapter 10.

Performing Work Not Practical for Humans to Perform

Some research is either too complex or impractical to carry out by conventional laboratory procedures. In the area of physics known as X-ray crystallography, the computer provides the only known practical technique for discovering the molecular structure of proteins, that group of chemical compounds so essential for life. In many types of scientific and engineering applications, the computer can accomplish computations in a few seconds which would take many man-years of effort without computers.

Expanding the Capacity of Employees

Crime is one of our major social concerns. Law enforcement is becoming increasingly sophisticated. The computer is used to analyze information about crimes and plot or pinpoint problem areas. A crime information system can provide rapid data about stolen property and wanted criminals.

Mass Data Processing Only Feasible by Automation

The Internal Revenue Service of the federal government handles over 100 million returns a year. The computer is used to process the returns, make refunds, check for irregularities, and catch mistakes. Some organizations must maintain records on many thousands of resources, customers, stockholders, etc., which would not be feasible to maintain by other than computerized systems.

Creation of Completely New Positions

Not many years ago, positions such as systems analyst, computer programmer, and management scientist were unknown. The rapidly growing importance of computers in our society has made computer-related work the fastest growing segment of our labor force. This was discussed in Chapter 7.

OCCUPATIONAL PATTERNS

The tendency towards a broader based college education for the general population, coupled with the reduced need for unskilled workers, will result in significant shifts in occupational patterns (Figure 11-1). The traditional pyramid occupational structure, with a large base of workers at the bottom and a small number of managers and well educated people at the top, is changing. The shape of the evolving structure is closer to a diamond form, with a reduction of the workers at the base and a substantial increase of well educated persons in the middle strata.

Because of the increased educational requirements of those in the upper two levels, the semi-skilled and unskilled workers may have growing difficulty in climbing the promotion ladder. Also, the uneducated will have greater difficulty in finding available jobs even at the semi-skilled and unskilled worker levels, since many of those tasks will be absorbed by automation and computers. These developments are bound to accentuate the problems faced by the aged, school dropouts, unemployed, and underemployed. Even for the

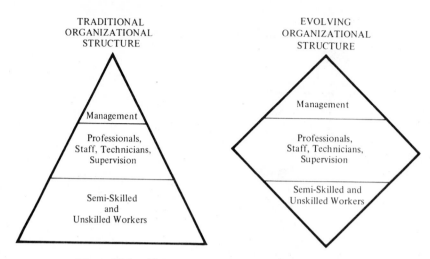

TRADITIONAL
ORGANIZATIONAL
STRUCTURE

EVOLVING
ORGANIZATIONAL
STRUCTURE

Management

Professionals,
Staff, Technicians,
Supervision

Semi-Skilled
and
Unskilled Workers

Management

Professionals,
Staff, Technicians,
Supervision

Semi-Skilled and
Unskilled Workers

Figure 11-1 Changing organizational patterns.

well educated, the future will be more demanding, since it will take a lifetime of learning to keep abreast of rapidly moving technology. The alternative is personal obsolescence.

THE COMPUTER AND CHANGING JOB PATTERNS

Effective computerization should include careful study of how it will affect work flows, jobs, and employees' morale. This calls for detailed and logical understanding of the composition of operations, the steps required to carry them out, and human nature.

Scientific Management

It appears that some of the classic lessons from history still have not been absorbed and implemented. Some decades ago, Frederick Taylor (1856–1915) and practitioners of the school of scientific management promoted the following ideas:

- There is a "one best way" of doing any work.

- Tools, techniques, and methods were the prime ways of improving operations.

- Management and supervisors should be completely rational in planning and making decisions.

- Most workers are like robots. If properly trained, supervised, motivated by financial gain or penalties—they will produce to reach the organization's objectives.

This school of thought is quite similar to that of the bureaucratic organization discussed in Chapter 2. While the tenets of the scientific management practitioners achieved some substantial achievements—the movement lost much respectability as society became more enlightened about human and social values. Still, vestiges of scientific management's views and practices persist in plants, offices, and in the computer profession.

Human Relations

Some years after Taylor's delineation of scientific management, Elton Mayo and Fritz J. Roethlisberger conducted the Hawthorne Experiments, at Western Electric Company, from 1927 to 1932. This work was to have profound effect upon the entire human relations movement. It challenged a number of prevalent assumptions as to the nature of the worker and his work, and served to discredit many of the underlying precepts of the scientific management school. The following are generalizations of some of Mayo's and Roethlisberger's main findings:

- There is no "one best way" of doing work; the "best way" is frequently situational.

- Human and group motivation are the prime variables for improving operations.

- People are not mere "economic-rational men"—but, rather "emotional-irrational men."

- Workers are individualistic, having subtle differences in attitudes, needs, and behavior. Formal and informal human relationships are critical factors influencing whether or not the organization will attain its goals.

The findings of Mayo and Roethlisberger have a close fit with the organic organization discussed in Chapter 2. *Although more than forty years have passed since the Hawthorne studies and the findings have gained wide acceptance by many thought leaders, the actual implementation of the ideas in everyday management and supervision seems inadequate.*
Some economists attribute the Japaneses successes in world trade to their high-levels of productivity which seems to result from a style of management that is not too dissimilar from that just described.

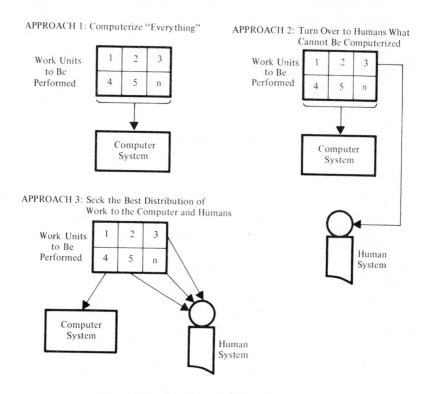

Figure 11-2   Interface of man and machine.

The Computer Field Attitude

The computer and management science fields, which are so absorbed with modern tools and techniques, too often seem to follow the principles of the school of scientific management while setting aside human relations concepts as ethereal and impractical to incorporate into computer systems and mathematical models. It is this very discounting of human nature and social systems that can bring discredit to the computer field—as the scientific management movement was stigmatized many years ago.

Systems should be designed to allocate work properly between humans and machines, and to assure a man/machine interface that is not inimical to people (Figure 11-2). *Too often in the past and present, the human system has been twisted to suit the machine system.* This has resulted in increased job boredom, reduced motivation and loyalty, and lowered productivity. Humanely designed systems can result in an enlightened distribution of work to man and machine, bringing job enrichment with its healthier and more productive possibilities.

Dickman indicates that any study of systems involves consideration of data, things, and people (Figure 11-3). Experience indicates that computer technicians stress data and things, and neglect people. This often results in deficient and mediocre systems.

Job Enrichment and Enlargement

Few computer systems are planned, designed, and implemented with any consideration whatsoever for job enhancement. The key to job enhancement theory is the "motivation-hygiene theory" of Frederick Herzberg. There is an important relationship between meaningful experience in work and mental health. According to this theory, man has two sets of basic needs: to avoid discomfort, and to grow psychologically.

Job experiences which lead to good reactions are most often related to the content of the jobs; that is, the task content. The bad reactions are most often related to the context in which the job is performed; that is, the surroundings and factors on the periphery of task content. The factors causing bad responses are related to avoidance of discomfort. The factors causing good responses are related to personal growth or fulfillment of psychological needs.

The factors identified as satisfiers and which are motivators in jobs, are: achievement, recognition, work itself, responsibility, advancement, and growth.

The factors identified as dissatisfiers and which are negative motivators in jobs, are: salary, company policy and administration, supervision, working conditions, and interpersonal relations. These are called "hygiene factors"—meaning preventive and environmental.

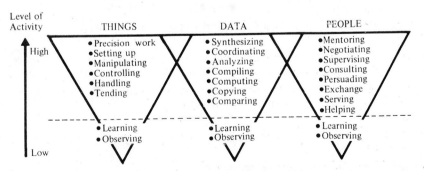

Figure 11-3   Functional job analysis. (Adapted from Robert A. Dickmann, *Personnel Implications for Business Data Processing*, New York: John Wiley & Sons, Inc., 1971, p. 5.)

There are three principles at the heart of the motivation-hygiene theory; they are:

- The factors involved in producing job satisfaction are separate and distinct from the factors that lead to job dissatisfaction. Growth occurs with achievement, and achievement requires a task to perform. Hygiene factors are relatively unrelated to tasks.

- The opposite of satisfaction on the job is not dissatisfaction; it is merely no job satisfaction. Satisfaction and dissatisfaction are discrete feelings. They are not opposite ends of the same continuum.

- The motivators have a much longer-lasting effect on sustaining satisfaction than the hygiene factors have on preventing dissatisfaction. The motivators in a work experience tend to be more self-sustaining and are not dependent upon constant supervisory attention. Hygiene needs, however, are related to things for which our appetites are never satisfied completely.[4]

Figure 11-4 indicates some of the practical approaches that can be used to strengthen positive motivators and result in job enrichment.

Job Enhancement and Computer Systems

The authors think that either systems designers should receive intensive training in psychology and sociology (in addition to technical skills), or

Change to Work	*Motivators Involved*
• Remove some controls while at the same time retaining accountability.	• Responsibility and personal achievement.
• Increase the accountability of individuals for their own work.	• Responsibility and recognition.
• Give a person a complete natural unit of .work.	• Responsibility, achievement, and recognition.
• Grant additional authority to an employee in his activity; more job freedom.	• Responsibility, achievement, and recognition.
• Make periodic reports of output and progress to the worker himself rather than to his supervisor only.	• Internal recognition.
• Introduce new and more difficult tasks not previously handled.	• Growth and learning.
• Assign individuals specific or specialized tasks, enabling them to become experts.	• Responsibility, growth, and advancement.

Figure 11-4 Job enhancement.

humanists (psychologists, sociologists, professional personnel staff, etc.) should be integral parts of major systems efforts. With a humanistic approach, the systems designer will design his or her system to assure that it is conducive to optimal performance—from the standpoint of combining human satisfaction and productivity. For instance,

- Rather than having the computer pace the work of humans, the humans might set the pace for the computer.

- Individuals affected by computerization would be deeply and sincerely invited to participate in the planning, designing, and implementation of computer applications.

- Rather than arbitrarily turning over work to computers, the designers would first study what would be the appropriate distribution between man and machine—so that employees will have a complete and natural unit of work.

- Determine with the employees affected by computerization how the new system will provide them with more job freedom.

- Design computer systems so information dissemination improves communication not only with managers—but also with workers.

- When work is absorbed by the computer, make certain that the affected workers are given more challenging (not more routine and boring) assignments.

- Use computerization as an opportunity to develop employees—not to reduce their importance or to get rid of them.

Unfortunately, the computer field has not yet sufficiently concentrated on the important need of developing ways of building provision for the human factor into their efforts. Job enrichment theory could be a very productive starting point for doing this. The lag of the young computer field in this regard is not surprising. The older field of plant automation has only recently been somewhat awakened, by "rebellions" of assembly line workers (e.g., Lordstown Syndrome), to the need of not only trying to achieve maximum production—but also to strive for maximum employee satisfaction!

USE OF THE COMPUTER IN MANPOWER PROGRAMS

The federal government has sponsored a number of efforts to try to use the computer as a viable instrument to improve various manpower programs. In this connection, an important means of facilitating the flow of information in the labor market is the attempt to increase the effectiveness of the U.S. Public Employment Service by computerization. The use of computer job banks, like the one now operated by the Employment Service in Baltimore, provides job-seekers with up-to-date records of job opportunities and valuable information about the nature of the jobs. Computerization of job information offers a number of advantages. It allows all employment offices in a given labor market to have essentially the same information about job openings, and it is possible to update this information daily. Even more important, the data-handling capabilities of the computer permit officials to collect and analyze information relating to the overall behavior of the local labor market and to maintain an audit of the operations of the employment offices' effectiveness. The success of existing job banks, especially in increasing the employment of the disadvantaged, has led to plans to expand this service to more than seventy cities in the early 1970's.

A companion activity, the Employment Service Automated Reporting Service (ESARS), will provide tracking information on persons as they move through the various manpower services. It becomes possible to find out exactly what kinds of services have been provided for any given applicant: interviewing, counseling, training, job referral, etc. This kind of information is useful to both Employment Service personnel and potential employers, and helps to reduce the time required to locate job opportunities that are mutually satisfactory to the employee and employer.

Computerized Job Matching

The final step in computerization of Employment Service operations is the establishment of computer programs that will match job-seekers with suitable job openings. While computer matching is still in the developmental stage, it holds a great deal of promise. Given the expanding capabilities of modern computers, it is not difficult to envision the day when computer job matching will be able to relate vast amounts of quantitative and qualitative information on applicants and employers. This will reduce the time needed to find and fill jobs, and enhance the likelihood that new hires will result in longer term employment and lower turnover rates.

The job banks are seen as the first stage in a computer-assisted matching system which will bring job-seekers and employment opportunities together. Experimental job matching systems are currently being tested in the states of Utah, Wisconsin, and New York. The system can be programmed, as it is in Utah, to find out quickly why certain applicants are repeatedly referred to jobs and then not hired. It may thus trigger re-examination of the need for particular kinds of training or other job preparation for applicants or even reveal staff deficiencies.

An Integrated Manpower System

The long-term goal of a community job market information center, stressing self-help and self-direction for those who are job ready, can be fully achieved only if there is a computerized job bank. Besides providing job order information, the computer can assist in integrating local information on employment, unemployment, labor turnover, job vacancies, and other labor market factors available through cooperative relationships with the Bureau of Labor Statistics. Early results of these experiments in computer operations raise the possibility that local public employment offices can indeed become a source of comprehensive current data for the job markets they serve.[5]

Figure 11-5 presents a model of an integrated manpower system toward which current incremental, disjointed efforts may ultimately gravitate. It is perhaps the absence of such an overview that causes so much haphazard and inefficient effort in our manpower programs to date.

In summary, it is quite apparent that the nation's manpower problems are among its most critical. The computer can be an integral part of an improved manpower planning system, and provide information and analysis currently unavailable or inadequate. It is already changing the patterns of employment and work in government and business—and has itself spawned one of the nation's largest industries, offering new career opportunities for many people.

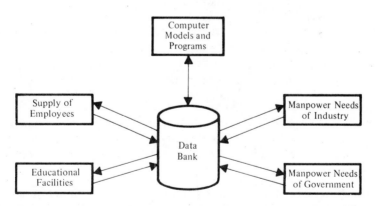

Figure 11-5   Model of an integrated manpower system.

PRIVACY AND THE COMPUTER*

The continued technological improvements in computer systems have reached a point where large-scale data banks have become economically and technically feasible. Data which previously were scattered, unintegrated, and uneconomic to collect, store, retrieve, and analyze, can now become centralized, integrated, and relatively inexpensive to obtain. This development has raised debate over the balance between the need for improved information by government and business, and the protection of the individual against invasion of privacy as well as other potential misuses of such concentrated information.

The computer joins a series of developments that potentially attack the principle of the individual's right to privacy: polygraphing, personality testing, truth drugs, wire tapping devices, electronic "bugs" and the possibilities of manipulating an individual's personality by drugs and brain surgery.

It would seem that the First Amendment of the American Constitution, which guarantees our rights to freedom of speech, press, and association, was intended to have a corollary: that we also have the right *not* to communicate. This would mean that we have the right to choose those to whom we do communicate and the terms on which we communicate.

There have been a number of federal government studies, by Congress and the Executive Branch, of the feasibility of establishing a national data bank which would integrate and expand the scattered government data files. This would correlate such data on individuals as: income tax, social security, military, criminal, welfare, employment, education, government loans, etc. To date, little has been done beyond the exploration stage, and increasingly vocal opposition to such a plan has been heard in Congress from groups and individuals concerned about protecting the rights of the individual.

Several examples of planned or operative data banks follow:

- Santa Clara County, in California, is implementing a data bank covering welfare, medical center, juvenile probation, adult probation, and health. The system will be able to locate and display information on any one of 180,000 individuals or 60,000 case files; the search by the computer will take a few seconds.

- The New York State Identification and Intelligence System provides a tracking system for criminal records of more than 600,000 persons. Among the features is the capability of searching incoming sets of fingerprints against a base file of 1.6 million fingerprints in no more than 25 seconds.

* For an excellent source of this material, refer to Alan F. Westin, ed. *Information Technology in a Democracy* (Cambridge, Massachusetts: Harvard University Press, 1971).

- The various large credit bureaus in the nation have computerized credit information on a large part of the population.

The individual organization using a data base for its personnel records may be faced with privacy problems. Some data might be included which is relatively objective and not controversial: name, profession or skills, education, and physical description. Even in this area, sensitive issues arise related to potential bias based on race, color, sex, religion, age, etc. Other data will be less public, yet hardly private, such as: maiden name, former spouse, job, hobbies. Certain data may contain private material ranging from the results of medical examinations, details of income, alimony, periodic performance reviews, etc. Finally, there may be records of personal details of which not even the employee may be aware: results of psychological tests, reference checks, career potential evaluations, etc.

An organization has a systems obligation to carefully consider who, and under what circumstances, has the right to such data. In such a data bank there must be confidence that,

- Data that is inserted into the data bank is correct, or have some level of confidence attached to it.

- Information, once inside the data bank, must be accessible only to individuals authorized to receive it.

Without such assurances, sensitive data can be misused. In the hands of an unauthorized person, the data can be used for gossiping and rumors, blacklisting, competitors' purposes, blackmailing, etc.

A related question is whether the employee has or does not have the right, periodically, to inspect his complete personnel record in the data bank. Only by permitting the employee to verify the record is there assurance that the data are indeed accurate and up-to-date. Further, by allowing the employee to have complete purview over the content of his record, it will dispel fear that the data bank is being manipulated for the organization's purposes.

There is a variety of methods that can improve the confidentiality and integrity of data banks; some of these entail manual controls while others are automated programmed controls. They include:

- Positive identification of persons accessing the data bank.

- Passwords or programmed locks on data files.

- Tight physical control over printed reports, computer programs, and data files.

- Security guards in the computer department.

- Purposefully fragmenting the data file.

"Well, it's come. The senator wants to investigate the brain's loyalty."

- Maintaining scrambled or coded data in files, and restricting access to the key for unscrambling and decoding the data.

- Establishing alarms in the physical computer facility, and in the computer programs.

- Periodically checking data transmission lines and data terminals for possible tapping.

- Establishing comprehensive audit procedures.

- Maintaining checks and balances in the computer department.

THE COMPUTER AS A CRIMINAL'S TOOL

The computer, in some ways, breaks down conventional methods of control. This opens avenues for illegal acts by employing the computer as an accomplice in crime.

Computerization has fostered the centralizing of data processing records. Paperwork that was once performed in a variety of offices (e.g., accounting, purchasing, payroll, personnel) is now processed in a single physical location—the computer department. This has eliminated the check and balance protection inherent when different departments and individuals perform different phases of an overall job. The centralization of control of information under one authority can be an inducement for taking unilateral steps to manipulate records.

When work is placed on the computer, many of the conventional visual records are modified or, indeed, no longer exist. A considerable amount of data, in a computer system, may be stored and processed in electronic form. The records are not visible to a human's sight. Traditional procedures for catching problem areas, often involving visual audits, are no longer as effective in many computer systems. In addition, computer technicians design computer applications and programs that are frequently not understood by managers and staffs who lack knowledge of computer technology. To an extent, the organization is at the "mercy" of the computer technocrats. Auditors, who are responsible for validating the accuracy and reasonableness of the organization's records, have only recently begun to adapt to computer data processing and applicable auditing procedures.

The complexity of the computer and its mysterious image have encouraged some employees, knowledgeable about computer techniques, to misuse their specialized skills. We hear of a growing number of computer-related crimes.

- A bank supervisor manipulates, for several months, the bank accounts in such a way that it permits him to remove over a million dollars of depositors' funds—which he uses to bet on horse races.

- The management of a large insurance company uses the computer to distort its financial records to make it appear that the organization's growth and size are considerably more formidable than they are. This distortion enables the organization to gain unjustified acceptance in the financial community and among investors.

- A computer technician writes a computer program in such a way that he is considered to be a supplier of goods to his organization. Besides collecting his normal salary, the computer technician is paid for non-existent merchandise and supplies. This situation remains undetected for several months.

- The vital records of an organization's time-sharing computer are illegally accessed by an ingenious young man who breaks the coding system that was intended to prevent unauthorized persons to access the computer. The culprit electronically steals valuable information, about proprietary computer programs, which he sells for tens-of-thousands of dollars.

A question is whether the rash of recent reports about computer-related crimes is merely the tip of an iceberg. Has the sophisticated computer encouraged a new and more sophisticated type of criminal and crime which are extremely evasive of discovery? This subject should undoubtedly be the subject of increasing study and research.

SUMMARY

A highly computerized organization or society is vulnerable to criticism that it is creating a dehumanized environment. This concern is undoubtedly the cause of the many fears and the resistance that people display towards automation and computerization.

The history of automation and computerization reveals that these developments have had, generally, more of a displacing effect rather than causing massive unemployment. However, there is little doubt that computerized applications and new systems result in considerable change in work patterns and in the qualifications required of employees. In this area, the computer field needs to build systems that enrich the tasks and environment of organizations—and not merely put work on the computer.

The federal government has been promoting a variety of manpower programs which facilitate making available information about job opportunities, and which assist persons in finding suitable work. A number of these manpower efforts use computer systems.

There is increasing concern about computerized data banks, containing extensive information about individuals, which may violate the constitutional rights of citizens to privacy. In this connection, organizations must be aware of this issue and how it might relate to data banks containing data about employees.

The computer has been used as a tool by employees in a number of sensational crimes, such as defalcations involving millions of dollars. The technical nature of such crimes may pose new problems to organizations and law enforcement officials.

Humanists, personnel staffs, and computer staffs have a considerable stake in the enlightened handling of these issues—both at the national level and in their own organizations. It is these broad issues, and how they are faced by leaders, that will largely determine the public's attitudes about the value of the computer to society. To date, the authors feel that the computer field has been less than effective in presenting a progressive and positive stance on these social issues.

Chapter 12, which follows, addresses itself to the staffing and organization of computer departments.

KEY CONCEPTS OF THE CHAPTER

1. The potential of the computer to change our style of life and work is considerable.

2. A coldly rational approach by computer technicians has undoubtedly created a widely held alienation of many people towards computers. Too little effort is made to bring a human touch to computer work.

3. Computerization and automation have caused considerable displacement of people, creating the need for extensive retraining and shifts of people into different occupations.

4. More attention should be devoted to developing ways of building human factors into computer systems. One theory that might be beneficially tested is that of including job enrichment concepts when designing new systems.

5. The federal government's computerized manpower systems that match jobs and applicants may serve as a nation-wide prototype that can help reduce unemployment.

6. The government and business organizations must be vigilant to assure that data banks are not violating the right to privacy of the individual, and that computer-related crimes receive necessary study by law enforcement experts so effective counter- and preventive-measures can be instituted.

DISCUSSION QUESTIONS

General Background (Seminar/Classroom Discussion)

1. What has made the issue of privacy and the computer of such strong public interest?
2. What type and degree of public intervention is necessary to attain socially desirable correction of some of the abuses attributed to computers (e.g., dehumanization, unemployment, invasion of privacy)?

Operational and Technical

1. Suggest ways that a computer department can overcome its image as a cold and mechanistic organization?
2. What role can personnel staffs play in computer projects to improve attainment of desirable social goals?
3. Consider your organization's controls over its personnel records. Are the controls adequate to protect against unauthorized access of records? How might the controls be made more secure?

Policy

1. Has top management considered the social responsibility issues raised by computer use? How do these social issues affect the particular organization?
2. Does your organization have formal policies and procedures that protect affected individuals during periods of technological change? For instance, what happens to an employee whose job is eliminated or downgraded by computerization?

Areas for Research

1. Ascertain what has happened to employees whose jobs have been absorbed by the computer. For instance, have they been retrained, moved to new jobs at a higher or lower level, taken early retirement, quit, been fired, etc. Talk with some of the employees. What are the reactions of the affected workers?
2. During your next computer application, try injecting a more "human touch" into the system. Try meaningfully to involve the persons who will be affected by the new system. Why can this approach make systems work more rewarding? Contrast the results of using the "human touch" with a project which followed a mechanistic path.

BIBLIOGRAPHY

Bowen, Howard R. and Garth L. Mangum. *Automation and Economic Progress.* Englewood Cliffs, New Jersey: Prentice-Hall, Inc., 1966.

Burke, John G., ed. *The New Technology and Human Values*. Belmont, California: Wadsworth Publishing Co., Inc., 1966.

Conference Board. Information Technology. New York: Conference Board, 1972.

Crosson, Frederick J. and Kenneth M. Sayre, eds. *Philosophy and Cybernetics*. Notre Dame, Indiana: University of Notre Dame Press, 1967.

Dechert, Charles R., ed. *The Social Impact of Cybernetics*. Notre Dame, Indiana: University of Notre Dame Press, 1966.

Harvard University. *Implications of Computer Technology*. Cambridge, Massachusetts: Harvard University Press, 1971.

Herzberg, Frederick, et al. *The Motivation to Work*. New York: John Wiley & Sons, Inc., 1959.

Kahn, Herman and Anthony J. Wiener. *The Year 2000*. New York: The Macmillan Company, 1967.

MacBride, Robert. *The Automated State*. Philadelphia: Chilton Book Co., 1967.

Martin, James and Adrian R. D. Norman. *The Computerized Society*. Englewood Cliffs, New Jersey: Prentice-Hall, Inc., 1970.

Mumford, Lois and Salkman. *Human Choice and Computers*. New York: North Holland Publishing Company, 1975.

National Commission on Technology, Automtion, and Economic Progress. *Technology and American Economy*. Washington, D.C.: U.S. Government Printing Office, 1966.

Silberman, Charles E. *The Myths of Automation*. New York: Harper & Row Publishers, Inc., 1966.

Taviss, Irene, ed. *The Computer Impact*. Englewood Cliffs, New Jersey: Prentice-Hall, Inc., 1970.

Terborgh, George. *The Automation Hysteria*. New York: W.W. Norton & Co. Inc., 1966.

Tomeski, Edward A. *The Computer Revolution*. New York: The Macmillan Company, 1970.

Tomeski, Edward A. *"Computer and Society Issues," in Computers in Business*. San Francisco: Holden-Day, Inc., 1979.

Walker, Charles R., ed. *Technology, Industry and Man*. New York: McGraw-Hill Book Co., 1968.

Westin, Alan F., ed. *Information Technology in a Democracy*. Cambridge, Massachusetts: Harvard University Press, 1971.

FOOTNOTES

[1] Herman Kahn and Anthony J. Wiener, *The Year 2000* (New York: The Macmillan Company, 1967), pp. 87–93.

[2] Harvey D. Shapiro, "IBM and All the Dwarfs," New York Times Magazine, July 29, 1973, pp. 10–11, 34–36.

[3] National Commission on Technology, Automation, and Economic Progress, *Technology and the American Economy* (Washington, D.C.: Government Printing Office, 1966), p. 109.

[4] Roy W. Walters and Kenneth Purdy, "Job Enrichment," *The Encyclopedia of Management*, ed., Carl Heyel (New York: Van Nostrand Reinhold Company, 1973), pp. 384–388.

[5] See the annual *Manpower Report of the President*, published by the U.S. Government Printing Office, available from 1963 on, which describe the evolution of these programs.

12

Organizing and Staffing the Computer Department

. . . the new utopians are concerned with non-people and with people substitutes. Their planning is done with computer hardware, systems procedures, functional analyses, and heuristics . . . The theoretical and practical solutions they seek call increasingly for decreases in the number and in the scope of responsibility of human beings within the operating structure of their new machines systems.

. . . the new utopians retain their aloofness from human and social problems presented by the fact or threat of machined systems and automation. They are concerned with neither souls nor stomachs. People problems are left to the after-the-facts efforts of social scientists.

Robert Boguslaw

OBJECTIVES OF THE CHAPTER

Organizational and staffing considerations in a computer facility are discussed. Particular attention is given to the need for maintaining and improving skills by providing training and educational programs for computer professionals and those affected by computers.

ORGANIZATIONAL STRUCTURE FOR COMPUTERS*

The organizational location of the computer function varies, depending upon such factors as: size of the organization, geographical dispersion, degree of delegation of authority, etc. However, two generalizations seem appropriate to the authors:

- The computer function should be apart from any traditional function.

- The computer function should report directly to a top administrator.

---

* The nomenclature given for the unit responsible for the computer activities varies. Some of the more frequent names used are: computer department, data processing department, management information systems department, automatic data processing department, among others.

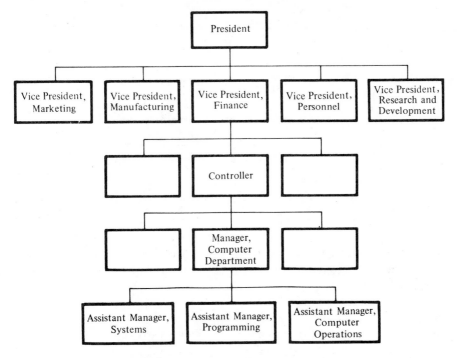

Figure 12-1   Traditional organization structure of computer function.

Traditionally, the computer used for business data processing was under the direction of the financial executive; this is still the most prevalent situation (Figure 12-1). Organizations with substantial engineering and scientific staffs usually provided separate computer facilities for such functions.

Today there is a trend towards placing the computer resource under an independent administrative executive (e.g., vice president, administration). (See Figure 12-2.) The reasoning here is that such a move will encourage diverse functional areas (marketing, manufacturing, personnel, etc.) of the organization to utilize computer services. When the computer function is under the financial executive, most applications tend to be of an accounting nature; this can impede other functional areas from utilizing the computer.

The problem of parochialism in having the computer within the jurisdiction of a single department was further compounded by having it, in many cases, report to a relatively low management level (e.g., assistant controller). However, experience has shown that for most effective use of computers, the manager in direct charge of the computer resources should report to someone of top management stature. This is necessary to gain acceptance of the

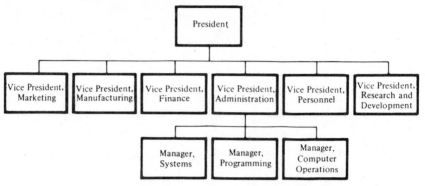

Figure 12-2   Emerging organization structure of computer function.

relatively new discipline and the change that is often inherent in its mission. And, of course, the independent status of a vice-president for administration facilitates the crossing of departmental barriers which is necessary in integrated MIS.

Figure 12-3 presents a position guide for a director of a management information and systems department. It is apparent from the description that the position calls for a highly competent executive capable of leadership and very broad organization-wide challenges.

"Technician Syndrome"

There has been a tendency to place technicians in the top managerial posts in computer departments. This has often not proven a successful experience. Computer departments are frequently significant budget items of an organization and, further, they are central service units for all parts of the organization. The managers of the computer department should, in addition to having a good grounding in computer technology and systems work, be competent administrators. The primary tasks of such managers are usually not of a technical nature; their main tasks are usually related to:

- Prudent allocation of resources that invariably are in short supply, and budgetary control of operations.

- Coordination with the diverse users of the computer facility.

- Development and retention of a competent staff.

- Planning to keep the organization abreast of computer developments.

- Justification (rate-of-return on investment) of proposed new or expanded computer installations or applications.

While not neglecting the internal computer department situation, the computer manager must continuously be aware of the various computer users' needs, expectations, and complaints. Since the computer manager's primary responsibility is to satisfy users' requirements, the manager must have a good grasp of the total organization's goals, operations, and basic policies.

Coordination

In large organizations a number of computers may be distributed among headquarters, divisions, subsidiaries, etc. (The largest organization, the federal government, has approximately 6,000 computers!) The computer installations may be located in decentralized locations and even overseas. The tightness of coordination of such dispersed computer facilities differs for different organizations; however, the headquarters' computer department usually serves as the coordination point. In the federal government, with thousands of computers located in many parts of the world, the ultimate coordination is exercised by three central units (Office of Management and Budget, General Service Administration, and the Department of Commerce's Bureau of Standards). These three units are respectively responsible for setting policy, procurement practices, and standards for all of the federal government's computer facilities. Such coordination facilitates an organization-wide approach to computers and information systems and interchangeability of computers, staffs, and computer programs, and makes for more effective negotiations with computer and software vendors.

STAFFING CHALLENGES

Staffing for the computer function is one of the most challenging activities of the personnel department. This is true for a number of reasons:

- The demand for well-trained and highly experienced computer personnel (particularly systems analysts and programmers) continues to exceed available supply. This was discussed in Chapter 7.

- As a consequence, there has been a pattern of high mobility of computer technicians. The turnover of systems analysts and programmers is likely to continue to be relatively high. One study indicated that this field has a turnover of about 21 per cent.[1]

- Developments in the high technology computer industry necessitate constant attention lest the computer staff become obsolete. There is need for close contact with sources of technicians as well as an active training and educational program.

Position Title—Director of Management Information and Systems Department

Reports to—Vice President, Administration

Function—Directs the Management Information and Systems Department in its development and application of business systems, technical computation, and management science essential to the company's continuing growth and profitability. Seeks out and develops techniques which facilitate management decisions and which contribute to the improvement of the company's competitive position.

Directs the department's efforts to provide effective commercial information systems and technical data processing including: computer programming, operating computer centers (at corporate headquarters and at other sites, worldwide), applying of mathematical methods, supporting communications systems (excluding mail and printed media), supplying management science assistance, and selecting computer and peripheral equipment.

Provides to company executives and to divisions and central departments specialized talents, assistance, and facilities in the foregoing areas. Evaluates the economic and other benefits of existing and proposed business systems, data processing programs, and communications systems (leased lines, radio systems and other equipment for voice, message, and data transmission and receipt) and monitors their continuing feasibility. Conducts a continuous program of education for all levels of management in these assigned areas. Coapproves with concerned members of operating management personnel assignments in his functional area of responsibility.

Duties

1. Plans and develops major programs and procedures for the effective coordination of functions and administration of the MISD. Orients MISD effort toward profit improvement through better business systems and more effective information processing.

2. Directs and coordinates business and applied mathematics functions and data processing and communications operations at the headquarters site and at regional centers in this country and overseas. Exercises functional direction over other computer, data processing, and communications systems and equipment throughout the company.

3. Directs the coordination of division and plant data processing and communication operations with the MISD data processing and communication operations and/or overall company requirements.

4. Directs data processing research activities, including analysis and solution of operating problems using data processing applications, design and installation of data processing systems,

Figure 12-3 Position Guide: Director, Management Information and Systems Department (A divisionalized chemical company). (Harold Stieglitz, "The Management Information Systems Unit," *The Conference Board Record*, October 1968, p. 35.)

supervision of programming of computer applications, analyses using operations research techniques and maintenance of a central information service for long-range planning and research into improved systems.

5. Directs communications systems research activities, including analysis and solution of operating problems, design and installation of communications systems, supervision of programming of communication systems applications and maintenance of a central information service for long-range planning and research into improved systems.

6. Obtains all Federal Communications Commission radio licenses (except for aircraft) required in the divisions and central departments and advises management throughout the company on operation of licensed radio systems in conformance with F.C.C. rules and regulations.

7. Consults with appropriate division and central department executives in the development, evaluation, and use of communications systems to meet the needs of the company.

8. Establishes codification, procedural and programming standards to be used uniformly throughout the company where necessary to serve corporate purposes; educates and instructs personnel throughout the company in understanding and use of such standards where required.

9. Consults with, advises and provides support to manufacturing, engineering, research and marketing representatives in the development of systems and application of data processing and mathematical techniques and communication systems for effective solution of technical and scientific problems and applications to manufacturing processes, quality control and other operating analysis and control areas.

10. Reviews and approves the schedules and implementation priorities of data processing and communications systems at all company locations. Approves, after evaluation, acquisition of major items of data processing equipment and communications hardware.

11. Approves all company requests for acquisition of data processing, computational and communication facilities; serves as the principal company contact with vendors of data processing and communications equipment and services; obtains required licenses for operation of company owned or leased radio communications systems.

12. Develops forward management information systems planning in keeping with planned company growth; develops policy recommendations regarding acquisition, usage and operating standards for the company's data processing activities.

Figure 12-3 (**Continued**)

- The foregoing make it particularly important to be sensitive to morale in computer departments and to do everything possible to maintain and improve motivation and loyalty.

Skills

A variety of different skills are required in a computer department. Figure 12-4 describes typical jobs found in the department. Of course, in a particular organization the position title may be somewhat different (e.g., systems engineer rather than systems analyst, or operations researcher rather than management scientist). Also, the general functions may differ from organization to organization. For instance, it is not rare that one technician will perform both the systems analysis and programming functions. This is particularly true in the organizations having a small computer staff, where the specialization that is possible in large organizations is not economically feasible.

Position	General Function
Systems Analyst/ Systems Designer	Analyzes existing organizational structure, activities, procedures, etc. Develops improved and new structures, activities, procedures, etc. Designs and guides implementation of improved systems and new systems.
Management Scientist	The management scientist normally concentrates effort on problems involving higher level mathematical skills, while performing tasks similar to the systems analyst.
Computer Programmer	An individual skilled in computer programming languages. Develops computer programs understandable to the computer equipment for improved systems and new ones.
Computer Operator	A person trained to operate any one of several pieces of equipment comprising the computer system.
Keypunch Operator	A person trained to operate a typewriter-like device used to prepare programs and data for input to the computer.
Control Clerk	Maintains controls of input data and computer output, in order to maximize accuracy and integrity of data processing.

Figure 12-4   Types of personnel in computer departments.

Dilemma of a Balanced Staff

Attaining a balanced computer staff can present a dilemma. Usually an organization needs particularly heavy computer support during peak periods (e.g., when getting a new computer, or converting from one computer to another). Some organizations have developed large staffs to cope with such conditions and then faced the problem of reducing the staff or reassigning the people to marginal projects or other parts of the organization.

Some organizations supplement their own staffs with outside assistance; a growing number of service and consulting firms offer a wide variety of computer-related capabilities to clients. These firms take on assignments on a fixed fee basis (if the job is well-defined) or otherwise on a daily or even hourly basis.

The disadvantages of the outside service approach are: loss by the company of real supervisory control, apparent higher cost, and a partial loss of the insights gained once the outside contractor completes the job and departs. On the other hand, the use of an outside contractor has some distinct advantages: the organization does not have to commit itself to a large internal staff, new perspectives are brought to the problem area, highly specialized experts can be obtained, independent judgment can be expected, and the organization's staff may be stimulated by the outside influence.

Recruitment

Sources of trained people are: computer manufacturers, employment agencies and executive recruiters (some of which now specialize in computer personnel), professional and technical societies, technical training institutes, universities and colleges and, of course, people working as computer technicians for other organizations. One has merely to scan the help wanted advertisements in newspapers and journals to be convinced of the large demand for computer-oriented personnel.

Besides the obvious attractions of salary, benefits, and locations, computer professionals and technicians are interested in organizations having:

- A professional reputation for leadership in computer use.

- Outstanding computer staffs from whom they can learn and so upgrade their own skills.

- Computer equipment that challenges the individual's technical ability.

- Stimulating computer plans and projects that will result in interesting assignments.

- An active and continuing training effort so that the staff can keep up with changes in the field.

- Adequate promotional paths.

- An organizational environment that provides acceptance for change and acceptance of the computer department's mission.

Selection

There is a wide range of quality in computer personnel. There are the relatively rare systems analysts and computer programmers, who not only have excellent command over the techniques of their field but who also understand the realities of organizations' operations and the relevance of the social system. The majority of computer practitioners primarily offer a command of some narrow aspect of computer technology, with limited sensitivities to an organization's operations and social system. Careful selection is needed to match the computer department's *real* staffing needs with the people available in the market. It is as unrewarding to hire a superior analyst for a mundane task as it is to hire a mediocre analyst for a complex assignment. Selection of personnel can be sharpened in the following ways:

- Multiple interviews and evaluation of applicants by several individuals.

- Careful reference checks from responsible persons knowing the applicant's technical capabilities, past performance, and organizational loyalties.

- Use of aptitude tests or related examinations.

- Assessment of academic work.

- Solution of short simulated computer problems by applicants.

From the applicant's side, the organization should be as candid as possible about the realities of the job being offered. Too often people take positions with mistaken ideas about the position, the opportunities, the limitations, and the organization involved.

A majority of the research on selection instruments for computer personnel has been devoted to designing or validating tests to predict success as a programmer. The apparent qualifications needed for the successful programmer are above-average intelligence, a logical mind, analytical ability, and an almost compulsive need for accuracy in detail. Also important are the ability to work under pressure and to work with people.

Several widely used tests for computer technicians are available. These include:

- IBM's Programmer Aptitude Test (PAT), which has been revised several times. It has three parts: number series, figure analogies, and arithmetic reasoning.
- General Aptitude Test Battery (GATB).
- Watson-Glaser Critical-Thinking Appraisal.

Several professional organizations in the computer field (e.g., Association for Computing Machinery, Data Processing Management Association) developed a method for testing and certifying computer personnel; to do this, an Institute for Certification of Computer Personnel (ICCP) has been established. The Educational Testing Service has also established tests to determine level of computer comprehension; such tests are increasingly used by colleges and universities where, in some cases, students must exhibit some basic competency in computer use.

Tests are of obvious value as an initial screening device for applicants. However, if an employer wishes to know how useful any given test is for selecting potential computer personnel for his own organization, there must be a validation of the instrument planned for use within the organization.

Evaluation

As with selection, many organizations have had difficulty in evaluating computer professionals and technicians. The ideal performance appraisal exists when the criteria, or demands of the job, can be objectively rated, are clearly understood by the employee, and the results of supervisory ratings are openly communicated at the end of each rating period. This requires three sets of information: Information about what the worker does on the job (the job description), about the standards required (management expectations), and finally, about how well the worker attains the standards set (performance appraisal). Too often, management's expectations are not clear or formalized, causing appraisal decisions to be arbitrary and inconsistent.

One of the chief methods of evaluation is a results-oriented review of the work of personnel. Adherence to work schedules and customer satisfaction with work performed are, of course, two key criteria of work well performed.

The U.S. Department of Agriculture uses the following criteria for rating its computer personnel:

- Carrying out assignments
  Performing tasks accurately
  Taking responsibility and initiating action
  Responding to need for extra effort

- Working with others
  Cooperating with others
  Getting along with others

- Planning and organizing work
  Motivating subordinates
  Training and developing subordinates
  Maintaining communications

It is interesting to note the heavy weight given to interpersonal relations in the evaluation of computer personnel; technical proficiency is not even explicitly identified as a criterion.

Weinberg's recent work gives promise that additional insight will be developing about the behavioral factors of computer personnel.

All too often we look at computer programming as a machine activity that just happens to involve human beings. This book inaugurates a radically new point of view by depicting the human element in computer programming—man over machine. It investigates, in detail and for the first time, the actual behavior and thought processes of programmers as they carry out their daily activities.[2]

EDUCATION FOR COMPUTER PROFESSIONALS

Increasingly, students in high schools (and even in some elementary schools), and colleges and universities are being given some background in computers. Some education is very broad (e.g., "Computer and Society") while other training is very specific (e.g., "Programming in the FORTRAN Language") and utilitarian. There is an increased requirement that students must have computer proficiency to attain entrance in some institutions (e.g., graduate schools of business). Computer training has long been accepted as necessary in certain fields such as mathematics, engineering, science, education, and business. Interest is growing in fields where it once was thought that the computer did not have much applicability; such fields include: medicine, social sciences, law, and others.

With college education so readily available to the general population, it is to be expected that most computer professionals will be college graduates. The analytical nature of the work, the requirement of being able to communicate with managers and others about business problems, and the need for continuing education—demand that such personnel be above average in ability and background.

In addition to formal educational background, the computer staff requires continuing training to remain abreast of the technical developments in the field. Such training can be obtained from various sources: internal training programs, courses offered by computer vendors, seminars conducted by professional societies (e.g., Association for Computing Machinery, Association for Systems Management, American Management Association), continuing education extensions of colleges and universities, and programmed instruction materials. These latter materials can be used by an individual in independent study or as part of one of the training programs identified.

Formalized Education in Computers

The Association for Computing Machinery (ACM) has made recommendations for graduate education in information systems (a number of colleges and universities already offer degrees—including at the Master's and Doctoral levels—in computer-related fields). It is encouraging that these recommendations give definitive recognition to the importance of human factors. The ACM report recommends that a Master's degree in information systems should consist of the following thirteen courses:

Course Group A: Analysis of Organizational Systems
  A1. Introduction to Systems Concepts
  A2. Organizational Functions
  A3. Information Systems for Operations and Management
  A4. Social Implications of Information Systems
Course Group B: Background for Systems Development
  B1. Operations Analysis and Modeling
  B2. Human and Organizational Behavior
Course Group C: Computer and Information Technology
  C1. Information Structures
  C2. Computer Systems
  C3. File and Communication Systems
  C4. Software Design
Course Group D: Development of Information Systems
  D1. Information Analysis
  D2. System Design
  D3. Systems Development Projects.[3]

The course relationships, recommended by ACM, are depicted in Figure 12-5. The recognition of the need to include attention to the social system in the education program is very apparent.

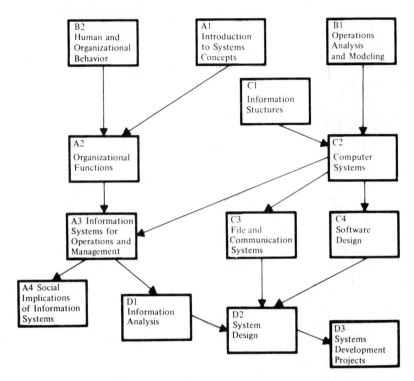

Figure 12-5   Relationship of information systems courses. (Adapted from R. L. Ashenhurst, ed., "Curriculum Recommendations for Graduate Professional Programs in Information Systems," *Communications of the ACM*, May 1972, p. 373.)

Ashenhurst indicates that:

Perhaps the most difficult task in program coordination is that of integrating the material on human behavior . . . with the rest of the curriculum material . . . If the program turns out practitioners who ignore or only pay lip service to the 'people problems'—which most experts agree pervade the information systems milieu of today—it will not have realized its aims.[4]

Internal Training Programs

To assure that employees can cope with increasingly sophisticated computers and applications, there is need for:

· Administrators who are sufficiently knowledgeable about the broad implications and potentials of computers to provide positive leadership to their staffs in the use of computers, and to be able to communicate what they wish to obtain from the computers.

- Technicians (systems analysts, computer programmers, computer operators, etc.) who are abreast of the dynamic advances in the computer field to assure sound and imaginative applications.

- Employees, as a whole, who are adequately briefed concerning the objectives of the computer plans and how they might be affected, to dispel fears of change and to gain their cooperation.

With respect to the last-named, proper indoctrination will increase the likelihood of acceptance and understanding for progressive use of computers. Conversely, lack of knowledge about computers can create negative results in terms of low morale, poor computer utilization, and unsatisfactory progress. While recognizing the truth of the above, under the pressure of "getting the job done," an administrator will frequently indicate his agreement about the desirability for training and yet contend that "there is no time for it!"

In addition to indoctrination, there must be a positive program with respect to all employees who might be displaced by computerization. In addition, there should be a program for training qualified people for computer-related positions. The training program can thus provide a path for upgrading some members of the organization. Obviously, an adequate training effort will minimize the number of people who must be recruited from outside. It goes without saying that outside recruiting for higher-paying computer-oriented positions can have an adverse impact on the morale of current employees.

In some instances it may not be possible to train people from within the organization, since many individuals do not have the aptitudes required for computer positions. However, an organization will do well to screen and give aptitude tests to existing personnel before seeking employees from outside sources. Insiders know the organization and its operations to a certain degree, and are more likely than outsiders to have loyalty to the organization. However, unqualified, old-time employees should not be foisted onto the computer department; such action can create a graveyard of mediocrity rather than a greenhouse for developing valuable talent.

An important point to keep in mind is that the apparently undeveloped road to general administration for computer personnel in many organizations can discourage some qualified, ambitious individuals from entering the field. There are some recent isolated instances of computer people attaining the top positions in business firms, government departments, and colleges and universities.

It should be apparent by now that training in the computer field is not a luxury. The following discussion between two employees will reinforce the need for adequate training:

Don said to Ray, "They want us to design sophisticated management information systems, but they don't even explain what is meant by MIS. I asked to go to a course about advanced systems techniques, and the boss said there wasn't time. He said 'get a good book on the subject, and read it on your own time.' "

Ray answered, "I am suppose to build some sophisticated mathematical techniques into my computer program about acquisition analysis. That's not my bag. I am told to do something for which I am not qualified. It's ridiculous."

The following series of internal training courses, developed for one organization, may be used as a general guide:

Technical Systems Courses
    Basic Systems Course
    Advanced Systems Course
    Systems Management Course

Technical Programming Courses
    Basic Programming Course
    Advanced Programming Course
    Programming Management Course

Computer Operations Courses
    Basic Operations Course
    Advanced Operations Course
    Operations Management Course

Non-technical Computer Courses
    Computers for Non-technical Personnel
    Computers for Supervision
    Computers for Management

While such a comprehensive training effort may be pertinent primarily to a large organization engaged in a major computer effort, an organization of any size can establish a training program on a scale suitable for its purposes.

The personnel department should assume an active service role in such a training effort. This should include:

- Determining and selecting eligible candidates for training.

- Scheduling courses and obtaining facilities.

- Conducting aptitude tests.

- Establishing testing procedures.

- Recording course completion, withdrawal, etc., by attendees.

- Assisting with pedagogical techniques.

· Evaluating training effort.

· Following-up to determine attendees' development as a result of training.

MOTIVATION AND THE SYSTEMS PROFESSIONAL*

Many systems professionals are dissatisfied with their jobs, for they ARE DEAD END ONES! By definition, a profession is a specialized field which (a) requires considerable training and education, and which is represented by colleges/universities offering degrees in the field (e.g., PhD in MIS, MS in Computer Science) and (b) which is represented by aknowledged professional societies/ publications (e.g., Association for Systems Management). Job satisfaction which contributes to productivity for the systems professionals is discussed extensively in articles and at meetings, but no answer to this issue has yet been found. Not only is this a concern for programmers and analysts, but also the MIS executives feel the same way[5]. Everyone wants to go ahead, almost everyone, but there is a minority which does not care about moving into management or moving into other areas within an organization. Within this minority are two groups. The first one, which is the majority within this minority, feels comfortable in what they are doing. They don't want any more responsibilities, or just don't want to learn something new; perhaps some of them wait for retirement.

The second group, the minority within the minority, are the professionals who do want to develop, but don't care for a management position. They are the core of any profession; they are more interested in contributing and advancing the profession. This article discusses this very special group which is very important for any organization and for the continuance of a profession, and their relationship to management. The following discussion does not limit itself to the systems profession but it holds true for all professions (Figure 12-6).

It is suggested that in many business professions there are a large number of transients. For instance, in a systems staff there are many who are barely earning a living—but who would be very interested in a promotion/new job at a managerial level which would bring them higher income and/or prestige/power. This situation is particularly true for young systems personnel including those just graduating from colleges and universities, and who enter the systems field; they are quite susceptible to opportunities, even those outside of their specialization. Of course, every profession has its marginal or low producers. Some of these marginal persons are tolerated, particularly if they have seniority in the organization; others use finesse to escape detection (i.e., team work, prevalent in

*Adapted from the author's article "Job Satisfaction and the Systems Professional", Journal of Systems Management, June 1980.

many systems projects, can hide individual ineptness). Last, as Figure 12-6 indicates there is a small number of core professionals who are dedicated to their technical profession. This article focuses on these persons in the systems field.

A Profile of Systems Staff

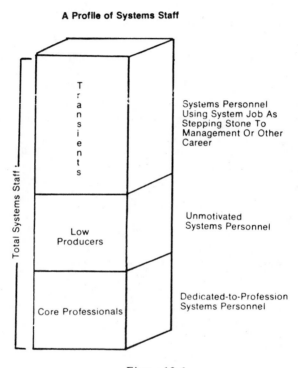

Figure 12-6

Management and Technical Professionals

Many seek a profession so they can be recognized by their peers, and perhaps most see in it economic security. Most organizations hire professionals for their more complex tasks, but it is also recognized that being hired as a technical-professional does not guarantee that one advances faster than a generalist. Some professionals with excellent specialized educational and practical know-how are frozen into their profession, and not infrequently a generalist is promoted to a more senior executive position. The systems professional who is forced to stay within his profession, and is not being promoted, is frustrated. For he feels that he has contributed to the organization's goals and is more capable of handling greater responsibilities than the generalist who gets promoted and who often gets more financial rewards. After all, some top general managers are getting around $1 million a year in compensation when one takes into account base salary and extra compensation. It is likely that some managers of MIS/Systems/Computers may be receiving salaries up to $50,000 to $70,000 per year. On the other hand, systems technicians are not likely to have any hope of earning much more than say $30,000 per year.

The art of managing and being a technical professional are two distinctly different professional paths. One can be excellent in one of these two professions but fail miserably in the other. Figure 12-7 illustrates the different job satisfactions which can be obtained by individuals. It would be well for an organization to know where each of its systems employees stand on such a grid. The organization could then develop paths for either (a) satisfying the employee's needs and thus increasing productivity and/or (b) redesigning the organizational variables to lead to greater productivity (i.e., training programs, job rotation, etc.).

**JOB SATISFACTION GRID FOR SYSTEMS
PROFESSIONALS**

Note: Adapted from the works of Robert Blake and Jane Mouten.

Figure 12-7

Too frequently a technically very competent person gets promoted to a management position for which he is not suited. The organization feels that if he is not promoted it will lose a technically well-qualified person, one who is a great resource to the organization. The organization has no plan, or it has not recognized one, of promoting and keeping the technical professional other than giving him a management position. Hence, when a technically oriented professional (e.g., systems analyst, accountant, engineer, etc., who does not manage human resources) is promoted to a management position for which he is not suited, he will bring harm to his career, the department which he should manage and the rest of the organization. No department is an island within the rest of the organization. All departments interrelate and have to complement each other for the continuance of an organization. If a department does not contribute to an organization's welfare, the department's need to exist will be decided by top management at one of their meetings.

A technically competent person who has been promoted to management, for which he is not suited, will find out sooner or later that he has made the wrong decision. He may start to criticize his staff, blames other departments for all of his shortcomings, and is very frustrated in everything he does. Naturally his staff starts to suffer, which affects other departments, and the total organization. His staff, realizing that he is unable to manage, will ask for transfers or leave the organization. The turnover of staff within the department might become great. Furthermore, each time a new member joins the department he has to go through a learning process (curve) until he is able to contribute to the department's productivity. The efficiency of the department, as well as the total organization, will suffer while he is going through a learning process. The cost of replacing a good employee may be in the range of $10,000 to $50,000 or more. This cost involves: loss of know-how, recruiting costs, a period of relatively reduced productivity during the period of training a new employee, etc.

One of the tragedies is that many competent professionals who attempt to work for this incompetent manager leave the organization before anything is done. Consequently, the organization's reputation within the industry suffers. The word goes around that firm X has a very poor MIS department and competent systems professionals do not want to associate themselves with the firm. The organization loses many technically well-qualified professionals who rather leave than work for this manager.

No one wants to be demoted, consequently the technically very competent person, whom is a failure in management, starts to look for another organization. When the manager leaves, or is fired, the management position has to be filled. It may take months or years to rebuild the MIS department before it can become a department from which the organization starts to receive benefits.

By the time the incompetent manager realizes that managing is not for him and attempts to go back into his profession, which he left years ago, he finds himself outdated. The technical proficiency he had many years ago is unacceptable today and since he is too old or does not want to be retrained, he has to stay in management the rest of his working life. Figure 12-8 shows the different characteristics of the systems and management professionals.

Too few organizations use realistic selection techniques to determine those who should be promoted. One method which offers promise is the assessment center concept where prospective candidates for new positions are carefully

Difference in Systems and Management Professionals

Systems Professional Characteristics	Management Professional Characteristics
• Technically oriented	• Management oriented
• Specialized interests	• Broad, general interests
• Problem solution oriented	• Action oriented
• Deals with all levels about problems	• Deals mostly with peers and upward
• Professional leadership based on competency	• Leadership partly based on authority
• Avoids politics and seeks best answer	• High degree of politics in job
• Tries to obtain opinions of others	• May make sole decisions or decisions with few management colleagues
• May like to work alone on some phases of project	• Must delegate to be effective

Figure 12-8

studied, under simulated realistic conditions, to determine their suitability for new positions. Such an assessment center approach should help in determining those persons who are not likely to succeed in management positions.[6]

The Dedicated "Professional"

A person may be satisfied with his position for many reasons, e.g., he will retire shortly and hence does not want his present work habits changed; technically he realizes that he has reached his level of competency (or level of incompetency per Peter's principles); or does not want any more challenges. Perhaps there are other reasons for not wanting more responsibilities, like extra hours which he must work when being promoted; not wanting to mediate conflicts, etc.

These are only a few examples, but many professionals feel very comfortable and secure with what they are doing and have no need to advance or seek new challenges as long as the present environment does not change.

The core of any profession, the minority within the minority which does not care to be promoted, are the ones which enjoy their work (i.e. work has become a hobby) and are more concerned in contributing to advancing the profession to which they belong. These professionals realize that the very moment they get promoted to management, even if they remain to lead fellow professionals, it is another branch of a profession. Take for example, a systems analyst whose main interest is to design and implement the best possible information system. If he becomes a manager of MIS, his responsibilities are to manage the MIS resources so that the organization receives the greatest benefits from it. But managing MIS resources if very different from designing a system. Managing people is to assu an organization which not necessarily fulfill the needs and wants of the individual member within the organization. Whereas in designing a system one works with other members of an organization to assure that the best possible system is designed which meets the systems user's needs and wants as well as the organization's objectives. The systems analyst is a member of a team, but he does not control it.

The professional does not want to be promoted because he is not capable of being a manager or dislikes administrative responsibilities, but he feels that his main function is for example, to design systems which benefit the organization. His technical know-how is very deep and he prides himself in it. Another way he can contribute is that he assists junior systems professionals so that they can learn from him and become good professionals. He is a leader and sets standards for others. When one of these junior professionals succeeds and receives recognition, the professional takes pride in it and feels joy that he was part of making this junior a leader. This professional is a leader not only withinin the organization he works for but also to the profession and society. The professional is also very active within his profession. He looks at new theories, tries to apply them and reports the success or failures of the applications so that the researchers can continue to enhance their work. He may even do his own applied research and report his findings. These professionals are needed since they are the ones who can translate theories into practice; they are a very special breed of people.

It is very difficult to translate theories into practice. A professional is one who sees his lifetime purpose in serving his professional community; without him the profession might decline or die.

A systems analyst may have been working for years in an area, has done his own research and may be more knowledgeable than the director of MIS in a specific area. The director of MIS may have implemented his last system five years ago, but since then approaches and theories have changed. The director of MIS speaks only out of a theoretical knowledge (i.e. what he reads about this subject in journals) or what he has done five years ago, which is outdated now. The systems analyst, on the other hand, speaks out of wisdom which combines theory, application and a very deep understanding of how the organization works. The director of MIS deals with people in his level of the hierarchy of the organization, whereas the systems analyst deals with all levels of the organization. Hence, when it comes to systems implementation, the systems analyst is really the one who has the greater knowledge.

A good professional also recognizes that in order to grow in his professional know-how, he has to go through hardships and is willing to accept them. He knows that through hardships one learns. He keeps an open mind through his trials and tribulations, for he knows if one does not stay objective he will become a cynic: one who criticizes everything and everyone. It is very important that the professional respect himself, for if he does not have self confidence in what he is doing it will affect his work. The professional listens to others, since if he becomes full of pride he may become arrogant and starts to ignore others.

A professional evaluates himself continually and in doing so evaluates his own work and seeks to improve it. Through this continuous self-examination, he attempts to find a better way of doing his work, or the work which benefits others. If he stands still and becomes part of the group of people who reached their level of incompetency, he is no more part of the professionals which seek to improve their professional knowledge.

Furthermore, a professional knows when his work at an organization is completed, i.e., when he realizes that he cannot contribute to the organization's welfare, or the proposals he recommends are not followed. He sees that he is wasting his time and hence he has to move on to another organization which needs his talents. It can become very frustrating to one who is seeking challenges to find out that the present organization does not care in advancing itself or developing its professionals.

Need for Organization Redesign

The systems professional who wants to remain within his job, i.e., does not care if he is promoted, is one who sees his main purpose as contributing to the profession. But many professionals and many organizations feel that one must get promoted to a management position, for if one does not want to be a manager he is not ambitious. This reflects itself in many organizations when the annual review time rolls around, or when one wants to change jobs. One of the authors had many experiences where he had to explain in length why he wanted to stay within his profession and did not want to be promoted to management. He frequently received the feeling and impressions that the interviewers thought he was not ambitious, or something was wrong with him. The organizations seldom recognized the contributions he made to an organization and the profession.

Many organizations put more emphasis on titles and how much one earns when one is interviewed for a job, as if they reveal the level responsibility. There is little relationship between these two variables and the job one performs. Some professionals continually seek jobs which are challenging and which will contribute in their growth. That is, sometimes they accept positions which are financially not as rewarding but which have great challenges. However, this is not recognized by many organizations. As a professional recognizes this, he may become a cynic, since he feels that he wasted many years and the know-how he gained. He becomes frustrated and loses his objectivity and purpose as to why he wanted to remain in the profession. He may become closed-minded and perhaps stop serving the organization and the profession.

An organization should and must recognize the contribution of a professional and find a way of recognizing his services by promotion and financial rewards. Some organizations have recognized these valuable human resources and have promoted them to internal consultants, consultants who serve the organization as well as the profession. New members of the profession and newly added staff in the organization receive great insight and wisdom from this consultant and learn great insight of how the organization functions. He can be called upon to do many difficult tasks, probe the latest theories and find out if they are workable. The organization, the researchers, as well as the profession benefit from this activity. They are indispensable members of the organization and the profession. Too frequently this valuable resource is ignored by organizations and by professions. Organizations feel it is cheaper to replace the competent person since he does not want to be promoted to a management post.

Professionals (e.g., systems analysts, management scientists, etc.) who must interface very heavily with all members of an organization, should be kept by an organization. The special relationship, and the respect the consultant earned over many years with all in the organization, is a valuable asset for any MIS department. The users listen to him, respect and feel very confident in his judgments. The professional brings stability into any MIS department.

Concluding Comments

Organizations should make a special effort to assist professionals who want to become very good specialists in their area of interests, e.g., materials management systems, to achieve their goal. When this goal has been achieved an organization should try to keep and promote the specialist to an inside consultant. This promotion will give a special status to the professional and the need of promoting to a management position or to a position outside the MIS area will not arise. He should be encouraged to interact within his profession, e.g., attend seminars and keep abreast with the newest developments. Perhaps he should be encouraged to do his own applied research. When this is accomplished, not only has the professional attained his goal and is satisfied with his career but also an organization, the profession, the researchers and society will benefit from him.

More attention must be devoted to advanced human resource techniques (assessment centers) to better understand the interest and attitudes of systems personnel, and to assess their potential. This potential may be to (a) become managers, (b) transfer to a non-management job outside of systems, or (c) develop into a highly qualified and valuable systems professional. At this time, most systems and MIS departments seem to take a "hit or miss" approach to knowing and understanding the things that motivate or "turn on" the individual systems person. Until this is corrected, our profession is likely to have more transients than dedicated systems professionals, which will limit the degree of influence of the systems field in the business community as well as the rewards given to systems persons.

SUMMARY

An organization with a powerful computer, but with a mediocre staff, will certainly not attain great success in computer operations. On the other hand, an organization with modest computer resources but with a skilled and highly motivated staff is likely to experience success in its use of computers.

Too much attention is directed to the technical aspects of computer systems, and not enough attention is devoted to one of the key elements in successful computer systems; i.e., the people who plan, design, develop, and install the applications processed by the computer.

The computer department should be so positioned as to provide it with the visibility and recognition needed to service computer users throughout the organization.

A vigorous personnel program is needed which integrates recruitment, selection, training, development, appraisal, and motivation of the computer staff. Without vigorous leadership, talented staffs, and high morale—computer departments will have continued difficulty in attaining the promises that have been delineated for the computer profession.

Chapter 13, which follows, describes some of the major aspects of designing an integrated personnel system.

KEY CONCEPTS OF THE CHAPTER

1. A computer department should, preferably, report directly to a member of top management. The computer activity is a central service and should not be organizationally positioned within one of the narrower functions (e.g., finance) that is a user of the central service.

2. Administrative skills and leadership qualities are more critical for success in managing computer resources than are technical skills.

3. Effective use of computers is highly dependent on a competent computer staff. Maintaining such a qualified staff is particularly troublesome because of the shortage of skilled systems analysts and computer programmers, and the problem is often compounded by lack of clear promotional paths.

4. Because of the dynamic nature of the computer field, it is essential to provide a continuous training program to maintain and strengthen the skills of the computer staff. There is need for training in interpersonal skills as well as technical ones.

5. Besides training computer technicians, it is often desirable to provide indoctrination for users in the capabilities and limitations of applying computers in work areas.

6. A retraining effort is needed to take care of those employees whose jobs are affected, or displaced by computerization.

DISCUSSION QUESTIONS

General Background (Seminar/Classroom Discussion)

1. What kinds of personality characteristics and skills do you think are required for a person to be a successful systems analyst? To be a successful computer programmer?
2. Why are there frequently great difficulties in staffing a computer department?

Operational and Technical

1. Do you feel that your organization provides you with the training needed to remain abreast of new developments in computer technology? How might existing training efforts be improved?
2. What suggestions do you have that might improve the motivation, morale, and productivity of the computer staff? Why haven't such ideas been adopted?

Policy

1. How might the organizational arrangement of your company's computer department be modified to improve its service to all parts of the firm? What prevents such new organizational patterns?
2. Is the manager of your computer and systems efforts primarily a technical expert or an administrator? Why are administrative skills so important in such a position?
3. Does your organization have a continuing training effort to prepare managers and workers to cope with new technology such as the computer? Why are such training programs desirable?

Areas for Research

1. Determine the turnover rate in your company for systems analysts and computer programmers. How does the rate compare with the company's overall turnover rate? How does it compare with other organizations? Try to explain any significant differences.
2. Study the training and educational curriculum in computers offered by your organization or local colleges/universities. How many courses in the curriculum are technical in nature? How many courses deal with administrative, social, and people-related issues in computer systems? What conclusions do you draw from your findings? What recommendations do you have about how the curriculum can be improved?

BIBLIOGRAPHY

Canning, Richard and Roger Sisson. *A Manager's Guide to Computer Processing.* New York: John Wiley & Sons, Inc., 1967.

Dickmann, Robert A. *Personnel Implications for Business Data Processing.* New York: John Wiley & Sons, Inc., 1971.

Orlicky, Joseph. *The Successful Computer System.* New York: McGraw-Hill Book Co., 1969.

Reichenbach, Robert R. and Charles A. Tasso. *Organizing for Data Processing.* New York: American Management Association, 1968.

Tomeski, Edward A. *The Computer Revolution.* New York: The Macmillan Company, 1970.

Tomeski, Edward A. *Computers in Business.* San Francisco: Holden-Day, Inc., 1979.

Weinberg, Gerald M. *The Psychology of Computer Programming.* New York: Van Nostrand Reinhold Company, 1971.

Withington, Frederic C. *The Real Computer.* Reading, Massachusetts: Addison-Wesley, 1969.

FOOTNOTES

[1] *Administrative and Technical Report.* (New York: American Management Association, 1968).

[2] Gerald M. Weinberg, *The Psychology of Computer Programming* (New York: Van Nostrand Reinhold Company, 1971).

[3] R. L. Ashenhurst, ed., "Curriculum Recommendations for Graduate Professional Programs in Information Systems," *Communications of the ACM,* May 1972, p. 373.

[4] Ibid., p. 381.

[5] Herbert Z. Halbrecht, "Managing Information for Profit," *MIS Quarterly,* September 1978, p. 56.

[6] Edward A. Tomeski, "Management of a Computer Department," *Computers in Business,* San Francisco: Holden-Day, Inc., 1979, pp. 408-425.

13

Designing the Human Resource Information System

To the extent that customers (and these may include government agencies or private industry) abdicate their power prerogatives because of ignorance of the details of system operation, *de facto* decisions are made by equipment manufacturers or information-processing specialists. The customers may find it impossible to specify all future situations; they may be unable to devise foolproof heuristics; they may fail to specify detailed operating unit characteristics; they may be unable to devise appropriate *ad hoc* plans. Under each of these conditions, *de facto* decisions are again made for them by systems designers or other technical specialists.

Robert Boguslaw

OBJECTIVES OF THE CHAPTER

An overview of the general stages and steps of planning and designing a system for a computer application is presented. A summary discussion of the design of an employee information system is provided to illustrate some of the concepts (e.g., integration, human involvement) discussed in earlier chapters. At several points, the authors highlight some of the human factors that can be critical during systems planning and design; such factors constitute a still largely undeveloped phase of systems work.

CONDUCT OF A SYSTEMS STUDY

A systems study should fit into the overall systems plans of the organization. Any particular new systems design should be viewed in relationship with other systems of the organization. The individual designing a new system should know the organization, its goals, policies, and operations. Without such background, proposed solutions are likely to be impractical. These observations might appear to be so obvious that they need not be said. However, the authors experienced situations where young technicians, having very limited seasoning in business, were given assignments involving the design and development of major systems.

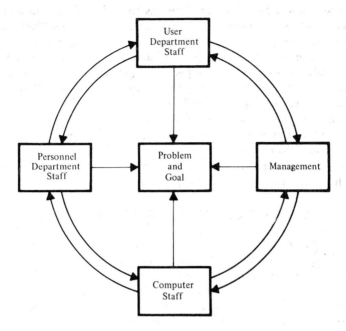

Figure 13-1 Task force approach to computer applications.

Too often a systems project is assigned to a member of the computer staff, and with minimal coordination the technician proceeds with the design of the new system. Preferably, a task force should be used in designing systems to be processed by computer. Such a task force should include a blend of technicians (systems analysts, management scientists, programmers) and representatives from the using departments involved. If the area affected involves organized or unionized employees, they too should be invited to have representation on the task force. In addition, the authors are of the belief that many such projects would greatly benefit by the insights of humanists (professional personnel staff, social scientists, psychologists). As stressed at numerous points throughout this book, it is the authors' view that one of the major causes of computer applications' deficiencies is that technicians develop systems which *may be* sound from a technical vantage point—but which overlook or mal-consider sociological and psychological aspects of new systems and related change (Figure 13-1).

As explored in Chapter 8, management involvement in major systems projects is essential to provide adequate backing, and to assure that such systems that evolve are consistent with the organization's policies and goals. Because of the highly technical nature of computer systems, too often general management has deferred major decisions to technocrats. The authors are convinced that some member of top management must have a sound administrative grasp of the broad implications of computer systems. At a number of points in the book (e.g., Chapters 8 and 11), the very major potential impacts of computers on people, organizations, and, indeed, society were identified. It was stressed that these require leadership attention which can effectively render high-level judgments.

Systems projects should be subject to careful planning and project management, covering target dates, allocation of resources to the project, and periodic reports on progress status.

The general concept of "systems" was treated in Chapter 5; this chapter brings the systems concept to a more operational focus.

UNDERSTANDING THE PRESENT SYSTEM

Systems work begins with an initial identification of the problem to be studied. This identification is usually subject to modification as the study progresses and as light is shed on the problem area. The required facts may be gathered by a number of means: observations, questionnaires, discussions, participating, etc. Part of the fact-gathering usually involves collecting salient details such as: forms used, statistics regarding work load, nature of the data used, peaks and valleys of work flow, how the work is currently performed, job descriptions of employees in the area being studied, etc. To make fact-gathering more orderly and to assure that desired data are collected, a data collection form of some kind is used.

After the facts have been gathered, the systems analyst studies the material collected, and develops a model (e.g., mathematical, visual, pictorial, written) which represents the existing problem area. Frequently, the model is represented as a system flowchart accompanied by a narrative description. As he develops the model of the existing system, the analyst appraises its strengths and weaknesses, in anticipation of the improved system to be recommended.

DETERMINING THE REQUIREMENT FOR A SYSTEM

Based upon the study of the existing system, the analyst begins anticipating critical parameters that will affect the overall design of the new system, i.e., the input, output, and files.

Input

The specification of each type of input of the system must detail: identification, content, format, frequency, volume, sequence in which it will be received, validation procedures, etc. A determination must be made about how the data will be captured and prepared. Ideally, the data will be recorded in a machine-processable form as a by-product of an actual transaction, e.g., punched paper tape automatically generated as a person types the details of a customer order. In some types of transactions, source data can be sent directly from a recording device to computer storage (referred to as direct entry into the computer). A determination must also be made as to type of processing: batch (groups of transactions that are gathered into an economic quantity before being processed by the computer) or on-line real-time (transactions that are not batched, but rather they are processed simultaneously at the time a transaction occurs). Batched transactions may be processed randomly (without rearranging the items in a particular order), or they may be sequenced into a particular pattern.

The analyst will usually have to design a series of input forms which serve as source documents for data, and forms that carry and store data through various stages of the input process. In addition, a variety of code design work is normally required. Numeric codes are frequently used to represent key data, since computers can more rapidly and efficiently process them. Examples are: account numbers, inventory numbers, location numbers, employee numbers, skill numbers, etc. There are numerous approaches to the design of such codes, some of which use self-checking digits (which help to minimize the recording and processing of incorrect codes). Also, the analyst should (but too frequently does not) develop a sound control and audit procedure to assure that accurate data will be processed in the system.

Output

Output must be intelligible not only to the analyst but also to the individuals who will actually use the output. The following points must be specified for each output: identification, content, format, frequency, schedule, volume, conditions that trigger output production, sequence in which output is to appear, etc. Although a printer is the most obvious output device, there are others such as cathode ray tubes and plotters. Cathode ray tubes are appealing from several standpoints, including the fact that the television-like display of information can overcome some of the existing paperwork pollution. Invariably, the analyst must design a series of output forms to be used both within the computer department and the departments interested in the particular application.

As stressed in Chapters 5, 6, 8, and 11—the analyst must be very sensitive to the users' output needs and coordinate closely with the users to assure that the output will answer real and not assumed needs. Further, the analyst must devote considerable attention to developing controls that will assure maximum accuracy of output information—since it obviously will be used by others for decisions. Increasing consideration must be devoted to designing a system that will protect the privacy of individuals and organizations; consequently, the system must provide certainty that only authorized persons will obtain output.

Files

The analyst must design the various data files of the system. This involves selecting the medium to hold data files: punched cards, paper tape, magnetic tape, magnetic drum, magnetic disk, magnetic cores, etc. To make decisions regarding file storage, the analyst must consider: degree of speed needed in accessing data, frequency of referral to data, size of the files, possible ways in which data records can be arranged, types of uses that will be made of the files, and the extent of maintenance required for the files.

As with input and output, the analyst should carefully plan control and audit techniques that will assure the integrity of the files, including the prevention of unauthorized access to them.

DESIGN OF THE NEW SYSTEM

As indicated in Chapters 5, 6, 8, and 11, the design of a new system requires consideration of such things as: kinds of decisions made at various organizational points, management styles, information requirements to support management decisions, delineation of the data elements for data bases, etc. These major considerations have a controlling influence over systems design.

By studying the system's input, output, and files—the analyst can determine the processing and computational requirements that are necessary. The analyst must deal with many technical system-design considerations such as: single input versus multiple input, media conversion, multi-programming and multi-processing, real-time versus batch mode, optimization, buffering, etc.

The most common form for representing and planning the new system is the flowchart (a pictorial representation that shows the major steps and sequence of data processing). The flowchart plots the flow of data and information throughout the system; it makes logical interrelationships clear, and shows the sequence of actions resulting from a set of conditions. Decision tables may be used to supplement the flowchart; the tables define actions to be taken when certain pre-specified conditions are fulfilled. They also make cause and effect relationships clear.

The analyst provides the program specifications that enable the programmer to develop the necessary computer programs. The systems analyst's specifications include: input, output, files, and flowcharts which indicate the processing requirements. Other relevant material must also be developed: clerical procedures, conversion procedures, equipment to be used, file retention schedule, parallel test period, etc.

When the computer programs are ready, they must be thoroughly tested ("debugged") to prove that they perform the intended tasks, and operate accurately. The new system must be well documented to provide a readily available record of the system. Procedures must be prepared for all phases of the computer system's operations, and necessary training must be organized.

New computer programs are usually run in parallel with the old procedure; such dual operations are desirable for a period to completely test the soundness of the new system. Organizations which have cut-over to new systems, without a parallel testing period, have experienced unexpected problems and sometimes chaos.

Computer programs are subject to improvement and change. Thus, it is not abnormal to have a considerable continuing program maintenance effort.

EXPECTATIONS FROM A COMPUTERIZED PERSONNEL SYSTEM

The aforementioned general principles regarding the design of systems apply to personnel applications as well as other systems. As stressed in Chapter 9, there has been a neglect of personnel systems. However, the benefits from procedures analysis, information need requirements, input and output determination, etc. just discussed can be applied to the personnel process.

Some of the reasonable expectations from the use of computers are:

1. Better ways of getting work done through reduced manual handling, increased accuracy of information, quicker availability of information, feedback of results for comparison with goals, etc.

2. Reduction in total cost by possibly containing growth of clerical and other staffs, combining or streamlining operations, decreasing paperwork, etc.

3. Extending the capability of management by providing information (e.g., manpower planning) not readily available previously, obtaining analyses that provide new insights about alternatives for the future, sharpening insights about the effects of certain decisions, facilitating the evaluation of performances, etc.

4. Improving the effectiveness of operations in such ways as: recruitment may be more efficiently handled, improved matching of people with positions, identification of employees with obsolete skills needing training, assigning human resources and work so as to maximize productivity, research that will keep the organization abreast of employee morale, etc.

PEOPLE-RELATED EFFECTS IN ALL SYSTEMS

In addition to computerizing the personnel function, management must consider a whole series of people-related impacts on *all* systems. Such impacts should be anticipated and be included as part of the systems study. The following list illustrates the kinds of impacts, involving the human system, which are too often not adequately considered in systems studies.

- As has been discussed frequently in this book—has the professional personnel staff been consulted and involved in matters of changes affecting employees and work?

- Will new staffing requirements upset the stability of current employees and result in increased turnover?

- Should an estimate be included for the disruptive effect that the computer may have on morale or operations?

- What will it cost to recruit the new staffing requirements?

- Is the required staff obtainable in the employment market?

- What will it cost to orient and train the new staff, and to retrain the existing staff?

- What new organizational units will be required? How will they affect existing organizational relations?

- Will management face up to terminating excess personnel? What will be the termination cost? Or does the organization have a higher ethical and social responsibility to such personnel? How will this effect morale?

- Can normal attrition (resignations, retirements, etc.) be counted on to achieve the required personnel reductions?

- Who will perform the tasks that cannot or should not be computerized? How will they interface with the computer application?

- Have adequate steps been taken to secure the cooperation of affected departments?

- Have effective controls been established to assure privacy of sensitive data?

- Has consideration been given to the tensions that will be created by loss of status, organizational change, and new and unfamiliar relationships and responsibilities?

Organization

A   Lack of documentation, controls, parallel operations; precipitous approach; turnover due to unreasonable management expectations; lack of management understanding of computers; no one given over-all control and responsibility from beginning of effort.

B   Management inexperience; hardware orientation; poor staffing; overambitious program.

C   Lack of management backing and involvement; unreasonable expectations; poor personnel policy; unclear management goals; extreme resistance to change by employees in a conservative environment; overambitious program set by computer department.

D   Not high enough reporting relationship; controller, in charge of computer effort, could not gain acceptance of other executives; friction between various systems and computer units; frequent change of personnel; ambitious plan; indecisiveness of computer committee.

E   Central control and guidance of computer effort was ineffective; insufficient talent in organization; overemphasis on research rather than useful applications; slowness in obtaining approvals of departments affected; slowness to implement computer applications.

Figure 13-2   Reasons for computer systems failures.

- Has any union representative been consulted about the changes?

- How will the new system make work conditions better for employees? Has this message been adequately communicated?

The issues outlined above indicate the desirability of human-relations experts in systems studies. Few computer technicians are qualified to cope with some of the areas.

An analysis, by the authors, of five organizations—that identify the apparent reasons for their computer failures—elicited the information summarized in Figure 13-2.

It is apparent from the above that people-related factors (e.g., lack of management involvement, weak staffing, etc.) were significant influences in determining whether a computer system was a success or failure. In this connection, three typical situations may be delineated:

1. When the application is originally proposed, the person who "defines" it does not set appropriate objectives or parameters. Rather than defining the

goal as A_1 it is defined as A_2. This type of misunderstanding can be attributed to the communication gap between the user (person with the problem to be computerized) and the computer personnel (the analyst who assumes he or she understands the need of the user).

2. The systems analyst designs a poor system, or the computer programmer writes a poor computer program. There may be correct understanding of the application and the goal desired by the user, but the technical analysis may result in a weak computer application. For instance, the system may lack provision for exceptional conditions (events outside of the normal routine), for effective controls, or for expansion. Relatedly, the technicians may not adequately check out their final product, the computer program. Because of the technical nature of systems analysis and computer programming, it may be difficult for the user to recognize weaknesses in the system—until the computer outputs some incorrect reports, bills, checks, etc. If the error is not immediately obvious, the organization can operate for long periods with incorrect information.

3. The data provided to the computer is faulty. The computer program may be very well designed to solve the user's problem, but if the computer is fed incorrect input data—the results will be GIGO (in the colorful phrase of the computer professionals, garbage-in, garbage-out). Inaccurate input data are a particularly difficult area, because organizations are frequently working with virtually mountains of data. At some point, in any system, humans activate the processing of data. Carelessness, fatigue, lack of interest in one's work, improper training, deliberate sabotage, etc. create situations that can result in faulty input.

If any of the above types of human failures have occurred, the computer will have obediently performed but yet will have generated "garbage." When the inaccurate outputs are discovered, the general reaction is to focus blame on the computer. A more thorough investigation of the cause of the breakdown will not infrequently trace the problem to one of the three kinds of human failures identified.

This is not to say that the computer equipment and software, supplied by vendors, are not sometimes responsible for malfunctioning systems. As indicated in Chapter 7, users have been known to experience faulty processing and output which can be attributed to product deficiencies of computer vendors. Some users have been able to substantiate considerable losses, and have won damage suits in court cases against computer manufacturers and suppliers of software.

DESCRIPTION OF AN EMPLOYEE INFORMATION SYSTEM

The following pages will present some summary highlights taken from an actual system study of personnel-related activities in large governmental units. The same general approach could apply to business organizations.

Findings

During the survey of the different agencies that compose the executive branch of the government, it was found that a number of problems existed regarding the administration of personnel record and payroll in general. Transactions took too long to be processed; a great deal of duplication existed in the personnel records kept by the Personnel Department and the various agencies; the payroll was mechanized in an elementary manner, thus causing an unnecessary work-load in the computer system; the loans and contribution status of accounts of organizations (such as the Teachers' Retirement Board) had backlogs of up to two and a half years; and the general procedures regarding personnel were slow, cumbersome and loaded with unnecessary controls which did not accomplish their main objectives and which contributed to delays.

The employee information system recommended was oriented towards the development of a master plan designed to apply advanced computer systems concepts and techniques in the government's activities.

Advantages

The principal advantages gained by implementation of the systems recommendations outlined included the following:

1. Elimination of automatic data processing equipment maintained in the personnel department.
2. Completely centralized personnel records.
3. Improvement of the computer system through:
   a. Decrease in computer runs, programs, setup time, etc.
   b. Elimination of dispersed files by centralizing them.
   c. Introduction of an on-line system for prompt information retrieval of personnel data.
   d. Manpower reduction at the agency level.
   e. Facilities to calculate personnel projections with the use of mathematical models.
   f. Improved service to employees and others.

Scope of the System

The system was designed to encompass all employees hired on a monthly basis working in the executive agencies of the government. Flexibility of design permits employees of municipalities and some public corporations to be included without incurring additional systems design or appreciable programming costs.

When fully implemented, the system will (1) provide up-to-date and complete information on each employee; (2) process the payroll for each agency (including all the computations related to it) and provide for its accounting; (3) provide information on vacant positions and eligible personnel to fill those vacancies; (4) provide budgeted position reports which will be used by each agency as the starting point for the preparation of annual budgets with respect to personnel needs; (5) maintain accounting records; and (6) provide up-to-date information on loans, insurance, employees' contributions to the several retirement systems, savings, employees' membership in organizations such as cooperatives, tax withholdings, and miscellaneous debts of each employee with the government.

System Description

The system was designed around four major files:

1. Employee master file.
2. Retired personnel file.
3. Eligibility register file.
4. Budgeted positions file.

The files could be expanded if so required by future information needs of the areas affected by the system.

The system as conceived took into consideration the fact that one input transaction may affect the contents of more than one file (e.g., when an employee retires, the notice of termination provided by the agency affects the contents of the employee master file, the retirement file, and the budgeted position file). When such a situation occurs, the system provides for the updating of all the files affected in one computer run, minimizing computer process and setup time. Consideration was also given to the fact that the contents of one file may originate several different reports. In order to make effective use of computer time, it was planned to have the necessary data for these reports processed with a minimum number of file scans.

Input data were to be processed following the batching method, with each batch of input documentation supported by a total for use by the computer in establishing zero balance controls.

The general premise was that the computer installation would balance all its outputs with control totals computed at the source of information and attached to the inputs. In the different programs required by the system, maintenance of accuracy would be maximized from run to run and within runs. Where precise arithmetic was not possible, order of magnitude and reasonableness tests would be applied, thus minimizing the possibilities of processing erroneous data.

The dynamic nature of a system like this—with master files being constantly updated—and the importance of the information maintained in those files, requires concentrated efforts in order to provide the maximum protection. Random access files are periodically dumped in high-density magnetic tapes, and the changes to the files are kept in their original computer form or also in high-density tape, thus providing a simple and rapid way of reconstructing a file should its contents be destroyed because of hardware failures or negligent handling. The possibility of this happening, however, is minimized through the use of file and core-protect features. There are control areas within the files so that important data items can be balanced periodically with corresponding fields in the control areas. Any transactions affecting those data items are also reflected in the appropriate control fields.

In spite of the controls mentioned above, some erroneous input data might be accepted by the computer system, because of compensating errors produced at the source of the data. Reports are produced covering all changes affecting the contents of the master files. These reports—showing the before picture, the transaction, and the after picture—are sent to the sources originating the transactions, and it is their responsibility to verify their correctness. The computer installation, if no further inputs are received, proceeds on the basis that the transactions have been correctly incorporated in the different files affected.

The system provides limited on-line capability for responses to inquiries. However, in order to take full advantage of the benefits derived from such a feature, the key fields to access the files have to remain constant. Otherwise, great efforts would have to be directed to the reorganization of the different files and the table necessary to cross-reference the information maintained in those files. For instance, the job number, which is part of the key field to access the budgeted positions file, should remain constant. Once a number is assigned to a specific position, that number should not be used for any other position, even if the first one is later deleted from the budget.

Employee Information

The employee information system is composed of the following subsystems: personnel, payroll, retirement, and budgetary.

A chart of the overall system, identifying the different subsystems and files, the runs where commonality of processing exists, and the interchange of information among the subsystems, is shown in Figure 13-3.

Personnel Subsystem

Personnel information processing and retrieval was partially mechanized (punched card equipment in the Personnel Department). However, the information needs were inadequately met because of slow and cumbersome processing of transactions, unnecessary controls, slow manual procedures, etc. A good example of delay caused by these problems was the time elapsed (often from two to three months) after an agency made a request to fill a vacancy until that vacancy was actually filled. Another very important problem that came to light during the survey of the personnel and different agencies was the extensive duplication existing between records. However,

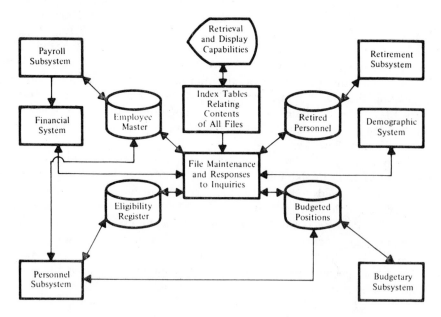

Figure 13-3   Employee information system—general chart.

paradoxical as it may seem, this duplication did not facilitate the retrieval of information regarding a specific employee, since the procedures were not specifically defined. An employee or a government official requiring certain personnel information was usually referred from one agency to another before the information could be located. This caused a waste of time and effort that could have been utilized elsewhere in more productive tasks.

The new personnel subsystem provided solutions to these problems by: (1) handling the transactions with speed and updating the different files; (2) providing the agencies with means to fill the vacancies as soon as the need arises; (3) providing complete, centralized personnel records; (4) eliminating duplication of information and manual work; and (5) simplifying and improving controls.

Remote terminals installed in the Personnel Department were included to provide a control tool and information retrieval capability of greater efficiency. By merely keying in a social security number or a budgeted position number and a code for the information desired, any of the data items sorted in the random access file is automatically available in a matter of seconds. This includes not only information regarding a specific employee— such as government service history, academic background, positions for which he (or she) is eligible, present salary, date of last salary increase, civil status, number of dependents, etc.—but also information such as how many persons are available to fill a certain position and who those persons are, how many positions of a specific job classification are available and vacant in each agency, what documentation is missing on employees recently hired, etc. Through the use of this information retrieval capability, the Personnel Department has, at any time, a close and accurate picture of the personnel situation in all agencies encompassed by the system.

Payroll Subsystem

The employee payrolls were being processed in the computer facilities of the Treasury Department. Complete computer processing was being provided for only some agencies. Partial computer processing was provided for agencies with more than 200 employees, and very limited computer processing was provided for the rest of the agencies. The new system provided that the complete payroll for all agencies be processed in the computer installation.

The study found that the payroll system was mechanized in a very unsophisticated manner. Even though third generation equipment was being used, powerful capabilities were not fully exploited because of lack of availability of qualified personnel. The equipment was operated under "emulation mode"; i.e., programs originally written for second generation (or in some cases first generation) equipment were "emulated" to run on newer equipment. While eliminating conversion costs, this greatly reduced the efficiency of data processing and decreased the capabilities and potential of the computer installation.

The new system was designed to improve substantially the existing automatic data processing situation, taking full advantage of the possibilities offered by modern computer equipment. Under this scheme, a fully automated payroll is processed for all agencies; complete and integrated loans accounting, statistics, and individual status of accounts are provided to the retirement organizations and the employees' association, and detailed reports on accumulated contributions to the retirement or compulsory savings plans are provided to the organizations responsible for the administration of those plans. The services to the employees were also improved since—through the information that the system maintains and quickly provides on request—the former delays in the processing and granting of loan requests and the backlogs in the recording of employees' accumulated contributions to different plans (retirement, savings) are greatly reduced or eliminated. Also, employees are placed on the payroll as soon as they start working.

Retirement Subsystem

The retirement subsystem encompasses all the employees retired from government service. Partial mechanization of transactions affecting retired personnel was being provided by the computer center of the Treasury Department to the central retirement organization and the Teachers' Retirement Board. The comments previously made (see Payroll Subsystem) about the former computer systems and equipment utilization, and how the new system was designed to improve them, also apply to this subsystem.

The new retirement subsystem was conceived as a logical extension of the payroll subsystem, providing for automatic transfer of information from one subsystem to the other. This means that when a person retires and is deleted from the active employees' payroll, he (or she) will be automatically placed in the pensioners' payments list. This will greatly reduce the volume of transactions and, consequently, the necessary manpower to originate those transactions.

The retirement subsystem produces pensioner payments checks, registers and accounting reports, pensioner deductions registers and pensioner loans accounting, statistics, and status-of-accounts reports. Payments coordination with F.I.C.A. can be performed automatically, and reports produced to that effect, as well as other statistical reports that the different retirement organizations consider necessary. Benefits to be paid to beneficiaries of deceased pensioners can also be reported automatically to the retirement organizations concerned.

Budgetary Subsystem

The budgetary subsystem is built around the budgeted positions file, and is designed to provide complete and updated information about each one of those positions. The on-line information retrieval capabilities permits instantaneous access to the information contained not only in the budgeted positions file, but also the information in all other files in the employee information system. This provides the Budget Bureau with an invaluable tool to exercise control functions in the area of personnel budget. Also, the information contained in the budgeted positions file and employee master file can provide the Budget Bureau with the necessary elements to make automatic and accurate projections of the personnel expenses of the government and to measure the impact of those expenses on policies and decisions regarding personnel.

The new system calls for providing each agency with a personnel budget work-sheet at the time of the annual budget preparation. Only the proposed changes in the last approved budget has to be posted, thus avoiding the tedious and time-consuming procedures previously used, whereby all the items included in the proposed budget had to be posted manually.

DIFFERENT APPROACHES TO INFORMATION SYSTEMS*

Economic models concern themselves with optimizing output, optimizing the utilization of resources, and the value of information. Models define a problem or problems and then give an answer or answers of how best to utilize the resources. Some of these models are very sophisticated and presuppose that an information systems practitioner has sufficient knowledge and skill to determine which model should be used and to implement it. Many intermediate steps have to be taken before a sophisticated economic model can be implemented. Furthermore, economic models without consideration of the behaviorial and technological variables are of very limited use to any information systems practitioner.

The behaviorists do not take economic and technological variables into consideration. They argue, "What if optimum output is achieved and the latest hardware is installed, but the systems user does not use the system?" Behaviorists deal with the needs, perceptions, wants, desires and cognitive styles of a systems user and the group interaction, power play and social structure of an organization and their influence on information systems design[1]. By not incor-

*Adapted from the author's article "Different Approaches to Information Systems," *Journal of Systems Management*, April 1981.

porating economic and technological variables into the behaviorists' models, the information systems practitioners receive only limited assistance in their day-to-day information systems design.

Technologists design equipment and software packages for a large and diverse group of users and consequently cannot consider the individual or the single organization. The human variables are therefore very general and limited. Technologists are defined as professionals who design hardware, telecommunications equipment, operating software (software packages needed to operate a computer) and predesigned software packages (applications programs sold on the market).

These three distinctly different approaches to information systems design, analyze, build models and try to predict certain outcomes. All three add to the body of knowledge of information systems and cannot be dealt with in isolation from one another. A systems practitioner deals with all three disciplines.

This article concerns itself with the knowledge/skill requirements of a system and its compatibility with the user. It is believed that in designing a more sophisticated system, the upgrading of the user has to be considered carefully. When the upgrading of the systems user is incorporated into the design, the economic, the technological and moreover the behaviorial variables can all be considered and satisfied. Development concepts and applications consider the various kinds of learning experiences which increase the value of an employee and contribute to individual and organizational effectiveness. Since many information systems span many different departments or divisions and incorporate different geographical regions, the design of effective information systems for large groups of users, is complex.

Conceptualizing versus Actual Design and Implementation

An information system does not just come into being, nor does the need for one; an individual first becomes conscious of desiring or needing additional or different information to support his activities. A desire is perceiving a want. A need, on the other hand, is perceived as important: unless it is met, one cannot perform a task effectively and efficiently. As one interacts with his/her environment the conscious needs or desires become reinforced in importance. When the conscious state becomes positively reinforced and one is assured that the need or desire is true, one starts to inquire how the need or desire can be satisfied. In information systems terms, one starts to conceptualize and to design a model. Conceptualizing is abstracting or reducing an idea (model) to a very few basic variables—variables which are readily understood, can be dealt with, and are important during this phase. Most variables of the system are ignored and are not yet known. At this stage one cannot say if the concepts are feasible and workable. To move a concept to something workable is a quite arduous and frustrating task, especially when it involves a large group with diverse backgrounds and from different environments.

During conceptualizing one also starts to determine whether one can take the concept through the design and implementation phases alone, or whether assistance is required. The user may feel, since he has the conceptual understanding and can visualize the interrelationships, that it is just a matter of putting the whole system—his ideas—together and that this is a simple task. Since the user is faced with many questions and details in getting a workable model, and this task is lengthy and time-consuming, he may start to lose interest in the design.

The user also, during the design stage, starts to go through a new conscious and conceptualizing phase. The systems designer through his experiences adds new ideas, which in turn cause the user to reevaluate his concepts. It may also happen that during this phase the user requests a different design from what was initially indicated. Some systems designers feel that the user does not know what he wants and that he is continually requesting changes. The designer should be ready when this happens to realize that the user has not yet understood what his actual information requirements are. It is the designer's responsibility to assist the user in determining the appropriate information needs. This is a continuing process for any individual.

When the information system is finally implemented, changes will be made in the system so it can become less of an abstraction than its initial conception. The user, on the other hand, keeps going through his evolutionary stages: consciousness and conceptualizing, and hence demanding new and more current changes to the information systems. As the user progresses and the environment changes, the user may have to work on a different level than where the information system functions and move back and forth between the environment and the information system. When the gap between the environment and the user is too wide, the information system cannot support the user and hence becomes ineffective and inefficient*.—not because the user is incapable of performing his task, but rather because the supporting information systems are performing at a level which does not complement the user.

Knowledge/Skill Requirements of a System

An information system is designed with a specific knowledge/skill requirements level. When the knowledge/skill level required by the system does not complement the user, the technological and social systems are in conflict. For

---

* Effectiveness and efficiency are only implied throughout the article. We have not yet found how these variables can be successfully defined and (more importantly) measured. An effective information system is very difficult to define and almost impossible to measure. Efficiency could mean optimizing hardware utilization, but this does not guarantee that the user will use the outputs. We could have used other words instead, but we are rather trying to show how loosely and indiscriminately "effective and efficient" are used by many. We ourselves have contributed to this.

example, to change an existing manual system to a computerized one may increase the complexity of the system. The increase in complexity may arise because the computer information system forces the user to structure his thinking in unaccustomed ways.

Skill is defined as effective use of knowledge. Therefore, skill is limited by knowledge obtained. Furthermore, one can have knowledge without any skills, but one cannot have skills without knowledge/skill is knowledge-dependent. Also, to obtain more knowledge one has to be systematically trained or self-trained, whereas a skill can be obtained through exposure to a system. Therefore, depending on the system, the user may have to increase his knowledge, but this does not imply that he can produce the desired output effectively and efficiently; for that the user also has to improve his systems skill. For example, to change from a manual to a computerized system does not require additional knowledge but merely an increase in systems skills. On the other hand, to move from a simple inventory system to a Material Requirements Planning system, the user who has never been exposed to one in a seminar or studied a book on this subject will first need systematic training. Then hands-on experience with the system will develop the adequate systems skills.

An increase in knowledge/skill requirements may also be demanded because the design team has a broad and detailed understanding of the new system, while the majority of users were never exposed to it. Perhaps some members of the design team have implemented a similar system in another organization and are now applying their expertise in the present one. Or the design team may not understand the users, since the system is nationwide and only a few selected people are on the team; here the technological system may lead the behavioral one. If the gap between these two systems is not closed, it will lead to an unsuccessful systems design.

There are other reasons for a mismatch of the knowledge/skills requirements level of a system with that of the user. One of them is that knowledge/skill represents power of one person or one department over others. Power has been defined as the ability to influence and control the utilization of resources and the ability of one decision-maker to direct another through a set of alternatives. The resources of a person or department are tangible ones, but even intangible resources may become more important than the tangible ones in bargaining**. Therefore, a systems designer has to give special attention during the design that certain members of the design team do not take advantage of this by increasing their knowledge/skills—power—over others are not part of the design team or cannot bargain for an equal share.

** For more discussion on "power," see Edward A. Tomeski and Konrad E. Sadek, "Utility Theory," *Journal of Systems Management,* July 1980, pp. 6-11.

Systems Design and its Relationship to the
Dynamic and Static Technological Subsystems

Information systems are composed of a technical subsystem which is relatively static and a social subsystem which is very dynamic. As a user interacts with the environment (often with departmental boundaries) as well as outside the organization and through reading journals, etc., he begins to adjust his expectations of a system and starts demanding new features from the information system. A system which today is ideal encounters questions and requested improvements tomorrow. The user learns as he interacts with the system and the environment; his knowledge/skill increases, and he has new expectations from a system.

Further, information systems are generally designed to serve a group of users. Not only does a system frequently serve a group of users in one department who share the same objectives and goals and communicate in the same language, but frequently an information system also crosses departmental boundaries, becoming interdivisional or even international. A Materials Requirements Planning system can be such a system.

Also, each individual has different needs for information to support his activities. For example, some decision-makers want reports to present certain situations in great detail, while others are comfortable with more generalized information about the same situation. But on other occasions the information needs of the same two decision-makers might be reversed. Consequently, the quantity and quality of information needed varies from one individual to the next and from one situation to the next. Particularly the quality of information can only be defined by each individual himself, since each one has his own standards.

The quality and quantity of information needed also changes as one gets to know and understand one's work. A more knowledgeable and skilled system user also demands different kinds of information than does one who has just entered the system. It has been shown that cognitive style influences the choices made by executives. A drastic change from one system to another (for example, the move from an informal to a sophisticated computerized system) also demands that the user must change his attitude toward the system, and hence the information needs will also change.

The user goes through a learning process until he is fully familiar with the system, and during this time additional information may be requested. This information may come from inquiries into the system, interaction with the systems designer, professional interaction, journal reading, etc. During this time the user's positive feelings toward the system either are strengthened or become unfavorable. Dickson et al., in their research, showed that more sophisticated information systems (model-based information systems) are not necessarily used by a manager, even if these models would improve his effectiveness and efficiency in decision-making[2].

When we speak of higher, more sophisticated systems, we include two factors: a) a user is able to work with more variables, and b) the predictability of a decision-maker has improved. The flow of information (i.e., the quality and quantity) to a decision-maker has improved and hence has reduced the amount of uncertainty.

A Design Strategy

Many organizations undertake systems projects with the expectation that certain operations will become more sophisticated and require increased knowledge and skill. This may come out of necessity. For example, a new executive has moved into the organization with a new and more sophisticated outlook on various operations. Ambitious projects are undertaken, man-years are spent in designing sophisticated systems, and sophisticated software packages are leased or purchased. Frequently, new and more sophisticated hardware is also leased or purchased. After two or more years have passed, management looks at the projects and starts to question how much has really changed. How much more sophisticated are the operations, how much has productivity increased, how much more effective and efficient are decision-makers today than two years ago? All too often it is realized that more hardware and software now supports the organization, but otherwise not too much has changed.

It must be recognized that if a system is implemented which demands a higher knowledge/skill level, many systems users may become frightened. The inference that one has to spend extra time or is not as quick as others in comprehending or, moreover, that someone else will be in control during the upgrading, might influence the users' attitude negatively toward the new system. As we learn a new skill, especially involving physical activities like working with a CRT, all complex adjustments and motor movements are painfully within our awareness. As one becomes familiar with the skill and the skill becomes automatic, the movements no longer enter consciousness. Also, as people become acquainted with a task or lock into it over a period of time, they start to feel comfortable and hence contribute in maintaining it and oppose innovation and change. An organization has to be watchful against too much stability, for this can become a liability later on.

An organization should first determine what its objectives and goals are for the next 5 years, then define what information systems are required to support these goals and objectives. When this has been achieved, the organization has to assess if an increase in knowledge/skill by the systems users and design team will be needed to achieve the objectives and goals, and what knowledge/skill will be needed to carry out the goals and objectives effectively and efficiently.

To achieve and maintain the goals and objectives may require different expertise. For example, a systems designer may have the knowledge/skills to achieve the desired goals and objectives and a programmer to code the computer programs, but the user has to have adequate knowledge/skill to maintain and use the new system. Any one of these three variables, if not considered and dealt with carefully, can lead to an unsuccessful design.

Most organizations know how to determine what information systems will be needed to achieve the goals and objectives but do not look at what knowledge/skill the information systems will require. Many organizations rather jump from what information systems are needed to what hardware and software will be needed to achieve and maintain the goals and objectives. An example of this has been reported by Millar:

> In one specialty apparel retailer, the chief executive officer (CEO) caused a problem by deciding that he should have point-of-sale (POS) terminals, and by hiring a Director of IS who has implemented a POS system in a much larger chain. The new director hired many people and bought a great deal of equipment. Unfortunately, the merchandising and store operations people had no idea of how to operate in a POS environment, and the POS Project never got off the ground. The Director of IS resigned and the company was back where it started, with a smaller bank balance[3].

When the knowledge/skill requirement has been established, the organization has to look at its human resources and evaluate if the knowledge/skill is present and, if not, what has to be done to achieve and maintain the desired goals and objectives. For example:

1. Human resources exist with adequate knowledge/skill in-house but people might have to be transferred to other positions in which their knowledge/skill is needed.
2. The organization does not have the required knowledge/skill in-house; can present personnel be systematically trained?
   a) Yes—Prepare systematic training plan (seminars, etc.).
   b) No—1) Hire personnel with adequate knowledge/skills;
      2) Hire personnel whose knowledge and skills will be developed in-house as they work with the system; or
      3) Hire outside, part-time help, or a consultant with adequate knowledge/skill, since their expertise will only be needed twice a year for 8 weeks.

The evaluation and analysis of the organizational human resources to determine whether the goals and objectives can be achieved and maintained is crucial to the success of an information system as well as any other project. For if the organizational goals and objectives are set too high (because the necessary knowledge/skill does not exist or cannot be obtained), they can never be reached.

Incorporating the Upgrading of the User

We really can only speak of a system when both the social and technological subsystems are designed as one. One cannot be designed in isolation from the other. But many information systems are designed in a dysfunctional fashion; many firms purchase software packages, hardware, even a Materials Requirements Planning system, and then design the organizational social subsystem to complement the technological one.

A system has to be designed so that the upgrading of the user is incorporated into the design. Perhaps a more sophisticated system is needed so that the organization can function more effectively and efficiently. The organization has first to evaluate if the user has the adequate knowledge/skill so both subsystems—social and technological—complement each other. If the subsystems do not match, it has to be determined what steps have to be taken and incorporated into the design so that the user can be upgraded to the system's knowledge/skill requirement level. But upgrading to a higher level implies not to have merely more knowledge without skills; the user will need time to work with the system until he fully understands and comprehends it. At this time the technological subsystem leads the user, so the social and technological subsystems are in conflict.

Many systems are implemented where the user only receives an introductory session on a CRT and perhaps a half-hour discussion with the systems designer. The user is then expected to operate within the system. Especially sophisticated systems, like Materials Requirements Planning systems and other planning systems, where many transactions and many different users interact with the same system, should and must be explained with supporting documents. In addition, reinforced training should take place—that is, letting the user get firsthand experience with the system, and a week or a month later, depending on the complexity of the system, go over the whole system in detail again—to assure that all users fully understand and comprehend all details of the system. Spielberg and De Nike found that reinforcing consequences were ineffective in modifying behavior as long as participants were unaware of the reinforcement contingency; but participants suddenly increased the appropriate behavior when they discovered which responses would be rewarded[4].

The starting point to determine what training program should be undertaken is to fully understand the original system. Put together examples of all calculations, show all the relations and interrelations of all steps from the beginning of a particular information system until the final output. The next step is to analyze the new system in great detail. Similarities, differences and all new features should be noted and documented. All the calculations, relations and interrelations of data, files and fields which are used by the new system should be documented, especially with computerized systems, since many of the operations are done automatically and are not visually seen by the user. User training is crucial in any move from a manual to a computerized system. With the manual system the user can trace and verify all steps, while with the computerized system many operations are done automatically, and the user frequently is not able to verify steps but is rather told to trust the system.

Making up physical examples has two functions: a) to convince the user that the system does arrive at the correct answers, and b) to provide the user with sound understanding as well as improve his skills on the new system through the use of teaching aids.

When all this has been accomplished, the user should get a very detailed briefing session on the overall system with accompanying examples. The user should also be encouraged to work out some examples to prove himself and to learn all the relations and interrelations from the beginning to the final outputs of the system. Similarities and differences between the old and new system should be explained clearly and in detail. There can be no ambiguities or doubts left in the user's mind. If doubts are left, if the user does not fully understand the differences between the systems, the user may start to expect things which are not within the capabilities of the new system and, perhaps more dangerously, may start to use the system differently at times than it was intended to be used. The user also should receive a very detailed introductory session on the hardware (not only the CRT) to thoroughly familiarize himself with the system and encourage him to use the system at least one hour per day one or more times per week, depending on the user's ability to improve his systems skills. It is crucial that the user be taught and his knowledge/skill be upgraded to the required level at a comfortable pace. If the upgrading is too fast and generalized, the user might not comprehend and understand the system; if the upgrading is too slow, he might become bored. Either case might give the user an unfavorable attitude to the design.

Depending on the complexity of the system, the user should be tested after the initial training period—not to penalize him if he does not fully understand the system, but rather to insure that he is familiar enough with the system to use it correctly. An instruction manual for the system and how it operates should be prepared. The instruction manual is not the same as a procedure. A procedure shows the sequence of steps (i.e. information flow) to complete the system's cycle but usually does not include the computer system's steps and operations. The procedure should be part of the instruction manual.

The instruction manual serves an even more important function. A user is initially thoroughly trained about how the whole system functions, but when different users perform different tasks, many times a user only performs a sub-task in a complex system. Hence, a user, through performing a given task like inventory control, will become very proficient in this task, but when transferred, for example, to planning, he may have to be refamiliarized with this function. The user may have had a thorough understanding of the planning subsystem when he was initially introduced, but he also may have forgotten or become less familiar with the planning subsystem after a few months or years. In addition, many systems, such as financial planning and other forecasting and modeling systems, are only infrequently used, perhaps once or twice a year. The user may have developed his knowledge and skills during the introduction and the first use of the system, but if he does not use it again for another six months, many details might be forgotten or become unclear.

It is interesting to note that systems professionals are continually being upgraded through seminars (especially soft/hardware professionals), to keep them current with all the new innovations and changes. It is also taken for granted that when one goes to a seminar, he needs more time to become proficient through hands-on experience of changes, new systems and applications. This philosophy does not always extend to the users: after they have been introduced to a new system, it is assumed that they should be working effectively and efficiently with the system after a short period of time. *This is a fallacy.* The user also needs time to get acquainted with a system through hands-on experience.

The design team during the design phase develops the systems skills. Especially the designer who works out every detail improves his system skills, and because of that he becomes the trainer of the system. Even if the designer does not possess sufficient skills at the beginning of the design, he usually becomes quite proficient after the task has been completed. The designer has to remember that many users were not involved in the design and hence could not develop an understanding of the system before implementation. These users, too, need time to familiarize themselves and develop the necessary skills to become effective and efficient in producing the desired output. Many designers become frustrated and cannot comprehend why it takes so long for some users to develop the necessary skills. Furthermore, it has to be recognized that each individual has his own time requirements of getting his systems skills, and for each individual each system has its own meaning; hence, a system has many different meanings.

Conclusions

Many variables have been identified which contribute to a successful systems design, but many more need to be identified. The understanding, conceptualizing versus a workable design, the learning process and the increase in knowledge/skill by the user also have to be considered as variables for a successful design. The designer's understanding of how systems are conceived in the user's mind and the dynamic change of an information system should provide for more effective systems. Upgrading the user's knowledge/skill as required by a system has to be carefully evaluated before a systems design is considered and implemented. Careful analysis of the user must determine if he has adequate knowledge/skill to operate within the designed system. The idea that a user will be able to upgrade himself, or could be upgraded by a few short sessions or seminars, has to be seriously questioned. Soundly designed information systems are tools which benefit any organization if the people within that organization understand and are ready for them. If people are to function effectively they must anticipate the probable consequences of different events and courses of actions and regulate their behaviour accordingly.

SUMMARY

Systems development for computers is a task that involves time-consuming, and complex challenges. In meeting these challenges, systems studies too often do not sufficiently take account of the human factors involved. When human factors are not adequately considered, faulty systems can be installed that cause serious malfunctions in organizational operations and managerial decision-making, as well as result in employees who resist or misuse the system.

The planning, design, and installation of personnel information systems involve detailed organizational analysis and integration of procedures, and call for considerable commitment of manpower and other resources.

KEY CONCEPTS OF THE CHAPTER

1. Experience has shown that a task force approach to computer applications is the most effective way to increase the likelihood of having a successful computer installation.

2. The determination of the requirements for a new system and the design of such a system require comprehensive and accurate supporting information and painstaking analysis. Too often, organizations rush applications to the computer without thorough systems analysis, and the results are almost inevitably disappointing.

3. A comprehensive employee information system is a substantial undertaking. Careful planning is required to incorporate good principles, as recommended in this book, into such a system. There is a mistaken notion that an employee information system is a simple undertaking when compared to other systems (e.g., manufacturing, marketing, financial).

4. The human factors in systems design, as discussed in many parts of this book, are frequently overlooked by computer professionals. The authors have repeatedly indicated this as one of the most notable gaps in systems theory and practice.

5. In addition to the personnel information system, the impact of *all* systems on people requires careful attention. This remains a largely undeveloped area that needs much more attention by researchers, educators, computer manufacturers, psychologists, sociologists, and computer professionals.

DISCUSSION QUESTIONS

General Background (Seminar/Classroom Discussion)

1. What difficulties does the computer technician face in designing information systems?
2. Outline the major steps that are required in the conduct of a systems study. What are the dangers of improvising and not using guidelines when conducting a systems study?

Operational and Technical

1. Does your organization provide analysts and programmers with guidelines and standards to be followed when designing new systems? How do such formal guidelines and standards help the technician?
2. Identify a system which you consider to be a poorly designed one. To what do you attribute the system's weaknesses? How can the weaknesses be eliminated? What barriers prevent such improvements?
3. Does your organization have a data base for personnel systems? What specific data elements should be in such a data base?

Policy

1. What are the benefits derived from a task force approach to systems problems? Are there any disadvantages to such an approach? Does your organization use the task force approach for systems work?
2. Review your organization's most recent computer feasibility study. Did the study, in your opinion, thoroughly take into account people-related issues?
3. Identify one computer project, with which you are familiar, which resulted in particularly disappointing results. Try to isolate the major causes of failure. Segregate the causes of failure by those which are primarily technical, and those which are primarily administrative or social. How can such failures be averted in future projects?

Areas for Research

1. Analyze the employee information system presented in this chapter. Suggest ways in which the system might be improved.
2. Study the overall systems design of an organization's personnel system. Develop a general systems chart depicting the current operations. Then prepare a general systems chart for an improved system. Present the two charts to the personnel administrator in the organization for his reactions.

BIBLIOGRAPHY

Blumenthal, Sherman C. *Management Information Systems*. Englewood Cliffs, New Jersey: Prentice-Hall, Inc., 1969.

Daniels, Alan and Donald Yeates. *Systems Analysis*. Palo Alto, California: Science Research Associates, Inc., 1971.

DeGreene, Kenyon B., ed. *Systems Psychology.* New York: McGraw-Hill Book Co., 1970.

Dukes, Carlton W. *Computerizing Personnel Resource Data.* New York: American Management Association, 1971.

Glans, Thomas, et. al. *Management Systems.* New York: Holt, Rinehart, and Winston, Inc., 1968.

Hartman, W., et. al. *Management Information Systems Handbook.* New York: McGraw-Hill Book Co., 1968.

Martino, R. L. *Personnel Management Systems.* Wayne, Pennsylvania: Management Development Institute, 1969.

Morrison, Edward J. *Developing Computer-Based Employee Information Systems.* New York: American Management Association, 1969.

Tomeski, Edward A. *The Computer Revolution.* New York: The Macmillan Company, 1970.

Tomeski, Edward A. *Computers in Business.* San Francisco: Holden-Day, Inc., 1979

Weinberg, Gerald M. *The Psychology of Computer Programming.* New York: Van Nostrand Reinhold Company, 1971.

FOOTNOTES

[1] Alexander M. Maish, "A User's Behavior Toward His MIS," *MIS Quarterly,* March 1979, pp. 39-52.

[2] Gary W. Dickson, and Senn and Chervany, "Research in MIS: The Minnesota Experiments," *Management Science,* May 1977, pp. 913-923.

[3] Robert E. Ornstein, *The Psychology of Consciousness,* (New York: Viking Press, 1972), pp. 41.

[4] C.D. Spielberg and L.D. De Nike, "Descriptive Behaviorism versus Cognitive Theory," *Psychological Review,* July 1966, pp. 306-326.

14

Case Examples: Integrated Human Resource Information Systems

OBJECTIVES OF THE CHAPTER

Three comprehensive descriptions of integrated human resource information systems, in wide use, are described. These case examples are intended to give the reader an appreciation of the actual state-of-the-art in using computers in the personnel function.

THE HUMAN RESOURCE SYSTEM*

The components of the Human Resource System (HRS) are:
- Personnel Record and Employee Profile
- Payroll
- Continuous Employment History
- Career Profile
- Expanded Career Profiling System
- Expanded EEO Compliance System
- Benefits Statement System—ERISA
- Expanded Benefits/ERISA Administration System
- Expanded OSHA System
- Attendance Option
- Position Control Option
- Job Evaluation Option

There is a General Retrieval System which makes it easy for non-data processing people to obtain data from computer files.

Figure 14-1 is a diagram of the Human Resource System and its components.

---

* *What's New, Tested and Available in Total Computerized Personnel Systems?*, Information Science Incorporated, Montvale, New Jersey 07645, 1976.

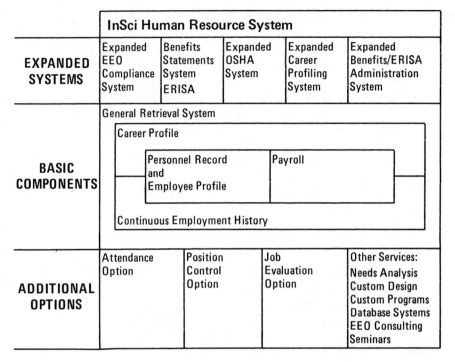

Figure 14-1   The Human Resource System

Personnel Record and Employee Profile

The heart of the Human Resource System is the Personnel Record. This is a computerized, fully-updated personnel file—capable of accepting, storing, and producing data on vital work-related facts about each individual in the company. For instance, it maintains accurate salary histories, automatically rejecting deviations from the pay scales established by the organization. It correlates salary and performance appraisals. It monitors salary and benefit programs. It will facilitate deductions and salary forecasts, and help track expenditures through the year.

Payroll

This module is flexible and can concurrently process payroll for multiple companies, and handle all types of payrolls or pay-groups within a company. It handles both salaried and hourly employees—with virtually any mix of earnings, taxes, and deductions—whatever their schedule of payment may be. Up to 999 different types of earnings, deductions, and taxes can be handled for each employee.

Continuous Employment History

This is a sophisticated, computerized information bank that accepts entries for every significant event in an employee's career and maintains these events indefinitely. The information in the file covers each employee's career—from "date hired" to "date terminated," or to the present time with the company. This allows for prompt comparison of the status of any employee or group of employees over any given period of time. These comparisons can be made in terms of pay, training, advancement, cause of termination, etc. This can be particularly helpful to meet the requirements of EEO, ERISA, and OSHA. Employers must be in a position to supply detailed, accurate information in response to charges, interrogatories, audits, complaints, suits or other actions related to these issues.

Career Profile

The Career Profile is ideal for the large company that wishes to be known as a "promote-from-within" organization. For it is really a unified, all-company individual capability inventory system. The Career Profile enables management to run a large company with much the same human touch that once prevailed when top executives could wander through an office or plant and greet every member of the staff on a first name basis.

Expanded Career Profiling System

The Expanded Career Profiling System is an expanded system which allows for virtually unlimited categories of career/talent information.

Expanded EEO Compliance System

The System is a fully automated instrument for gathering, manipulating and mainatining all data required for a complete utilization analysis—a study of the employment policies of a company, relative to EEO legislation. With it you can also get a precise picture of on-going progress toward Affirmative Action goals—and zero in on problem areas which require adjustment in policy and practice. This System is used in conjunction with the Continuous Employment History.

Benefits Statement System—ERISA

The Employee Retirement Income Security Act (ERISA) makes necessary accurate reports. With this System, a statement can be generated showing any or all benefits coverage for each employee. Data may be maintained to calculate accrued and vested benefits.

Expanded Benefits/ERISA Administration System

This system will automatically produce reports related to retirement/pension administration, group insurance administration, thrift plans, stock purchase and profit sharing administration, etc.

Expanded OSHA System

The Occupational Safety and Health Act requires records and reports be maintained. The OSHA System helps avoid violation of legislation by constantly updating a log of OSHA-reportable cases, by scheduling employee physical examinations on an orderly basis, and by identifying hazardous jobs and automatically monitoring health and safety conditions.

Attendance Option

The Attendance Option can provide useful information for analyzing such areas as: absentee-prone days, cumulative absentee costs by unit, and for establishing ways to cope with attendance problems.

Position Control Option

With this option every position within an organization can be monitored on an individual basis. One report produced by this option summarizes all authorized positions and compares them to actual positions filled. It compares budgeted salaries to actual salaries.

Evaluation Option

This unit has been designed to assist in the maintenance and use of data required to evaluate the relative status of jobs within the organization. One report prepares a detailed analysis of each organizational unit by salary grade and/or by job evaluation level. It shows individual position number and indicates incumbents and/or unfilled positions, with appropriate totals. It tells whether a position is inactive, over-quota, or if there is an error in allocating the position.

THE PERSONNEL MANAGEMENT AND REPORTING SYSTEM*

The Personnel Management and Reporting System maintains and reports on data in the following areas:
- Personnel Information

* *Personnel Management and Reporting System*, Management Science America, Inc., 1975.

- Educational Background
- Skills Inventory
- Current Job Information
- Performance and Salary Reviews
- Qualifications and Preferences
- Benefits
- Health and Safety

There are also "add-on" modules which include:

- Position Control
- Benefits (Expanded)
- Life-to-Date History
- Lost Time or Leave and Absence
- Applicant Flow
- Manpower Development
- Labor Relations
- Rating

The Personnel Management and Reporting System is structured so that it is completely compatible with a Payroll System.

Personnel Information

This includes birth date, place, and country of citizenship, military information, marital data, emergency notification data, physical characteristics, blood type, credit card data, driver's license information are among the elements which are maintained.

Educational Background

The Educational data maintained for each employee includes highest number of years completed, degrees and certificates, school, type of degree, date of degree, major and minor fields of study, professional licenses and memberships. There are also provisions to indicate education in progress and projected year of completion.

Skills Inventory

It is possible to maintain, for each employee, information on as many as twenty skills. Each individual history includes both general and specific job categories or skill functions, an indication of supervisory and/or non-supervisory experience at that job or skill, the number of years experience, proficiency level, the last year worked using that skill, and an indication whether the skill experience was obtained with the present employer or a previous employer. One use of this skills bank is to provide reports that list the employees with a particular mix of skills that match a new job function.

Current Job Information

All current job information, including job title, annual salary, date assigned to present position, supervisor, office extension, position control number, etc. is maintained by the System. Additionally, all transfer information and an indication of promotion readiness are maintained.

Performance and Salary Reviews

The ten most recent performance reviews can be recorded using the Basic Personnel System. Each review includes the rating given the employee; an indication of the supervisor making the review, the date on which the review was made, and the job being performed when the review was made. As with the performance history, it is possible to record the ten most recent rates or salaries. The date, the amount, the reason, and the job being performed when the increases were applied are indicated. The user may coordinate the rate/salary and performance reviews as desired.

Qualifications and Preferences

The System maintains in addition to the present job, three jobs for which the employee is qualified, three jobs for which the employee is recommended, as well as the job which is preferred. The employee's geographical preference is also maintained.

Benefits

Selected information in the area of benefits is maintained by the System.

Health and Safety

The System maintains selected information in the area of health and safety.

Position Control

This module provides the ability to keep track of and report on each position within the organization. The available information includes the position control number, the associated title, salary range, authorized or unauthorized status, vacant or filled status, part-time, full-time status, skills and/or limitations associated with the position, employee identification of employee(s) filling the position, etc.

Benefits (Expanded)

The Benefits module is primarily a reporting module providing various benefits reports including some reports required by ERISA. One of the reports the module provides is an annual or periodic statement of employer-paid benefits received by an employee. An analysis of vacation, holidays, and credit union benefits is also reported upon in this module, and projected pension and/or retirement incomes are calculated.

Life-to-Date History

This module provides complete history information for any data elements selected by the user. The user specifies which data elements are to be carried in the history file as well as the number of times the data element is to be carried. For example, five year, ten year, or life-to-date details on job positions, salaries, reviews, ratings, increases, location and transfer information, addresses, etc. may be specified. The module is intended to contain extended history information that is not contained on the basic file. It is useful in extensive employee reviews, pension calculations based on years of service and salary, and union and governmental reporting on types of positions held over a specified period of time by any or a designated number of employees.

Lost Time or Leave and Absence

This module provides detailed reporting on all absences and other lost time. Specialized reporting on the type and number of employee absences including total length, dates and days involved, connection with holidays or weekend, pay to the employee, lost time to the department, compensation involved, and other statistical data that may be relevant to the absence is available. This module further provides all loss reporting including the log information for OSHA. Accidents, on the job injuries, the resulting lost time, related expenses, associated dates, workmen's compensation, etc. are reported.

Applicant Flow

The applicant flow module maintains applicant data such as applicant number, name, address, telephone number, EEO code, date and location at which application was made, the source of applicant awareness of the position, position for which application is being made, test information, primary skills, interviewer, hire/not hired code with associated reasons, and disposition of application.

Manpower Development

This module provides reports on the formal, special and additional education, licenses, memberships, skills and qualifications of each employee for the purpose of internal job selection. Career objectives, job preferences, and special training can be matched so that employees who are both qualified and interested can be prepared for future jobs. Career paths can be structured with this module and goals and timetables for career development can be established. Career paths leading to a particular position, as well as paths planned for an employee, can be plotted. Through this module executive level positions can be planned for and potential executives can be prepared through lateral progression to occupy these key positions.

Labor Relations

This module provides reports on union information including seniority by job, date, department and shift. Dates of union membership, number of employees per union, withdrawal dates and reasons, grievance data, arbitration results, cease and desist orders, strike and walk-out data with the associated reasons, duration, and resultion are all maintained and reported upon.

Rating

This module will be used to evaluate an employee relative to the qualifications for a position and relative to the corresponding evaluation of his peers. The supervisor rating the employee, and the rating of his peers would be maintained. This module will create a series of graphic portraits of an individual relative to his peers and to the group average. One report will produce a simple bar graph of traits or rating factors for the individual employee and for the average of all others.

SUPER PERSONNEL*

Functionally, the System is divided into four processing segments: Labor Relations, Skills Inventory, Benefits, and Manpower Planning and Budget Analysis.

The basic processing flow of the System is illustrated in Figure 14-2. All personnel transactions are validity checked for accuracy of content and of existence of an employee record. Absence of an employee record will cause

* *Super Personnel,* Wang Laboratories Inc., Tewksbury, Massachusetts 01876, 1975.

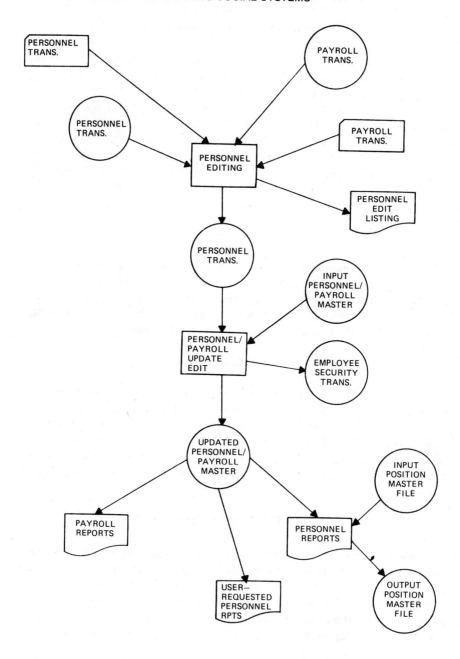

Figure 14-2   Super Personnel System Flowchart

the transaction(s) to be rejected and an appropriate message to be printed on the edit listing. The edited personnel transactions are then passed to the personnel/payroll update edit file along with the previous personnel/payroll master file. The System generates an employee security transaction file which is updated whenever a transaction is processed for an employee. Once the personnel/payroll master file is updated, the reports are then generated. The Systems produces personnel reports for each module in addition to user-requested reports produced by a Personnel Report Generator. During report generation, the manpower planning module checks the job positions master file against the updated personnel master scanning for available, filled, or new positions, updating the file as is necessary.

Labor Relations

This module produces an employee profile report which is a complete employee document for use by management. This is printed on a convenient turnaround form which can be corrected by the employee and sent back to update the data base. Equal Employment Opportunity reporting, salary classification and history, and a variety of employee rosters are also produced by this module.

Examples of reports which can be generated by this module are:

Figure 14-3 which is the basic employee profile document.

Figure 14-4 which is an example of a report for EEO.

Figure 14-5 which indicates persons hired or terminated by job classification.

Skills Inventory

The Skills Inventory module is a tool which enables management to utilize human resources in skills searches, as well as to track and guide individual employee career paths. A variety of useful reports on skills, education, promotability, and career counseling are produced.

Examples of reports which can be generated by this module include:

Figure 14-6 which is a basic skills information form.

Figure 14-7 which reports on promotable persons by skill code.

Benefits

This module helps management to track indirect employee expenses as well as to display to employees the benefits that the organization provides. Insurance, dependency, retirement, pensions, and profit-sharing listings are all available.

Illustrations of reports which can be generated by this module are:

Figure 14-8 which is a benefits status report.

Figure 14-9 which is an employee's benefits statement.

EMPLOYEE PROFILE

RUN DATE	PAGE	EMPLOYEE KEY		COMPANY NAME
04-26-75	29	001/21/WCS1/067324851		WANG COMPUTER SERVICES

NAME	EMPLOYEE NAME	FIRST NAME	SFX	FLO OCC	MARITAL M STATUS	DEP	STATUS	DATE CHANGE MADE
	G J MCCADDEN	GEORGE	M	C	M	3	A	

ADDR	STREET ADDRESS	DATE OF HIRE	JOB CODE	WHEN IN JOB		JOB TITLE	SALY GRADE	RANGE MINIMUM
	10 CAMBRIDGE ROAD	08-01-68	CS125	02-01-74		PROGRAMMER ANALYST	C1101	12000.00

APT # PO BOX	DATE OF BIRTH	HRLY RATE	P P SALY	AN SALARY	NORMAL HOURS	RANGE MIDPOINT
APT #9	06-09-47		579.17	13900.08	86.66	13000.00

CITY	STATE	ZIP	TERMINATION DATE	REASON	REHIRE	NEXT EVAL	SUPERVISOR	RANGE MAXIMUM
ARLINGTON	MA	02174				02-75	GUSTIN	14000.00

SALARY, JOB AND EVALUATION HISTORY CHRONOLOGICALLY

EFFECTIVE DATE	TYPE CHANGE	EVAL CODE	NEW P P SALY RATE	AMOUNT OF CHANGE	% CHANGE	JOB CODE	JOB TITLE	SUPERVISOR
02-01-74	AN	EXC	579.17	700.00	5.3%	CS125	PROGRAMMER ANALYST	GUSTIN
02-01-73	AN	EXC	550.00	1200.00	10.0%	CS126	SR. PROGRAMMER	GUSTIN
02-01-72	AN	EXC	500.00	1000.00	9.1%	CS126	SR. PROGRAMMER	WALKER
02-01-71	AN	GOO	458.34	800.00	7.8%	CS150	PROGRAMMER	BARTLETT
02-01-70	AN	EXC	425.00	900.00	9.7%	CS150	PROGRAMMER	BARTLETT
02-01-69	SM	GOO	387.50	600.00	6.9%	CS175	JR. PROGRAMMER	WALLACE
08-01-68	NP		362.50			CS200	PROGRAMMER TRAINEE	WALLACE

EMPLOYEE KEY   EMPLOYEE NAME   DATE CHANGE MADE

001/21/WCS1/067324851   G J MCCADDEN

SPOUSE NAME	DATE OF BIRTH	HOME TELEPHONE #	WORK EXT.	EMERGENCY CONTACT NAME	RELATIONSHIP	EMERGENCY TEL #
BARBARA	10-15-47	617 648-8550	1524	BARBARA MCCADDEN	WIFE	617-648-8550

EMERGENCY ADDRESS IF DIFFERENT FROM EMPLOYEES

EDUCATION INFORMATION

LEVEL	NAME	YR	MAJOR	SUBJECT	DATE	LENGTH	GRADE
111	W ON MSTRS		MATH	IBM/OS	02-71	1-WK	NGD
110	BS	68	MATH	COBOL PGMNG	10-68	1-WK	NGD

BENEFITS (EMPLOYER AND EMPLOYEE CONTRIBUTIONS)

	COVERAGE	BENEFICIARY	RELATIONSHIP		COVERAGE
13.60	8.00	50,000	BARBARA MCCADDEN	WIFE	7.92	6.32	FAML

Figure 14-3 Employee Profile

COMPANY RPT 125 1 DATE 04-12-75 PP 15 PAGE 1 EQUAL EMPLOYMENT OPPORTUNITY REPORT SUPER TEST COMPANY 836 NORTH STREET, TEWKSBURY MA 01876

	TOTAL EMPLOYEES	TOTAL MALES	NEGRO	ORIENTAL	AMERICAN INDIAN	SPANISH SURNAMED	TOTAL FEMALES	NEGRO	ORIENTAL	AMERICAN INDIAN	SPANISH SURNAMED
OFFICIALS & MANAGERS	6	5					1				
PROFESSIONALS	10	6			1		4		1		
TECHNICIANS	3	1				1	2				1
SALES WORKERS	3	3				1					
OFFICE & CLERICAL	10	2	1			1	8	1		1	
CRAFTSMEN (SKILLED)	6	5	2								
OPERATIVES (SEMI-SKLD)	3	3		1		1					
LABORERS	1	1				1	1				1
••••• TOTALS •••••	41	26	4	1	2	4	15	2	1	1	
OJT PRODUCTION	2	2				1					
••••• TOTALS •••••	2	2				1					

Figure 14-4 Equal Employment Opportunity (EEO)

```
                                                                                                    SUPER TEST COMPANY
COMPANY  RPT    DATE     PP   PAGE
 123      6   04-12-75   15     1  "HIRED OR TERMINATED" WITHIN QTR. BY JOB CLASS     836 NORTH STREET, TEWKSBURY  MA 01876

EMPLOYEE NAME            SOC SEC NUM    HIRED    TERMINATED    TERMINATION REASON        SUPERVISOR     EEOC  EEOJ  SEXC

R T PETERSON             201-21-3420   01-16-75                                           HENDERSON       C     S     F
T M PRODNEY              000-00-0000   01-04-75   03-31-75     OTHER JOB                  HENDERSON       C     A     M

        # OF PEOPLE TERMINATED     # OF PEOPLE HIRED FOR JOB CLASS     CS050
                    1                          2

J L FERNANDEZ            232-41-1918              03-31-75     MARRIAGE                   CUMMINGS        S     5     F

        # OF PEOPLE TERMINATED     # OF PEOPLE HIRED FOR JOB CLASS     OF150
                    1

R N CRABB                216-98-4017   01-15-75   02-28-75     EXCESSIVE ABSENTEEISM      CURRAN          C     8     M

        # OF PEOPLE TERMINATED     # OF PEOPLE HIRED FOR JOB CLASS     PR025
                    1                          1

J A BAILEY               478-31-6420              02-15-75     DISSATISFIED WITH SALARY   VINCENT         C     7     M

        # OF PEOPLE TERMINATED     # OF PEOPLE HIRED FOR JOB CLASS     PR100
                    1

COMPANY  TOTALS
                    4                          3

50829
```

Figure 14-5 Hired or terminated within quarter by job class.

EMPLOYEE NAME
J S LOPEZ

RUN DATE
09-04-75

PAGE
01

SKILLS INFORMATION

CHECK 1: 32 ___ NEW
33 ___ REPLACE
34 ___ CHANGE

EMPLOYEE KEY
123-22-20020-00127h277

REPORT DATE
08-28-75

SKILLS HISTORY

SKILL	YRS OF	LAST R/		SKILL	YRS OF	LAST R/		SKILL	YRS OF	LAST R/		SKILL	YRS OF	LAST R/		CHECK
CODE	EXPERE	USED CD		CODE	EXPERE	USED CD		CODE	EXPERE	USED CD		CODE	EXPERE	USED CD		IF CHG
CS200	3	75 E		CS195	3	75 E		CS190	2	73 E		CS189	1	71 E		
CS185	1	70 G		CS180	2	69 A		CS175	1	67 E						

INTERVIEWS/COUNSELING

INTERVIEWER/	DATE	PROMTBLE	SKILL PREFERRED			DATE	REASN	INTERVIEWER/	DATE	PROMTBLE	SKILL PREFERRED			CHECK
COUNSELOR	INTER	1 2 3	OR SKILL OR RESULTS OF			AVAIL	CODES	COUNSELOR	INTER	1 2 3	OR SKILL OR RESULTS OF			IF CG
			INTERVED INTERVIEW								INTERVED INTERVIEW			DATE AVAIL
J L HAYE	06-75 1		CS225 CS220 CS210	06-76	A - A	J L HAYES	06-74 1		CS210 CS200 CS190	12-74	
M R SMITH	06-73 2		CS190 CS180 CS179	12-73	A - A	M R SMITH	06-72	3	CS180 CS175 CS170	12-72	

EDUCATION

LEVEL	MO/YR	MAJOR	MINOR	SCH	CHECK		TRAINING				CHECK		TECHNICAL EXPERTISE/HOBBIES			
ATTND	CMPLD			CDE	IF CHG		TYPE	DATE	TYPE	DATE	IF CHG		TYPE	PRO	YR LAST	CHECK
							TNG	CMPLD	TNG	CMPLD				CDE	USED	IF CHG
BS	06-72	MIS	MKT				ACAL	04-75	SPAN	10-74			CHES	1	75	
HS	06-68												VOLB	2	75	
													SRED	1	71	

GEOGRAPIC PREFERENCE			LANGUAGES			
AREA	CHECK IF CHG		LANG CODE	PRO CDE	CHECK IF CHG		KEYED BY: _____ DATE: _____
NE			02	1			PERSONNEL AUTHORIZATION: _____ DATE: _____
EC			09	2			EMPLOYEE AUTHORIZATION: _____ DATE: _____
US							SUPERVISORS AUTHORIZATION: _____ DATE: _____

Figure 14-6 Skills Information

COMPANY	RPT	DATE	PP	PAGE				SUPER TEST COMPANY	
123	6	09-04-75	40	10	PROMOTABLES BY SKILL CODE			836 NORTH STREET, TEWKSBURY, MA 01876	

EMPLOYEE NAME	EMPLOYEE KEY	SKILL TITLE	DATE AVAILABLE	DATE OF HIRE	SEX	EEO	SKILL PREFER	PROMOTABILITY
E D FERRARA	123-11-10010-783254056	ASSEMBLER/CIRCUIT	09-30-75	03-09-74	M	C	ASMBL	YES
M L AVILA	123-11-10010-064792781	ASSEMBLER/CIRCUIT	10-30-75	05-18-74	M	C	ASMBL	YES

NUMBER OF PEOPLE   PROMOTABLE FOR SKILL CODE ASMBL

   2

R C HOWARD	123-22-20020-413652100	TESTER/CIRCUITS	01-01-76	06-16-74	M	C	TESTG	YES
F L LIGHTFEATHER	123-22-20000-091004352	TESTER/SMALL PARTS	11-01-75	06-23-69	F	A	TESTG	YES
J S LOPEZ	123-22-20020-064826483	ASSEMBLER	08-01-75	01-16-75	F	S	TESTG	YES

NUMBER OF PEOPLE   PROMOTABLE FOR SKILL CODE TESTG

   3

Figure 14-7   Promotables by Skill Code

EMPLOYEE NAME
J L THORNTON

DATE 08-30-75   PAGE 01

CHECK II 32 ___ NEW
33 ___ REPLACE
34 ___ CHANGE

BENEFITS
STATUS REPORT

EMPLOYEE KEY
123-11-10010-10664220

LIFE INSURANCE

DATE OF ENTRY	INS AMOUNT	RENF SWTH	CO ID	A/C NO	CO CONTR	EMPL CONTR	CHECK IF CHG	BENEFICIARIES/DEPENDENTS BENEFICIARY NAME	RELA CODE	DATE OF BIRTH	CHECK IF CHG
01-01-75	17500	A C	10	42367000	450	100		B L THORNTON	01	10-16-40	—
01-01-74	5000	A C	20	04141100	100	10		P N THORNTON	02	11-15-60	—
								B T THORNTON	03	06-18-62	—

MEDICAL INSURANCE CLAIMS

DATE OF PAYMENT	DEP SWT	PLAN CODE	TYPE CODE	PAYMENT AMOUNT	CHECK IF CHG
08-01-75	B	1	2	140.00	—
06-15-75	D	1	3	1800.00	—
04-18-75	A	2	1	15.68	—
02-28-76	A	3	1	156.70	

KEYED BY: _____ DATE: _____
REVIEWED BY: _____ DATE: _____
PERSONNEL AUTHORIZATION: _____ DATE: _____
EMPLOYEE AUTHORIZATION: _____ DATE: _____
SUPERVISOR AUTHORIZATION: _____ DATE: _____

MEDICAL INSURANCE

DATE OF ENTRY	CERTIFICATE NUMBER	CO ID	PL CD	DEPENDENT SWITCHES	COMP CONTR	EMPL CONTR	CHECK IF CHG
01-01-70	672866444	01	1	A C	450.00	250.00	
01-01-70	846709121	01	2	A B C	260.00	100.00	
01-01-70	426679678	01	3	A B C	750.00	400.00	

RETIREMENT/PENSION/PROFIT SHARING

US PL CD	DATE OF ENTRY	RENE SWTH	COMPANY-CONTRIBUTION PERIOD	TO/DATE	EMPLOYEE-CONTRIBUTION PERIOD	TO/DATE	CO-PER	OPTION 1	2	3	OPTION AMOUNTS 1	2	3	CHECK IF CHG
01 01	01-01-71	A B C	1800.00	11250.00	450.00	3500.00	A BB				450.00			
04 02	01-01-72	B C	500.00	2500.00	110.00	560.00	D EE				120.00			

Figure 14-8 Benefits Status Report

```
COMPANY      RUN DATE 09-23-75     REPORT DATE 09-30-75     COMPANY AND EMPLOYEE CONTRIBUTIONS FOR                    PAGE 10
NO.  NAME                                                   RETIREMENT AND/OR PENSION AND/OR PROFIT SHARING
123  SUPER TEST COMPANY

       PLAN 1:          PLAN 2:          PLAN 3:          PLAN 4:          PLAN 5:
       EMPLOYEE         EMPLOYEE         EMPLOYEE         EMPLOYEE         EMPLOYEE
       1000.00          3000.00                           4000.00          2000.00
                                         1000.00


                  RETIREMENT        PENSION         PROFIT SHARING       GRAND TOTALS
TOTALS
       COMPANY    14000.00          15000.00        12000.00             41000.00

       EMPLOYEE   1000.00           3000.00         1000.00              5000.00
```

Figure 14-9 Employee Benefits Statement

Manpower Planning and Budget Analysis

The MPBA module gives users the ability to plan, implement and monitor company-wide human resource allocations and budgets. Thus, the personnel department can locate employees for jobs, jobs for employees, provide career planning for key personnel, and measure the impact of increased salary demands on corporate budgets. Position analysis, qualification reports, salary trends, and career-path mapping are all produced by this module.

Illustrations of reports which can be generated by this module include:

Figure 14-10 which is a manpower budget analysis report.

Figure 14-11 is a career path map report.

SUMMARY

Three fairly comprehensive integrated personnel information systems were described. They indicate the types of files, reports, and processing that can actually exist with current state-of-the-art advances.

REPORT DATE 06-26-75
RUN DATE 09-04-75

SUPER TEST COMPANY
CORPORATE MANPOWER BUDGET ANALYSIS

PAGE 1

STAFF BUDGET UNIT	DIRECTOR/MANAGER	ACTIVE EMPLOY	ON LEAVE	APPR. REQS. REPL./INCR.	TOTAL	BUDGET #	(OVER)/UNDER BUDGET #	REMARKS
CORPORATE R & D	R K HARRIS	40	1	2/3	44	0/1	2/2	STARTED MIS PROJECT
PROGRAMMING/MINI	C R SMITH	20	0	1/0	20	0/0	1/0	NEW PROD ASSIGN.
QUALITY CONTROL	C A MORGAN	11	0	0/0	11	0/0	0/0	
CUSTOMER SERVICES	R E MOORE	9	1	1/3	13	0/1	1/2	INCREASE CUST. BASE

Figure 14-10 Corporate Manpower Budget Analysis

```
REPORT DATE 08/28/75                                                    PAGE 10
RUN DATE 09/04/75

                              SUPER TEST COMPANY
                              CAREER PATH MAP

UNIT NUMBER  123                      GROUP NUMBER  1110
UNIT NAME  CORPORATE R&D              GROUP NAME  PROGRAMMING/MINICOMPUTERS
DIRECTOR/MANAGER R K HARRIS           DIRECTOR/MANAGER S C SMITH


                                      CURRENT    EXPERIENCE  EDUCATION  SKILL   CURRENT  ------PERTINENT SKILLS------   CURRENT
EMPLOYEE NAME       EMPLOYEE KEY      JOB KEY    RATING      RATING     RATING  SALARY                                  STATUS

J L CALLAHAN    123111001033241191B  CS125      AAAA        CCCC       AAAA    920000   COBL ASMB PL/1

                                                                                       INTERVIEWER COMMENTS

ADVANCEMENT POTENTIAL - CURRENT POSITION   JOB NAME PROGRAMMER/ANALYST
ESTIMATED DATE FOR OPTIMAL  EXPERIENCE RATING 01/02/76  EXPECTED RATING AAAA
REQUIRES ADDITIONAL EDUCATION FOR OPTIMUM RATING        NO EXPECTED RATING
REQUIRES SKILL IMPROVEMENT FOR OPTIMUM RATING          YES EXPECTED RATING AAAA
POSSIBLE ADDITIONAL SKILLS AS FOLLOWS - FORT
POSSIBLE JOB GRADE IMPROVEMENT FROM CS12 TO CS15
MAXIMUM SALARY IMPROVEMENT 14,000

ADVANCEMENT POTENTIAL - NEW POSITION   JOB NAME SYSTEMS ANALYST
                                       JOB KEY  CS145
ESTIMATED DATE FOR PROMOTIONAL EXPERIENCE RATING 01/02/76  EXPECTED RATING AAAA
REQUIRES ADDITIONAL EDUCATION FOR PROMOTION RATING     NO EXPECTED RATING
REQUIRES SKILL IMPROVEMENT FOR PROMOTION RATING        NO EXPECTED RATING
POSSIBLE ADDITIONAL SKILLS AS FOLLOWS
POSSIBLE JOB GRADE IMPROVEMENT FROM CS15 TO CSP5
PROMOTIONAL SALARY IMPROVEMENT TO 20,000
```

Figure 14-11 Career Path Map Report

Part III Cases

DENVER CONTROLS

SUBURBAN BANK

NO-FAIL COMPANY

CROWN COMPANY

CARTER PRODUCTS

DENVER CONTROLS

Mike Reid, 43, is the president and major stockholder of Denver Controls. Mr. Reid described his major tasks as president as follows:

> I have to ensure coordination among the diverse units of the company. Also, I set overall goals for the enterprise and try to encourage planning on the part of our managers. Currently, our planning horizon consists of a 12-month budget, but we will eventually have a five-year horizon. In addition, it is my responsibility to identify talented employees and to motivate them.

Mr. Reid feels the weaknesses in his organization are the lack of long-range planning and a very thin management. There are few promising young managers to back up the current top managers.

The president foresees that the nature of his responsibilities will be changing, and the computer will be instrumental in the change.

> I see myself spending less time with day-to-day decisions, and more time with long-range planning and external relations.

> I need to recruit entrepreneurial-type managers, and get them involved with the future of the company.

Our company needs improved communications and information. This will involve an integrated data base and a computer-communications system. We need a system which will permit us to identify marketing opportunities anywhere in the world, facilitate product planning, and manufacture quality products at the lowest possible cost. The computer can digest a mountain of data to pinpoint untapped markets and optimize profitable production (taking into account differential labor rates, transportation costs, material costs, etc.).

QUESTIONS

1. What do you think of Mr. Reid's concept of his current and future role as chief executive officer of Denver Controls?
2. Is Mr. Reid's vision, of his company's computer effort, realistic?
3. What kinds of problems will be faced by Denver Controls if they proceed with Mr. Reid's computer plans?

SUBURBAN BANK

Suburban Bank had total deposits of 135 million dollars, and was staffed by 200 employees. The Bank was composed of eight main departments: commercial loans, real estate, cashier's office, investment, trust, personnel, computer center, and installment loans. Each department was headed by a vice president or a director, and all reported to the executive vice president, who in turn reported to the president.

Top management set and reviewed the goals of the personnel department. For example, top management reviewed the staffing of departments and salary/promotion recommendations. The individual department officer sent recommendations on staffing, salary adjustments, and promotions to the personnel department. The personnel department normally routinely approved such recommendations if they were within the Bank's policies and procedures. The personnel director then sent all such personnel change recommendations to the executive vice president who channeled the paperwork to the board of directors.

The Bank has had a computer for a number of years. It is mainly used for deposit and check accounting, loan accounting, and trust accounts. Only the payroll phase of personnel work has been computerized. All other personnel paperwork is handled manually in the personnel department. The personnel officer thinks this is essential to maintain confidentiality of records.

The Bank has also offered its computer services to its customers, and the computer department now handles data processing jobs for manufacturing firms, a few hospitals and schools, a government agency, and a number of professional people (e.g., doctors, lawyers). This has caused some problems, since the computer department is under pressure to meet the deadlines of the Bank's customers but also must meet the deadlines for the Bank's internal reports.

QUESTIONS

1. Why do you think the Bank's personnel work has not been computerized?
2. Which areas of personnel work seem ripe for computerization? How could

such computerization help management, and improve conditions for employees?
3. What roles should the following individuals play in computerizing personnel work: Bank workers, personnel director, computer center director, supervisors of work areas, vice presidents of main departments, the executive vice president, the president?
4. Suggest ways of improving the computer center's scheduling and coordination problems.
5. How can the computer center improve its relations with top management? With inside users? With external users? With Bank workers?

NO-FAIL COMPANY

The systems department of the No-Fail Company was in the final stages of testing the spread-sheets. The spread-sheets are the vital financial reports used by the top management of No-Fail. Up to this time, the spread-sheets were produced on a panic basis by a large staff of analysts and clerks.

The systems department promised that the computer program would be operative by December. Ray, of the systems department, and Bob, of the financial analysis department, had been working feverishly to get the job done. It proved more difficult than imagined due to the many interrelated computations and refinements requested as the systems work progressed.

In December, test runs of the spread-sheets uncovered some erroneous results. Bob and his boss, the vice president of financial analysis, became very disturbed since they had promised the president that the spread-sheets would be produced by computer in time for a top management meeting to be held early in January. Alex, the manager of the systems department, entered the picture and began a thorough review of the logic of the computer program. Also, he assigned Duane,—a young, but brilliant computer programmer—to help Ray on the project.

When Ray learned of the new developments, he said:

This implies criticism of my work. I just followed the specifications of Bob and the financial people. The program works as they defined the problem. Now I have people taking over my job after I have done all the work, and they will get credit for it. Why should I be criticized? I don't have to put up with this. I quit.

QUESTIONS

1. What are some of the probable underlying causes for Ray's blowup?
2. How should Alex handle the situation with Ray?
3. What role, if any, might the personnel department play on such a project?
4. How would you react to the situation if you were the superior of both Alex and Ray?
5. Suggest a plan, for No-Fail, to improve employees' morale, cooperation, and motivation in the systems department.

CROWN COMPANY

On January 2, Mr. Pipps, personnel staff assistant, was asked to review and improve procedures used to evaluate and control the overall performance of the data processing center (DPC) and its individual employees. Mr. Checkers, manager of the data processing center, asked for this review. He wondered if the present procedures provided the most useful measures of performance, and what improved measures might be used.

The Crown Company has eight manufacturing plants at various locations throughout the South and a central office located in Miami, Florida. At each plant, there is also a warehouse from which products are distributed.

The data processing requirements of the company are extensive. Payroll preparation, customer billings and collections, and disbursements to suppliers are the major large volume data processing tasks. Crown Company has nine data processing units; each of these units (one at each plant location) are responsible for the routine, repetitive, high volume tasks described above. Their work can be carried out satisfactorily with a small staff and with machine operators who have little or no previous training or experience. No programming is done at these units.

The ninth unit, the data processing center (DPC), is located in the central office at Miami, and its work is quite different from the other eight units. This work consists principally of many small, difficult, one-time jobs. The unit is primarily concerned with providing management information reports requested by various departments of Crown Company. At any given time during the year, the center is responsible for nearly 300 different projects. The DPC has about 50 employees, including: systems analysts, computer programmers, keypunch operators, console operators, and some administrative personnel.

QUESTIONS

1. How would you go about appraising the adequacy of existing performance evaluation methods?
2. What methods could be recommended to evaluate the performance of the DPC and each of the various classifications of employees?
3. What are the differences that Pipps must be aware of, between the Miami DPC and the eight plant data processing units, that might call for different performance evaluation methods?
4. How can Mr. Checkers determine if Pipps' recommendations are sound?

CARTER PRODUCTS

Carter Product's computer had been used primarily to process routine paperwork rather than information for management. The president set up a management information systems committee for the following purposes:

1. Review the firm's current and proposed computer uses.
2. Propose computer plans for the next three to five years.

Particular attention was directed towards the type of computer equipment required, the manpower levels needed in the computer department, and the allocation of such manpower among the various computer projects.

The committee set up sub-committees to study and report on existing and proposed computer applications in the various functional areas: manufacturing, marketing, accounting, personnel, research and development, etc. The sub-committees were asked to give priorities to each of the applications. Consolidation of the various sub-committee reports indicated the necessity for at least 40 man-years of systems and programming effort to do all of the work needed to achieve a management information system.

When the president learned of this, he disbanded the management information systems committee and decided to replace the current computer manager. He said,

We have used computers for five years. Now I learn that we haven't been using them effectively. What have we been doing for five years? We can't afford to reprogram everything and devote 40 man-years and more than half-a-million dollars on developing a MIS. There must be a simpler and cheaper way of getting a MIS.

QUESTIONS

1. What are the overall problems in planning for an information system?
2. What is your opinion of the MIS committee's analysis? Do you agree with the president's actions?
3. What would you do if you were the incoming manager of the computer center? How would you approach your new responsibilities?
4. How should an organization decide the type and quantity of computer equipment needed for its purpose?

PART 4
EPILOGUE

All things excellent are as difficult as they are rare.

Spinoza

Based on extensive research and experience, the authors call attention to an impending *crisis in computers* which they attribute to a *neglect of the human factors in computer systems.*

Many of the troubles with computers stem largely from over-concentration on the technical aspects of this powerful modern tool. As a consequence, there has been a pronounced under-concern about the human dimension—in the selling of computers by computer manufacturers, and in the development of systems by business, government, and academic and institutional organizations.

Computer professionals are hypnotized by computer technology. Conversely, social scientists have not been sufficiently involved in the planning, design, and implementation of computers—notwithstanding their great impact on organizations and society.

While the computer industry has enjoyed the euphoria of unparalleled growth, fissures were developing in its foundation. As a result, the industry today faces a host of difficulties:

- Paperwork pollution (both in volume and inaccuracies) is generated by the prolific computer printers.

- Dehumanization and alienation result from the requirement that employees adjust to machines.

- Socially unacceptable uses are made of computers (e.g., "snooping" by use of data banks, harassing mailings).

- The computer interdicts communication between human beings.

- Cost savings anticipated from computers are not achieved.

- Management feels uncomfortable due to dependency on computer systems and technocrats they do not understand.

- Rapid growth, concentration of market power, and indifference to social concerns have created an environment of court battles, government investigations, and may well result in government regulation of the computer industry.

The authors are concerned, for they fear the computer industry could experience a loss of credibility comparable to that suffered by the school of scientific management several decades ago.

Today, a scant three decades after the invention of the modern computer, it is difficult to attribute any social or economic "miracles" to the computer. Our businesses have difficulty in competing in the world markets, and at home many of our products and services seem to decline in quality while, relatively speaking, prices increase. In government, the Department of Defense is still blatantly wasteful, although it is the largest single user of computers and advanced management science methods. Notwithstanding the use of thousands of computers, the bureaucratic tangle in the Executive, Legislative, and Judicial branches of government is hardly becoming less tangled. And in the public and private sectors alike, the relations of people with organizations, and people with people, seem to be less satisfactory than they were B.C. (before computers).

Not all of the above shortcomings, of course, are attributable in whole or even primarily to computers, but it would be encouraging to be able to point to more examples of the computer's making *fundamental* contributions to the improvement of our society.

In fact, recently the authors are finding a disturbing number of instances of drastic action being taken against computer systems. In at least a few organizations (both large and small) the decision has been to decomputerize —and to return the work to people! The reasons for these actions range from costs to communications breakdowns between executives.

The authors urge that it is time for a new generation of computers—a generation not of mere exotic technology, but one involving computers that are:

- Designed to be easily comprehended and used by most people, and not just technocrats.

- Marketed only when they are thoroughly "debugged" and within a code of ethics that prevents over-selling and withholding pertinent facts and support from the user.

- Planned primarily to benefit people and society, and not profits and productivity at the cost of harming the human system.

- Installed to serve the social system—and not for the social system to be twisted to serve the computer.

The computer industry is at a pivotal point in its development. It needs revitalization if it is to build on and sustain its past growth and acceptance. It will take a major effort for computer vendors and users genuinely to adopt the human approaches to computers that are developed in this book. If such change does not occur, it is highly likely that there will be increasing confrontations between government and the computer industry, computer vendors amongst themselves, computer vendors and users, computer users and employees and unions, and technocrats and non-technocrats. More importantly, there may be a ground-swell of public reaction against computers. Notwithstanding the broadened use of computers in society, there is considerable sarcasm about computers and their utility.

For the "people-oriented computer systems" we must shift our focus. Up to now, we have too often required that people be "bent, stapled, and mutilated."

Subject Index

automation
and employment, 238-239
and systems, 131-134

behavioral science, 21-26, 93-100, 125-126

Cargo data interchange system, 120-121
centralization, 179-185
change
and computers, 1-2, 26-29
and employees, 57-60
and gaining acceptance, 95-96
and problems, 19-21
computers
and automation, 238-239
and cargo data interchange system,
120-121
and change, 26-29
and communication, 4, 152
and computer industry, 136-138, 341-342
and computer users, 139-145
and decentralization/centralization, 179-
185
and decision-making, 176-179
and distributed data processing, 26
and education and training, 142-144
and effect on management, 171-189
and electronic fund transfer system,
118-119
and employment patterns, 141-142,
242-247
highlights and features, 144-148
history of, 134-136
and management information systems,
105-110, 179-184, 341-343

management responsibilities, 174-175
and man-machine interface, 182-184
and manpower programs, 247-249
and organization structure, 21-27, 179-
185
and organizing and staffing, 258-283
and personnel applications, 190-211
and personnel department, 6, 60-61, 190-
211
and personnel systems, 6-7, 190-211,
284-311, 312-337
and point-of-sale system, 119-120
and simulation, 123
problems with, 8-9, 155-159, 171-174,
190-193
and programming, 4-5
pros and cons of, 171-174, 190-193
and social issues, 232-257, 341-343
and training and development, 212-231
trends, 148-151
and types of processing systems, 131-134
criminal uses of computers, 253-254

decentralization, 179-185
decision-making, 116-120, 176-179
designing personnel information systems,
284-311
distributed data processing, 26

economy, U.S., 43-44
education and training, 142-144, 212-229,
269-273, 273-281
Electronic fund transfer system, 118-119
employees
and change, 53

and work patterns, 44, 141-142, 239-242, 273-281
employment
  and automation, 238-239
  and computers, 141-142
errors and computers, 157-160

Human resource system, 284-311, 312-337

information systems, 65-75, 104-123, 284-311, 312-337

job patterns, 242-247, 273-281

management
  affected by computers, 171-189
  computer responsibilities, 174-175
  and decision-making, 176-179
management information systems, 100-129
  computer-based MIS, 105-110
  and decision-making, 176-179
  and management science, 110-112
  planning and implementing, 112-117, 284-311
  and people, 116-117, 299-309
  status and trends, 100-105, 341-343
management science, 110-112
manpower
  and change, 44
  and computers and automation, 238-239
  forecasts, 50-51, 65-67
  goals, 38-39
  national policy, 33-37
  planning, 39-40, 62-65, 67, 199-200
  programs, 247-249
  projections, 45-46
  supply and demand, 33-37
  systems, 249
Motivation and systems personnel, 273-281

occupational patterns, 44-45, 141-142, 238-242
organic organization, 23, 90-92
organization
  and change, 179-185
  and computers, 18-19, 179-185
  concept of, 77-78
  and systems, 86-88
  and technology, 15-30

organizing the computer department, 258-283

people
  and computers, 28-29
  and management information systems, 116-117
  and systems, 289-292
personnel departments, 50-53
  and the computer, 60-61
  computer applications, 190-211
  impediments and opportunities, 56-60
  personnel information systems, 284-311, 312-337
  systems approach to computers, 190-211
  and use of computers, 190-211
personnel systems, 6, 284-311, 312-337
Point-of-sale system, 119-120
privacy and the computer, 250-253

simulation, 123
social issues and the computer, 5-6, 7-8, 232-257, 341-343
  and criminal acts, 253-254
  and dehumanization, 236-237
  and manpower programs, 238-249
  and privacy, 250-253
  and unemployment, 238-249
  and work patterns, 239-242, 273-281
Space odyssey, 151-155
staffing the computer department, 258-283
systems approach, 6-7, 77-99, 196-198
  gaining acceptance of change, 95-97
  integration, 83-86, 249
  and manpower, 249
  and organizations, 86-88
  people-related effects, 289-292
  personnel systems, 197-199, 284-311
  and processing, 131-134
  study, design and implementation, 88-91
  total systems, 81-83
  weaknesses in computer systems, 94-96
technology
  and change, 15-16
  and computers, 19
  and problems, 19-26
  and work patterns, 239-242, 273-281
training and development
  and computers, 212-231, 273-281

Name Index

Ackoff, Russell, 114
Aiken, Howard, 134
Argyris, Chris, 94, 190
Ashenhurst, R.L., 270
Atanasoff, John V., 134
Aurelius, Marcus, iii

Babbage, Charles, 134
Bennis, Warren, 213
Blake and Mouton, 217
Boguslaw, Robert, 258, 284
Boulding, Kenneth, 79
Bush, Vannevar, 134

Dearden, John, 179
Diebold, John, 172, 185
Downs, Anthony, 115
Drucker, Peter, 50, 101, 171

Eckert, J. Prosper, 134

Forrester, Jay, 178
Freeman, Gaylord, 104
Fromm, Erich, 232

Galbraith, John Kenneth, 17
Gardner, John, 104-105
Greenlaw, Paul S., 213
Gross, Bertram, 89

Hammer, Carl, 155

Hanold, Terrance, 100, 184
Hertz, David, 179
Herzberg, Frederick, 245
Hollerith, Herman, 134

Kahn and Wiener, 130, 236
Kast and Rosenzweig, 179
Kennedy, John Fitzgerald, 33
Kepner and Tregoe, 217

Liebtag, Wesley R., 200

Mauchley, John, 134
Mayo and Roethlisberger, 243
Mesthene, Emmanuel G., 15
Montagu, Ashley, 18

Orwell, George, 234

Schlesinger, James, 115
Simon, Herbert, 18, 177, 179
Steiner, George A., 100

Taylor, Frederick, 242
Toffler, Alvin, 212

von Bertalanffy, Ludwig, 77, 79, 110
von Neumann, John, 134

Whistler, Thomas L., 26, 179
Wiener, Norbert, 1